Social Constructivism and the Philosophy of Science

Social constructivists maintain that we invent the properties of the world rather than discover them. Is reality constructed by our own activity? Or, more provocatively, are *scientific facts* constructed? Is *everything* constructed?

André Kukla presents a comprehensive discussion of the philosophical issues that arise out of this controversial debate, analysing the various strengths and weaknesses of a range of constructivist positions. He argues that current philosophical objections to constructivism are drastically inconclusive, while offering and developing new objections. Kukla shows that the strongest constructivist arguments still suffer from conceptual difficulties, illustrating the divide between the sociology and the philosophy of science through examples as varied as laboratory science, time and criminality. Throughout, Kukla distinguishes between the social causes of scientific beliefs and the view that all ascertainable facts are constructed.

Social Constructivism and the Philosophy of Science is a clear assessment of this critical debate which has become increasingly important to many in science studies and sociology. It will be of interest to anyone who is looking for a clear introduction to the range of philosophical arguments surrounding this key question in science.

André Kukla is a Professor in the Departments of Psychology and Philosophy at the University of Toronto. He is the author of *Studies in Scientific Realism*.

Philosophical issues in science
Edited by W. H. Newton-Smith
Balliol College, Oxford

Social Constructivism and the Philosophy of Science

André Kukla

London and New York

First published 2000
by Routledge
11 New Fetter Lane, London EC4P 4EE

Simultaneously published in the USA and Canada
by Routledge
29 West 35th Street, New York, NY 10001

Routledge is an imprint of the Taylor & Francis Group

© 2000 André Kukla

Typeset in Times by Taylor & Francis Books Ltd
Printed and bound in Great Britain by TJ International Ltd, Padstow,
Cornwall

British Library Cataloguing in Publication Data
A catalogue record for this book is available from the British Library

Library of Congress Cataloging in Publication Data
Kukla, André, 1942–
    Social Constructivism and the Philosophy of Science / André Kukla
    (Philosophical issues in science)
    Includes bibliographical references and index.
    1. Science – philosophy. 2. Constructivism (philosophy).
    I. Title. II. Series.
    Q175 .K952 2000   00-020063
    501–dc21

ISBN 0–415–23418–2 (hbk)
ISBN 0–415–23419–0 (pbk)

To the Three who know the Secret of the Ring

Contents

viii *Contents*

Preface

Is reality constructed by our own activity? Do we collectively invent the world rather than discover it? Those who are prone to answer these questions in the affirmative go by the generic name of *social constructivists*. The constructivist thesis is amenable to a great variety of interpretations, ranging from the banal to the literally earth-shattering. One might suspect, on general grounds, that the newsworthiness of each version would turn out to be inversely proportional to the strength of the case that can be mounted in its favour. I aim to find out whether this is so. In this book, I will try to distinguish various points of view that go by the name of constructivism, and to assess the import and merit of each. I'll be particularly interested in the thesis that *scientific facts* are constructed. But I'll also deal with several other related constructivisms. The most adventurous of these is the thesis that *everything* is constructed.

The literature of (scientific) constructivism has been generated both by sociologists, who tend to be enthusiastic supporters, and by philosophers of science, who tend to be incredulous critics. I will discuss both literatures. I won't, however, spend much time going over or criticizing the details of the constructivists' analyses of specific scientific facts. For the most part, I'll take the empirical pronouncements of sociologists at face value. My question is whether these data can be made to sustain the metaphysical, epistemological, and (to a far lesser extent) ethical conclusions that have been drawn from them.

The issue of constructivism seems to raise philosophical passions to a high pitch. Some become livid at the very mention of the c-word; others are unbridled enthusiasts for the extremely counter-intuitive conclusions of half-baked analyses. In the end, these *a priori* predilections turn on whether one is endowed with a conservative or a radical intellectual temperament. There are two types of professional thinkers: normal scientists and paradigm-busters. The former derive their job satisfaction from sustaining and refining an established tradition; the latter are professional trouble-makers whose objective is to shake up the status quo. The former insist that the case for a radically new idea be extremely compelling before it earns the right to be taken seriously. The latter are willing to tolerate a greater risk of being wrong for the sake of putting forward a provocative thesis. The former are repelled *ab initio* by the iconoclastic agenda of constructivism. The latter are attracted to it – there's an unmistakable glee that accompanies constructivists' suggestions that the world does not exist. Where along this continuum do my predilections lie? I'll let the reader decide.

An important part of this work is to make clear which versions of constructivism fall within the scope of some of the standard arguments in the field. The literature of constructivism commits more than the usual number of philosophical sins that I call *switcheroos*. One commits a switcheroo by starting with a hypothesis that's amenable to a range of interpretations, giving arguments that support a weak version, and thenceforth pretending that one of the stronger versions has been established. For example, one gives reasons for supposing that scientific facts are socially constructed and pretends that reasons have been given for supposing that there is no independent world. The news that scientists uniformly invent rather than discover scientific facts would unquestionably warrant a large headline – but not in such a large typeface as the report that there isn't any unconstructed reality besides or behind the scientifically constructed one. The field also abounds in *reverse switcheroos*: you put forth a strong version of the hypothesis, and when it gets into trouble, you retreat to a weaker version, pretending that it was the weaker thesis that you had in mind all along. Switcheroos and reverse switcheroos can be performed in tandem, and the cycle can be repeated *ad infinitum*. A judicious application of this strategy enables one to maintain an indefensible position forever.

The primary audience I have in mind for this book is the community of philosophers of science. However, I have tried to make it accessible both to students of philosophy and to social scientists with philosophical interests. The result is a work which I think would be suitable as a primary text for a graduate or advanced undergraduate course in the philosophy of constructivism.

Acknowledgements

A preliminary version of Chapter 8 was presented to a 1996 conference on constructive empiricism at Tilburg University, Netherlands. An early version of Chapter 12 was presented in 1999 at the 11th International Congress of Logic, Methodology and Philosophy of Science in Cracow, Poland.

The writing of this book was supported by a research grant from the Social Sciences and Humanities Research Council of Canada. I also profited from the conversation and correspondence of Rebecca Kukla, Richard Manning, and Harvey Siegel.

1   Defining constructivism

To say that 'social construction' and 'constructivism' are vogue words is to understate an extraordinary situation. In a recent survey of the field Hacking (1999) mentions sixty-odd items that have recently been described in print as socially constructed. Here's a haphazardly selected sample: gender (of course), illness, women refugees, quarks, Zulu nationalism, Indian forests, Japan, Ireland, the past, emotions, reality, serial homicide, authorship, the child viewer of television, the Landsat satellite system, dolomite and the self. Hacking notes that the class of putative constructions is not only numerous, but remarkably heterogeneous. Among the items for which constructivist claims have been made, we find people, inanimate objects, states and conditions, events, practices, actions, experiences, relations, substances, concepts and an assortment of what Hacking calls 'elevator words' (because they raise the level of discourse, both rhetorically and semantically): reality, truth, facts, knowledge.

What do women refugees, the Landsat satellite system and reality supposedly have in common by virtue of which they're all socially constructed? 'Don't ask for the meaning,' Hacking tells us, 'ask what's the point' (1999: 5). He describes the point in three clauses:

Social constructionists about X tend to hold that:

1   X need not have existed, or need not be at all as it is. X, or X as it is at present, is not determined by the nature of things; it is not inevitable.

Very often they go further and urge that:

2   X is quite bad as it is.
3   We would be much better off if X were done away with, or at least radically transformed.

(1999: 6)

Later on, Hacking adds a zeroth clause:

0   In the present state of affairs, X is taken for granted, X appears to be inevitable.

(1999: 12)

In brief, X is asserted to be constructed when we want to call attention to the currently invisible evitability of X for the purpose of mobilizing efforts to evade it.

I can see why conditions (2), (3) and (0) may be said to give the 'point' of constructivist claims rather than their 'meaning'. But what about condition (1)? On even the most traditional accounts of the matter, (1) seems to be a straightforward, necessary condition for the truth of 'X is constructed'. Hacking himself tells us that condition (1) is something that constructivists about X 'hold', as opposed to (2) and (3) which merely specify what they 'urge', and (0) which stipulates what they 'take for granted'. Moreover, Hacking also tells us that conditions (2), (3) and (0) are not absolutely essential prerequisites for constructivist claims. They're merely satisfied 'very often'. So, despite his disclaimer, Hacking does say something substantial about the meaning of 'X is constructed', as opposed to the pragmatic purpose that might be served by asserting it. He says that 'X is constructed' entails that X is not inevitable. This may not yet be a full definition; but it is a necessary condition for the validity of constructivist claims.

But is that all that can be said about the truth-conditions for 'X is constructed'? To say that X is not inevitable is to assert that not-X is *possible*, and, as every student of philosophy knows, there are various grades and flavours of possibility. Which variety of possibility is at stake here? Hacking is disinclined to pursue this question. His view seems to be that the relevant notion of evitability is *not* further explicated in constructivist writings: if philosophers want to get clear about what constructivists say without putting words in their mouths, they're going to have to work with the unexplicated notion.

I'm in sympathy with the general Wittgensteinian point that the use of vague concepts doesn't automatically call for remedial treatment. But condition (1) simply doesn't exhaust what can be said about the truth-conditions of 'X is constructed', as that phrase is used by those who claim that women refugees, reality and the Landsat satellite system are constructed. Consider: if anything is not inevitable in the vague, unexplicated, everyday sense of the word, it's a freakish accident, like the destruction of New York by a falling asteroid. But nobody would be inclined to say that the freakish accidentality of an event is evidence of its social construction. The possibility of not-X which is relevant to constructivist claims must be delimited in a way that excludes the possible non-occurrence of events of this type.

The needed elaboration of Hacking's condition (1) is given by Nelson (1994). Discussing the special case of the construction of scientific facts,

Nelson writes that constructivists endorse the following 'Constructivist Counterfactual Argument':

> If scientists had chosen to confer facthood otherwise than they actually did, then subsequent history would reflect this in a world-view consistent with the choice they counterfactually made. Therefore, the 'facts' are determined by scientists' choices, not by 'objective reality'.
>
> (Nelson 1994: 541)

This formulation is consistent with Hacking's condition (1): the Constructivist Counterfactual Argument entails that the facts of science are not inevitable – they could have been other than what they are. But Nelson further specifies that the evitability is due to the fact that *scientists could have made other choices*. More generally, the type of possibility at issue in constructivist claims is *the option of free agents to do something other than what they actually did*. It's true that the social construction of gender differences is predicated on the idea that these differences could have been different from what they are – this much is what Hacking's condition (1) tells us. But that's only part of the constructivist story. In addition, the constructivist thesis about gender entails that gender differences would have been different from what they are if human agents had made different choices. The fact that they could have been different *tout court* isn't enough. So the whole issue of constructivism versus 'realism' arises only in a context where both sides in the dispute accept the good old-fashioned metaphysics of freedom of the will.

In sum, X is said to be constructed if it's produced by intentional human activity. This is more or less what a dictionary would have told us in the first place. It follows that pianos, television sets, cheese sandwiches and all other artifacts qualify as constructed. To be sure, everybody has always known this – Hacking's condition (0) fails to be satisfied by cheese sandwiches. But it's nonetheless a truth, albeit a humble one, that cheese sandwiches are constructed. It should be only slightly less obvious that *all our concepts are constructed*. The fact that we conceptualize some people as women wouldn't be a fact if we acted differently – e.g., if we *didn't* conceptualize anybody as a woman. But there's no point making that argument specifically for the concept of a woman. It's just as true for the concept of the colour blue, or for the concept of a quark. The view that concepts are human constructions is sometimes contrasted with the doctrine of *natural kinds*, according to which only some conceptual schemes manage to carve nature at its preexisting joints (see for example Hacking 1999: 82–4). But the two claims are orthogonal. Suppose that nature has joints. Then one of our concepts may succeed while another fails to carve nature at its joints. But that doesn't make the first concept any less of a construction: if a complex pattern of human activity had been different, we wouldn't have fashioned that particular natural-kinds concept. The fact that it carves nature at its joints is neither here nor there. Trying to carve nature at its joints is just another optional project which we might or might not undertake.

Of course to say that the concept of a woman or a quark is constructed is not yet to say that women themselves, or quarks themselves, are constructed. The claim that these entities themselves are produced by intentional human activity is substantially stronger. In the case of women, it's easy to see how women might turn out to be constructed. Here is one possible (and entirely unoriginal) scenario. We begin by constructing the concept of a woman. We include in this concept all the traditional appurtenances of femininity: nurturance, seductiveness, social intelligence, a poor sense of direction, and so on. Naturally, those to whom this concept is applied come to know that the concept is applied to them. This knowledge leads them to behave in ways that are different from how they *would* have behaved if they had not been so categorized. Perhaps it causes them to have a poor sense of direction by undermining their self-confidence. The result is the social construction, not just of the concept 'woman', but of women. Women turn out to be a type of being that wouldn't exist if a certain pattern of intentional human activity had not taken place.

It's not so easy to devise an equally commonsensical scenario whereby the facts about quarks (not just our concept of a quark) turn out to be socially constructed. But it's precisely claims of this type – more generally, claims that the facts of so-called natural science are constructed – that I'll be dealing with in this book.

Before we start, it's necessary to distinguish three issues that receive a great deal of play in the constructivist literature. People who call themselves constructivists sometimes argue for a *metaphysical* thesis about some or all facts about the world we live in, sometimes for an *epistemological* thesis concerning what can be known about the world, and sometimes for a *semantic* thesis concerning what can be said about the world. The characterization of constructivism immediately preceding this paragraph equates it with the metaphysical claim: women, or quarks, are invented rather than discovered. Most of the chapters in this book are devoted to an examination of various grades of this metaphysical hypothesis.

The epistemological claim associated with constructivism is the thesis of *epistemic relativism*. This is the view that there is no absolute warrant for any belief – that rational warrant makes sense only relative to a culture, or an individual, or a paradigm. Both the metaphysical thesis and the epistemological thesis are often regarded as two sides of one and the same 'constructivist' coin. Thus Fine states that the two doctrines of 'constructivism' that give it its philosophical interest are 'its anti-realism and its relativism' (Fine 1996: 232). And Nelson writes:

> philosophical constructivism … is relativistic in two senses. First, there
> is an ontological relativism about entities and processes. We are not to

think of the phenomena studied by scientists as the inevitable manifestations of objectively existing entities and processes; instead, theoretical
entities and processes are constituted or constructed by scientists *post
hoc* ... The second relativistic facet of constructivism concerns scientific
rationality. According to non-relativistic rationalists ... defensible
scientific decisions, if not correct ones, should be made ... in accord
with universal standards governing the use of appropriate scientific
evidence ... Constructivists, holding as they do a sort of relativism
about rationality, deny the universality of such standards.

(Nelson 1994: 535–6)

My nomenclature is different from Nelson's. I usually reserve the term
'constructivism' for what he calls 'ontological relativism', and I use
'epistemic relativism' to refer to his 'relativism about rationality'. When
there's a danger of being misunderstood, I sometimes refer to Nelson's
'ontological relativism' as the thesis of *metaphysical* constructivism.

Despite their frequently being espoused by the same individuals,
(metaphysical) constructivism and epistemic relativism are, at least *prima
facie*, independent doctrines. To begin with, constructivism doesn't
obviously entail epistemic relativism. It's (*prima facie*) possible to combine
the constructivist view that facts are socially constructed with the anti-
relativist idea that we can nevertheless have absolutely true or absolutely
false ideas about them. The fairly uncontroversial thesis that at least some
aspects of *social* reality are constructed provides an apt illustration. The
value of money is a socially constructed fact: the pieces of paper that we call
money enable us to buy things only because it's widely acknowledged that
they enable us to buy things. Nevertheless, an isolated individual who
believed that dollar bills have no purchasing power would be absolutely
wrong. By the same token, it could be maintained that scientific facts are
socially constructed, but that once they've been constructed, it's a mistake
for anyone to disbelieve them. The conceptual option of avowing constructivism while denying relativism seems to have been taken up by some
constructivist authors. Latour and Woolgar, whose *Laboratory Life* is one
of the most influential documents in the literature of constructivism,
caution the reader that their position 'is not relativist' (1986: 180).

Conversely, it's possible to combine the view that beliefs are only relatively warranted with the anti-constructivist hypothesis that there is an
independent reality. This is the position that Devitt (1991) calls 'fig-leaf
realism'. Fig-leaf realists admit only that something exists independently of
human activity, but they deny that we can have absolute knowledge of any
of its properties. Kant was a fig-leaf realist. So is the contemporary
sociologist and relativist Karin Knorr-Cetina (1993: 557). Knorr-Cetina still
counts herself among the 'constructivists', however, partly on the basis of
her relativism, and partly on the grounds that she regards the relativized
facts of science as constructed.

The second type of claim to be distinguished from the metaphysical thesis is a semantic hypothesis. Constructivists are wont to say that nature 'plays no role' in the acceptance of scientific claims. When they say this, they sometimes have in mind the metaphysical thesis: nature plays no role in scientific acceptance because it's prior acceptance that constitutes, as it were, the nature of nature. At other times, however, the argument takes a decidedly semantic turn. Harry Collins (1985), for instance, maintains that past verbal usage doesn't determine the future application of words. It follows that sentences have no determinate empirical content: there is no fact of the matter whether an event confirms or disconfirms a hypothesis. The outcome can be negotiated either way. On this account, nature plays no role in scientific acceptance because it fails to hook up to language in the requisite manner. This *semantic constructivism* is, at least *prima facie*, independent of both (epistemic) relativism and (metaphysical) constructivism. The semantic thesis refers to sentences, while the relativist thesis refers to beliefs. It's possible to reconcile semantic constructivism with the denial of relativism via the notion of *tacit* knowledge: sentences have no determinate empirical content, but we may still have non-propositional knowledge about the world that's absolutely correct. That is to say, we may tacitly know what happens next and act accordingly, even if we're unable, even in principle, to *say* what happens next. The converse proposition – that relativism doesn't entail semantic constructivism – is intuitively compelling. The fact that warrants for belief are all relative doesn't mean that there aren't any absolutely true sentences. It just means that, even if there are absolutely true sentences, we can never absolutely know which ones they are. It's also compelling that semantic constructivism is independent of metaphysical constructivism. The world might be socially constructed even if sentences have determinate empirical content; and the world might be independent of our constructive activity even if the limitations of language render us impotent to describe it.

I emphasize that the foregoing remarks provide merely a *prima facie* case for the independence of the three constructivist theses. My point is only that these theses don't obviously comprise a package that must be accepted or rejected in one piece. Nevertheless, there are intricate connections among the three doctrines. These connections will be traced in some of the later chapters.

2 Constructivism and the sociology of scientific knowledge

There's a standardized bit of history that (scientific) constructivists tell about their antecedents. Students are regaled with it on the first day of countless courses dealing with the social study of science. The story is told in print by Woolgar (1988) and by Ashmore (1989). According to Ashmore, its main purpose is to establish the originality of the new research programme. The story tries to achieve this end by 'a strategy of dissociating [the] new research programme from others' (Ashmore 1989: 3). It would be begging the question raised by constructivism to ask whether this story is objectively correct. Non-constructivist historians of ideas would at the very least accuse it of oversimplification. Everyone will agree, however, that it tells us something useful about the face that constructivists wish to present to the world. The story goes like this.

Constructivism stands at the confluence of two streams in the history of sociology: the sociology of knowledge and the sociology of science. The first was shaped by the vision of three seminal thinkers: Marx, Mannheim and Durkheim. All of them emphasized the causal role of social factors in shaping individual belief. Marx famously argued that social class determined various intellectual attitudes (Marx and Engels 1963). Mannheim (1936) and Durkheim (1915) broadened both the range of causally relevant social factors and the range of intellectual attitudes that fall under their sway. But, like Marx before them, they exempted the beliefs generated by mathematics and the natural sciences from their social analysis. Scientific belief was thought to be rationally rather than causally determined, and thus to transcend social and cultural influence. This epistemic dualism is what distinguishes the classical period in the sociology of knowledge from its more modern manifestations.

Setting the question of scientific knowledge aside (and stepping momentarily out of the story), the general thesis that some beliefs are socially determined can hardly be denied. It's amply demonstrated by the enormous ideological differences that exist between societies, as compared to the ideological variation to be found within each individual society. Compare the prevalence of Moslem ideology in Riyadh and nearby Tel Aviv, or of communism in Leningrad and Atlanta circa 1955. Statistically speaking, it would be absurd to attribute these differences to the hypothesis that the two groups of individuals assessed the claims of the Koran or Karl Marx independently of their social milieu, and that they just happened to come to the same conclusions as the other members of their society. The precise extent of social determination is a question for ordinary empirical research – so long as scientific beliefs continue to be exempted. As will be seen shortly, things get more complicated when sociologists try to do altogether without a privileged class of beliefs. Now back to the story.

Another precursor of constructivism is the 'sociology of science' of Robert Merton (1973) and his followers. Its name might lead one to suppose that the sociology of science is the subdiscipline of the sociology of knowledge that deals with scientific knowledge. But this is not what Merton *et al.* did. They studied how the *institution* of science is organized. They tried to elucidate the various social roles that are created by the profession of scientist, the reward system that drives scientific activity, and so on. As has often been remarked, Mertonian sociology of science is aptly described as the social study of *scientists*. Scientific *knowledge*, however, continued to lie beyond the scope of sociological analysis.

More recently, sociologists have tried to apply the types of social explanations that figure in the classical sociology-of-knowledge tradition to the intellectual content of science. The inspiration for this move is often said to be Thomas Kuhn (1962). Kuhn famously argued that the course of scientific activity is shaped by the scientific community's choice of a paradigm. In Kuhn's account, this choice is not rationally dictated by the content of prior science. It's an irrational, or arational, leap. Now Kuhn didn't have anything systematic to say about the determinants of the direction of that leap. But his analysis opened the door for an account in terms of social causes: if rational considerations don't determine paradigm choice, where else is there to look for determinants? The elaboration of a social account of the content of science might very well have been called sociology of science. However, feeling the need to distinguish their enterprise from the Mertonian brand of sociology of science, researchers in the new field have dubbed it the *sociology of scientific knowledge* (Woolgar 1988: 41). Mercifully, this dodecasyllabic monstrosity (compare: physics) is usually referred to as SSK. End of story.

At this point, I begin to construct my own story. Note that the story of origins just related ends with the creation of SSK. Where does constructivism come in? Well, if scientific belief is socially caused, then it's 'constructed', in the broad sense of the term which was introduced in Chapter 1: it wouldn't be what it is if the social activities of scientists, officers of granting agencies and other players had been sufficiently different. Indeed, SSKists are often called constructivists on no more basis than that they regard scientific beliefs as having social causes. However, *some* SSKists – by no means all of them – have advanced a far more adventurous thesis. According to Latour, Woolgar, Knorr-Cetina, Collins and Pickering (*inter alia*), it's not only scientific *beliefs* that are socially constructed – it's scientific *facts*. If the social history of science had been sufficiently different, we wouldn't, according to SSKists in general, have the beliefs that we do have about quarks. This is a thesis which is relatively easy to swallow. But Latour *et al.* go further. They claim that if social history had been appropriately different, *there wouldn't be any quarks*. When philosophers of science talk about constructivism, they usually have this stronger thesis in mind. The characterization of constructivism by Fine and by Nelson quoted in Chapter 1 are examples of this usage. My own linguistic habits have been shaped by this philosophical literature. This accounts for the perceptible equivocation in my discussion between the social scientist's omnibus notion of constructivism and the philosopher of science's more circumscribed notion. According to Fine, Nelson and me, merely positing that scientific beliefs have social causes doesn't yet make you a constructivist about science. Constructivism about science involves the claim that social processes produce scientific facts.

It's easy to come up with the names of SSKists who explicitly deny the validity of constructivism in the sense in which Fine, Nelson and I understand that term. It's also easy to come up with SSKists who don't espouse the view that I called *semantic* constructivism – the view that sentences have no determinate empirical content – I'll reveal the names below. It's not so easy to name an SSKist who repudiates both these constructivisms and epistemic relativism as well. The main point I want to make in this chapter is that SSK is conceptually independent of relativism, as well as of metaphysical and semantic constructivism. There may not be any SSKists who subscribe to an absolutist epistemology, but there are no obvious reasons why there couldn't be.

The most influential formulation of the main tenets of SSK is David Bloor's (1976) 'strong programme' for the sociology of knowledge. According to Bloor, theory and research in the sociology of knowledge should conform to the following methodological precepts:

1   It would be causal, that is, concerned with the conditions which would bring about belief or states of knowledge. Naturally, there will be other types of causes apart from social ones which will co-operate in bringing about belief.
2   It would be impartial with respect to truth and falsity, rationality or irrationality, success or failure. Both sides of these dichotomies will require explanation.
3   It would be symmetrical in its style of explanation. The same types of cause would explain, say, true and false beliefs.
4   It would be reflexive. In principle its patterns of explanation would have to be applicable to sociology itself.

(Bloor 1976: 4–5)

Bloor doesn't lay claim to any methodological novelties. On the contrary, he insists that the four planks of the strong programme are what you get if you approach the sociology of knowledge 'scientifically'. They 'embody the same values which are taken for granted in other scientific disciplines' (4). Evidently, just being scientific buys you the conclusion that there are social explanations of scientific beliefs – for there are indubitably social explanations of some *non*-scientific beliefs, and the third principle tells us that the same types of explanations are to be provided for all classes of beliefs. According to Bloor, simply being scientific about the sociology of knowledge also dictates an epistemic relativist stance (Barnes and Bloor 1982). How, exactly, relativism is supposed to flow out of Bloor's four principles will be dealt with in due time.

Bloor's programmatic statement has been subjected to a barrage of criticisms by Laudan (1981). To begin with, Laudan notes that Bloor doesn't provide any explicit criteria for distinguishing between the 'scientific' and the 'unscientific'. The result is that it's impossible to evaluate the claim that the strong programme is scientific. Moreover, Principles 1, 2 and 4 are trivial and their truth is uncontested, except by Bloor's straw men. Most importantly, the third principle is said to be untenable on a copious variety of grounds:

1   the claim that all beliefs are to be explained by the 'same type' of cause is hopelessly vague (what counts as the same type?);
2   even if the symmetry principle made a determinate claim, it would still commit the sin of trying to settle an empirical issue by *a priori* fiat – whatever we mean by the 'same type', we surely need to look and see whether any two classes of phenomena have the same type of cause;
3   the established sciences don't exhibit any trace of utilizing anything like the symmetry principle;
4   there are unproblematic ways to distinguish between rational and irrational beliefs such that they compellingly *do* have different types of causes.

Bloor (1981) has responded to Laudan with, I think, considerable success. For instance, here's how he deflects the accusation that there's no substance to the claim that the strong programme is scientific. He admits that he can't formulate an explicit criterion for distinguishing the scientific from the non-scientific, but correctly points out that this doesn't mean that the distinction can't be made. Indeed, Laudan himself seems to rely on the science versus non-science distinction when he tells us that *science* makes no use of the symmetry principle. In further (but only partial) defence of Bloor, I would add that the first criticism of the symmetry principle – that it's not clear what counts as the 'same type' of cause – effectively disarms the next three criticisms. Without knowing what counts as the same type of cause, it really isn't informative to be told that the established sciences *don't* seek to postulate the same type of cause for all the phenomena in their domain, or that rational and irrational beliefs don't have the same type of cause. It isn't even possible to say with any certainty that the issue needs to be settled empirically: if any two naturalistic causes count as being of the same type (in contrast with non-naturalistic causes, like God's will), then it might be argued that the natural sciences have an *a priori* commitment to provide the same type of explanation for all their phenomena. At worst, the critique of Bloor's four planks comes to this: they're a collection of vague pronouncements and uncontested platitudes. This is not yet to say that they're false.

In fact, vague pronouncements and uncontested platitudes are enough for Bloor to secure half of the results he wants to obtain. The four planks of the strong programme were an attempt to ground two theses. The first is that, in contrast with the classical *weak* programme of Marx, Mannheim and Durkheim, the sociology of knowledge has unrestricted scope: all beliefs, those of the natural sciences included, are candidates for social explanation. The second is relativism. It's my contention that the validity or invalidity of Laudan's criticisms has no bearing on the disposition of these two core theses. The first thesis is secure even if Laudan's criticisms are accepted, for it takes no more than a collection of platitudes to secure it. The second thesis doesn't follow from Bloor's four planks, even if Laudan's criticisms are *in*valid. Let's see why this is so.

The first core thesis is that all beliefs, the rational as well as the irrational, are candidates for explanation in social terms. Laudan candidly admits that this thesis is true: the causal determinants of any type of belief can only be ascertained by empirical research, and it's inappropriate to rule out any possible cause on *a priori* grounds. He notes, however, that even if all beliefs turn out to have social causes, it's still possible that there are also *additional* causal factors which are different for rational and irrational beliefs, and which presumably would warrant different assessments of their epistemic status. In fact, he claims that this is bound to be the case on at least one common conception of the rational. Recognizing that other conceptions exist, Laudan stipulates that the rationality of an agent

> consists in his engaging in a process of ratiocination in order to ascertain what course of action his goals and prior beliefs commit him to. To adopt a belief rationally, the agent must be able to specify reasons ... for adopting that belief rather than its negation.
>
> (187)

Presumably, a belief is deemed to be *ir*rational if it's adopted without regard to prior ratiocination – i.e., impulsively. Laudan continues:

> Suppose there were a group of rational agents. Suppose we were to identify the rules by which this group of individuals 'fixes' its beliefs ...

Suppose, further, that these rules require agents to subject prospective beliefs to certain forms of scrutiny and analysis prior to their adoption. Imagine, finally, a very different community of, say, epistemic anarchists. Their view, insofar as there is assent about these matters, is that one adopts beliefs independently of any shared cognitive policy. One may or may not have reasons for one's beliefs; one may or may not have evidence for them, etc. Now, the sociologist who wants to explain beliefs in these two societies will in both cases refer in his explanation to the belief-governing policies in each society. That is the common core. But the 'causes' in the two cases are apt to be radically different ... what this hypothetical example illustrates is that both rational and irrational behavior may have significant social components, even when the causal mechanisms productive of rational and irrational belief are very different.

(190–1)

Here Laudan grants the viability of a sociology of knowledge that has unrestricted scope. So what's his disagreement with Bloor? It's that his scenario of the two communities supposedly shows the symmetry principle to be unwarranted. The passage quoted above continues:

A program for the sociologizing of all forms of knowledge *need* not be committed to the thesis of causal symmetry ... [P]reliminary evidence ... suggests that different kinds of causal mechanisms are involved in rational and irrational actions. That fact, if it is a fact, is no obstacle to a global view of the prospective scope of sociology. But it is, and I suspect will remain, a source of grave reservations about the Bloor–Barnes version of the strong program for the sociology of knowledge.

(191)

But, once again, in light of Laudan's *other* criticism of the symmetry principle – namely, that it's so vague as to be without substance – one has to conclude that the 'grave reservations' expressed in the last passage are themselves without substance. There's no difference worth preserving between 'a global view of the prospective scope of sociology' and 'the Bloor–Barnes version of the strong program'. The objection to the four planks isn't epistemological – it's *aesthetic*. At worst, the four planks are merely ugly and useless.

The second thesis that Bloor wants to establish is relativism. Laudan announces that he will argue that the 'relativism entailed by the symmetry thesis' is 'without warrant' (1981: 184). What follows this announcement is the story of the two communities quoted above. Now the conclusion of this argument says nothing about relativism: the conclusion is that the symmetry thesis is false. This is rather curious. If, as Laudan tells us, relativism is entailed by the symmetry principle, then purporting to show that relativism is without warrant by arguing against the symmetry principle is to commit the fallacy of denying the antecedent. There are, however, other passages that cast Laudan's argumentative strategy in a more favourable light. Sometimes he writes as though relativism is more than merely *entailed* by the symmetry principle – he suggests that the symmetry principle is already a statement of a relativist position:

> Boldly put, the thesis of symmetry is a strong formulation of *cognitive relativism* ...
>
> (Laudan 1981: 184)

This identification of the symmetry principle and relativism is a point on which Laudan and Bloor concur. I will have more to say about it when I discuss Bloor's defence of relativism. In any case, it explains why one and the same argument is able to do double duty for Laudan. For the time being, let's accept that the symmetry principle is identical to, or immediately entails, relativism. Let's also suppose, contrary to fact, that Bloor's strong programme and the SSK of global scope that Laudan finds acceptable are significantly different enterprises. (This amounts to the assumption that Bloor and Laudan have settled on a definite interpretation of the symmetry principle, and that they disagree over its truth value.) Even so, I don't see how Laudan's conception of SSK can be free of relativism if Bloor's original programme entails it. Presumably, it's because of its assumption that beliefs are socially caused that the strong programme leads to relativism. According to Laudan, rational beliefs are the outcome of a process of deliberation. Now Laudan admits that the rules deployed in our deliberations can be socially caused. But surely, if the direct social causation of belief relativizes these beliefs, then the social causation of our deliberative rules must at one remove relativize the beliefs that issue from the deliberative processes determined by those rules.

Laudan's use of the word 'rational' can easily mislead us here. After all, one of the two societies in his story has absolutely rational beliefs and the other doesn't – and isn't the existence of absolutely rational beliefs immediately incompatible with the thesis of epistemic relativism? This is of course a mere play on words. As Bloor points out in his reply, the rationality of a belief, as Laudan defines it, has no connection of meaning with the epistemic warrant that's at stake in epistemic relativism. Laudan's 'rationality' is a purely descriptive concept, devoid of normative implications. This is clearly seen by the fact that it's logically open for someone to maintain that it's the deliberating society in Laudan's story that's making the epistemic mistake, and that the impulsive society is epistemically on track. Such a view could be part of a romantic epistemology that counsels spontaneity and regards deliberation as always obsessive and unproductive. On this view, the 'rational' (i.e., deliberative) beliefs of the first society would be irrational (i.e., unwarranted), whereas the 'irrational' (impulsive) beliefs of the second society would be rational (warranted). So the 'rationality' or 'irrationality' of beliefs in Laudan's sense doesn't speak to the issue of epistemic relativism versus absolutism. The conclusion of the previous paragraph stands: if the strong programme includes or entails relativism, then so does Laudan's medium programme.

But do the four planks of the strong programme include or entail relativism? Like Laudan, Bloor writes as though the espousal of relativism is not so much *based* on the adoption of the four planks as it is *constituted* by that adoption. Sometimes he directly equates relativism with the symmetry principle:

> The form of relativism that we shall defend – is that all beliefs are on a par with one another with respect to the causes of their credibility.
>
> (Barnes and Bloor 1982: 22–3)

I have no objection to this eccentric use of the term 'relativism' – so long as it's kept in mind that we're not talking about the doctrine of *epistemic* relativism, according to which there is no warranted belief *tout court*, but only warranted belief relative to a society. If Barnes and Bloor want to migrate from their 'relativism' to epistemic relativism, they need an argument. But they take this conceptual journey without a ticket. Soon after defining 'relativism' as the symmetry principle, and without any intervening attempts to justify the transition, they write:

> For the relativist there is no sense attached to the idea that some standards or beliefs are really rational as distinct from being locally accepted as such.
>
> (27)

Why is this so? Friedman has recently asked the same rhetorical question:

> Why ... should the enterprise of empirically and naturalistically describing how beliefs become locally credible as a matter of fact compete or stand in conflict with the enterprise of articulating the non-empirical and prescriptive structure in virtue of which beliefs ought to be accepted as a matter of norm?
>
> (Friedman 1998: 244)

For instance, why can't we say both that all our beliefs have social causes, and that certain configurations of social forces produce an epistemic climate in which our opinions are absolutely warranted? To suppose that we *can't* say this is tantamount to claiming that the sheer fact of its being socially caused renders a belief ineligible for absolute warrant. Even if this ultimately turns out to be so, it certainly isn't obvious that it is so. At least it requires an argument.

What might such an argument be like? When I try to think of one, I can only come up with the following idea: there's no essential connection (whatever that means) between the social cause of the belief and its epistemic status. Even if certain social configurations caused us to get our beliefs right, we would have no more epistemic *warrant* for them than if we had merely guessed right. In contrast, when the causes of our beliefs are *reasons*, there's a direct conceptual connection between their cause and their epistemic status. This line of thinking runs up against a brick wall, however. If 'reasons' are conceptualized as providing causal explanations, then there's no more 'essential connection' between cause and epistemic status when the cause is a reason than when it's a state of society. Consider the following explanation of my belief in Q: I believe it because I have prior beliefs that P, that P implies Q, and that *modus ponens* is a valid form of inference. If this is understood as a *causal* explanation, then it's just a matter of contingent luck that the world is so constructed that my prior beliefs happen to produce the right epistemic effect. In another possible world, my beliefs that P, that P implies Q, and that *modus ponens* is valid could cause me to adopt the belief in an entirely unrelated R. The fact that these beliefs produce the correct conclusion is no less adventitious in this case than if a certain state of society produced it. So there can't be anything particularly debilitating about *social* causation as compared to any other sort. We must say either that the bare fact of their being caused negates the epistemic warrant of *all* our beliefs, or that *every* type of causation is compatible with being warranted.

If we take the view that every type of causation is compatible with being warranted, then, of course, we have no reason to suppose that the strong programme entails relativism. What if we say that causation always negates epistemic warrant? Then we must choose between the following two options:

1   adopt the antinaturalist view that some beliefs (the rationally warranted ones) stand outside the causal nexus – i.e., retreat to the weak programme of Marx *et al.*; or
2   adopt a blanket scepticism according to which no belief is ever warranted.

Now the epistemic relativism that Barnes and Bloor champion is *compatible* with the second option; but it's not *entailed* by it. For all we know, *relative* epistemic warrants of the type that relativists accept may be just as incompatible with causation, in which case we will have to settle either for the weak programme or for a scepticism so deep that it undoes even relativized knowledge claims. There's no way of knowing whether this is so until we actually see the argument that shows that causation negates absolute warrant. Far from being automatically committed to epistemic relativism, adherents to the strong programme who want to embrace relativism owe us two arguments:

1   that causation negates absolute warrant, and
2   that it *doesn't* negate relative warrant.

Perhaps the reflexivity postulate of the strong programme will do the job that the symmetry postulate couldn't do. Relativistic SSKists need to deny that some causal configurations may produce epistemically warranted opinions. Let X be the proposition that they need to deny. If all beliefs are caused, then, by reflexivity, belief in X must also be caused – and then we're not warranted in accepting X unless we *already* believe that we're warranted in accepting some caused beliefs. That is to say, we're not warranted in accepting X unless we already accept it. Does this mean that we're not warranted in accepting it? It depends on the empirical details. We do get into trouble if the cause of belief in X is of the type that our hypothesis says *doesn't* lead to warranted belief. This situation is akin to a Biblical fundamentalist finding a passage in the Bible that tells him *not* to believe anything just because it's written in a book. In such cases, the hypothesis is revealed to be untenable. But there's no tenability problem if the cause of belief in X is of the type that, according to X itself, does lead to warranted belief. This situation is akin to the Biblical fundamentalist finding a passage in the Bible proclaiming that everything in the Bible is true. To be sure, such a discovery doesn't *confirm* the hypothesis. But neither does it make trouble for it. On the contrary, it indicates that the hypothesis has passed at least one test – the test of internal consistency – that not every point of view is able to pass. So while an anti-relativist proponent of the strong programme may be admonished for adopting a belief on the basis of insufficient evidence, it can't be maintained, as both Bloor and Laudan do, that proponents of the strong programme are automatically committed to relativism.

Despite their migrating without prior comment from the symmetry principle to epistemic relativism, Barnes and Bloor do eventually get around to providing some motivation for the move. Here's what they say about the possibility that some beliefs may be absolutely warranted even though all of them are caused:

> the charge would be that the sociologists had conflated validity and credibility. But – validity detached from credibility is nothing … [C]onsider again the two tribes T1 and T2. For a member of T1 examining what is to him a peculiar belief from the culture of T2, there is a clear point to the distinction between the validity and the credibility of a belief. He will say that just because the misguided members of T2 believe something, that doesn't make it true. Its rightness or wrongness, he may add, must be established independently of belief. But, of course,

what he will mean by 'independently of belief' is independently of the belief of others, such as the members of T2. For his own part, he has no option but to use the accepted methods and assumptions of his own group ...

If our imaginary tribesman was dialectically sophisticated, he might realize that he is open to the charge of special pleading, and that he had, in his own case, collapsed the distinction upon which he had been insisting. How could he reply to the accusation that he had equated the validity and credibility of his own beliefs? As a more careful statement of his position, he might claim that not even the fact that his own tribe believes something is, *in itself*, sufficient to make it true. But he would then have to mend the damage of this admission by adding that it just was a fact that what his tribe believed *was* true. A kindly providence, perhaps, had here united these two essentially different things.

(Barnes and Bloor 1982: 29–30)

What Barnes and Bloor seem to be claiming is that the absolutist's distinction between validity and credibility is a conceptual complexification that doesn't buy you anything. It's worth noting that, even if this is right, it's not the same thing as claiming that relativism is contained in, or is logically entailed by, the strong programme. Barnes and Bloor's analysis doesn't call into question the *coherence* of an anti-relativist strong programme. It merely suggests that the relativist strong programme is a better metatheory than the anti-relativist programme. The absolutist tribesman of T1 who cleaves to a distinction between validity and credibility has a sensible story to tell. It's just that the relativist story is simpler – it cuts out the part about his beliefs being absolutely true, which seems to be doing no work anyway.

Here's an absolutist rejoinder. I grant that the relativist story is simpler (though this is by no means obvious). But I don't grant that the distinction between validity and credibility doesn't accomplish anything useful. In Chapter 15 I will argue that relativism is, as many writers before me have averred, irretrievably incoherent. If this is true, then the loss of simplicity attendant on absolutism is more than adequately compensated for by the escape from incoherence. If the tribesman's asserting that what he believes happens to be true helps him to avoid talking nonsense, then he has a good reason for asserting it. To be sure, until we come to Chapter 15, this rebuttal of Barnes and Bloor is based on a promissory note. Nonetheless, the point can be made now that the purportedly greater simplicity of relativism doesn't settle the issue in its favour. There may be other forms of theoretical compensation.

To summarize the result of the last few pages: the acceptance of an SSK with unrestricted scope doesn't entail a commitment to relativism. In light of the coming revelation that relativism is incoherent, this is a lucky thing for SSK. It's also obvious that a relativistic stance doesn't dictate one's opinion about SSK. One could, like Bloor and Barnes, be both a relativist and an SSKist; or one could be a relativist and deny that social factors cause anything at all. Relativism and SSK are two different topics.

It's rather more obvious that you can be an SSKist without being a metaphysical constructivist. All you have to say is that scientific acceptance is socially caused, but that at least some scientific hypotheses are true or false, depending on what the independent, pre-existing world is like. Barnes and Bloor belong to this class of SSKist. In fact, they concede that non-social facts about the independent world may play a role, along with social forces, in shaping our beliefs:

> There is no need for a relativist sociology of knowledge to take any-thing other than a completely open and matter-of-fact stance toward the role of sensory stimulation. The same applies to any other of the physical, genetic or psychological and non-social causes that must eventually find a place in an overall account of knowledge. The stimula-tion by material objects when the eye is turned in a given direction is indeed a causal factor in knowledge and its role is to be understood by seeing how this cause interacts with other causes. There is no question of denying the effect on belief of the facts
>
> (Barnes and Bloor 1982: 33)

Compare this with what Steve Woolgar, an extremist among metaphysical constructivists, has to say:

> there is no sense in which we can claim that the phenomenon ... has an existence independent of its means of expression ... There is no object beyond discourse ... the organization of discourse is the object. Facts and objects in the world are inescapably textual constructions.
>
> (Woolgar 1988: 73)

Clear enough?

There are also SSKists who endorse semantic constructivism and others who don't. Knorr-Cetina doesn't. Barnes and Bloor do, as does Harry Collins (Barnes 1982; Collins 1985). In sum, the sociology of scientific knowledge can be – and is – practised both with and without adherence to any of the three constructivist theses. Constructivism is an idea (really three ideas) that arises in the course of conducting and thinking about sociologi-cal investigations of science. But, at least as I use the term, its claims go significantly beyond the basic assertion that all scientific decisions have social causes. This conclusion should be kept in mind. I'll be discussing some severe criticisms of constructivism in subsequent chapters. However damaging these criticisms may turn out to be, they will have no effect on the status of SSK.

3 The varieties of dependence

To say that facts are 'constructed' is, roughly, to say that their being facts is dependent on the occurrence of certain human actions. The negation of constructivism is thus the view that the facts are *in*dependent of human activity. According to Boyd, this is one of several theses which characterize the philosophical position of *realism*. Realism about the theoretical entities of science, for instance, entails that

> [t]he reality which scientific theories describe is largely independent of our thoughts or theoretical commitments.
>
> (Boyd 1984: 42)

In Boyd's formulation, the constructive human activity is cognitive ('thoughts or theoretical commitments'). Most (but not all) of the recently influential forms of constructivism single out social activities, such as negotiations, as the determinants of the facts about the world. As it happens, the discussion in this book is pitched at a level that doesn't require an exact specification of which human activities are supposed to be responsible for the facts. My conclusions are robust in the face of large changes to the constructans. But there's no avoiding the need to get clearer about what it means to say that facts are 'dependent' on acts.

Constructivists have had several different relations in mind when they've talked about the dependence of facts on human activity. For the moment, let's restrict the discussion to the construction of scientific facts. One sense in which scientific facts have been said to 'depend' upon human activity – the most straightforward – is that the facts are about entities and processes which are *made to take place* by the activities of scientists, and which wouldn't occur without them. Knorr-Cetina reminds us of the extent to which the events that comprise the data of science are literally and uncontroversially produced by scientists and those in their pay:

> In the laboratory, scientists operate upon (and within) a highly precon-structed artificial reality ... the source materials with which scientists work are also preconstructed. Plant and assay rats are specially grown

and selectively bred. Most of the substances and chemicals used are purified and are obtained from the industry which serves the science or from other laboratories ... In short, nowhere in the laboratory do we find the 'nature' or 'reality' which is so crucial to the descriptivist inter-pretation of inquiry: To the observer from the outside world, the labo-ratory displays itself as a site of action from which 'nature' is as much as possible excluded rather than included.

(Knorr-Cetina 1983: 119)

Let's call this thesis *material constructivism.*

Three points need to be made about material constructivism. The first is that it's incontrovertible. If the independence of scientific facts from human activity means no more than that the facts wouldn't be what they are if people didn't do certain things, then it has to be admitted all round that scientific facts are constructed. Moreover, I think it has to be admitted that the *extent* to which scientists surround themselves with entities and processes of their own making was, until recently, radically underappreci-ated by philosophers of science. One might unreflectively have supposed that the materials used by scientists in their constructions come directly from unconstructed nature. But Knorr-Cetina points out that even these materials are generally made to order by scientific suppliers. Even the use of laboratory rats doesn't constitute an intrusion of raw nature into the artificial world of the laboratory.

The second point is that it's just as obvious that there are *some* scientific facts which are *not* materially constructed in this straightforward sense. In her catalogue of scientific materials, Knorr-Cetina emphasizes the point that even the 'source materials' are preconstructed; but she strategically chooses not to carry the account further backward in time. Laboratory rats may all be constructed, but what about the mother of the first laboratory rat? The chemicals used in experiments are purified, but what are they purified *from*? At some point or other, every material-constructive recipe calls for a scoop of unreconstructed nature – or so we must say, unless and until far more drastic considerations are brought into play. Thus, even if the difference between materially constructed and unconstructed reality were of great metaphysical import, there would still be no general conclusions about the world that could be drawn from the defensible versions of material constructivism. This point is underscored by the fact that one of the foremost proponents of material constructivism – Ian Hacking (1983) – is a self-declared scientific realist.

The final point is that the distinction between materially constructed and unconstructed reality is not very interesting from a metaphysical point of view – i.e., from the perspective of wondering about what the constituents of the world may be. The hypothesis that scientific facts are materially constructed may engage our epistemological concerns: there may be reasons for suspicion about a process whereby one arrives at opinions about unconstructed nature by means of immersing oneself in a humanly constructed world. Hans Radder (1993) attributes the discovery of this epistemological problem to Bachelard. Metaphysically speaking, however, materially constructed objects are very much like natural objects. The only difference between them is that the former have a human origin. But so what? If that's what the 'construction of reality' comes to, then it's a very compelling but not very arresting hypothesis.

Let's turn to a more interesting notion of human dependence. Materially constructed objects need humans to come into existence; but they share with natural objects the property that their *continued* existence doesn't depend on the continued existence of humans. If all of humanity suddenly ceased to exist, there would still be lasers and specially bred rats – at least for a while. If a laser were to be left on at the moment of our mass extinction, there could even be laser *beams* in a world without humans. At least, this is the common-sense view of the matter. Constructivisms begin to get interesting when they assert that features of reality have this stronger form of human dependency – that they would *cease to exist* without the continued presence (and appropriate behaviour) of human agents. There are two very different types of scenarios which satisfy this criterion, which I'll call *causal* and *constitutive* constructivism. In the case of causal constructivism, ongoing human activity produces and sustains the facts about the world; in the case of constitutive constructivism, what we call 'facts about the world' are revealed to be facts about human activity.

For illustrative purposes, let's consider a particularly simple version of a causal constructivist hypothesis – the thesis that facts about the world are the products of self-fulfilling prophecies. According to this thesis, the general acceptance of a proposition by society initiates a causal process which renders the proposition true. There can be little doubt that *some* facts about the world are the products of self-fulfilling prophecies of this type. Robert Merton (1948), who invented the term 'self-fulfilling prophecy', gives the classic example of a run on the banks: if everybody thinks that there will be a run on the banks, then everybody wants to get money out of the banks before it's too late, as a result of which there's a run on the banks. Moreover, the lifetime of the phenomenon produced – the run on the banks – is coextensive with the duration of the social process that produces it: when people cease to believe that there's a run on the banks, there ceases to be a run on the banks. In this case, what's produced is itself another social fact. But it can't be ruled out *a priori* that everybody's believing in the existence of electrons somehow produces electrons. In any case, the causal constructivist thesis is clearly true for some facts. The interesting question is whether it's true for *all* facts, or for entire classes of facts whose causal construction we might not have suspected.

Like causal constructivism, the constitutive constructivist thesis is undoubtedly true of some facts. For instance, the fact that there's a social convention about stopping at red lights is *constituted* by everyone's believing that there's a social convention about stopping at red lights. The difference between such a convention and a Mertonian self-fulfilling prophecy is clear enough. Everybody's believing that there's going to be a run on the banks may *result* in that event's taking place; but the belief doesn't *constitute* a run on the banks. Something else has to happen. But for everybody to believe that there's a convention about stopping at red lights *is* for such a convention to be in place. Nothing else needs to happen. (Actually, there are many other things that need to happen. Conventions are undoubtedly more complicated than this cartoon-like characterization suggests. But the necessary additions and qualifications are themselves going to be social. The point is that for a given convention, there is a state of society which constitutes the existence of that convention.) Once again, it's at least *prima facie* possible that so-called physical facts turn out to have the same character as social conventions.

(There's a position which is intermediate between the causal and the constitutive theses: the view that the physical *supervenes* on the social, in the same sense as it is sometimes claimed that the mental supervenes on the physical. Roughly, a class of properties A supervenes on a class B if every A-type difference between events entails the existence of a corresponding B-type difference. Supervenience is a relation between phenomena which, like identity, are conceptual rather than causal; but it's weaker than out-and-out identity. I enclose this brief disquisition in parentheses because, so far as I know, no constructivist has ever suggested that the physical supervenes on the social. Moreover, I think that the issues that I'm going to discuss aren't significantly affected by the existence of this intermediate type of constructivism. But I must admit that I haven't kept this possibility unswervingly in mind as I've worked out what I wanted to say.)

For the most part, the constructivist literature seems to concern itself with the constitutive as opposed to the causal thesis. The quotation from Woolgar in the previous chapter ('there is no object beyond discourse') expresses an unambiguously constitutive point of view. Latour and Knorr-Cetina also have the constitutive thesis in mind most of the time. But all these authors occasionally lapse into causal language and imagery. Latour and Woolgar jointly write:

> We do not wish to say that facts do not exist nor that there is no such thing as reality. In this simple sense our position is not relativist. Our point is that 'out-there-ness' is the *consequence* of scientific work rather than its *cause*.
>
> (1986: 180)

Similarly, Knorr-Cetina tells us that 'science secretes an unending stream of entities and relations that make up "the world" ' (1993: 557). Secretion is, of course, a causal rather than a constitutive relation: if scientific activity secretes entities, these entities can't be *composed* of scientific activity, any more than hormones are composed of glands (nor do hormones supervene on glands). The same confounding of the causal and the constitutive occurs in the writings of some realist critics:

> A second objection concerns the strange causal powers that construc-tivism seems to assign to the mind, allowing it to ontologically consti-tute a world that doubtless existed before there even were minds.
>
> (Trout 1994: 47)

Despite frequent confoundings with both causal and material construc-tivism, it seems to me that it's the constitutive thesis that's at stake in the debate about constructivism. Moreover, although it's true that causal and constitutive constructivism make radically different claims about the world, their confounding is usually benign in practice. For the most part, the issues and arguments that arise in the analysis of either one of them have their homologous counterparts in the analysis of the other. For instance, Trout's objection, quoted above, plays itself out in much the same way whether we talk about causality or constitution (Trout's objection will be taken up in Chapter 7). This being the case, I'll restrict the subsequent discussion to the constitutive thesis.

Causal
Constitutive.   Constructive

of rule

4   The varieties of constitutive constructivisms

Constructivisms may also be distinguished by the types of facts to which they apply. Virtually everybody is a constructivist about *some* things. It's almost universally believed that certain social facts – facts about social institutions, languages, social classes, governments, legal systems, economic systems and kinship systems – are what they are by virtue of our own actions, beliefs and intentions. Non-constructivist views of these aspects of social reality are conceivable. We might, in a Platonistic vein, regard the grammar of our language as a description of a pre-existing abstract entity whose properties are discovered (rather than invented) by a special mental act. This view is at least plausible enough to have warranted an explicit repudiation by Chomsky (1986). But virtually all the self-proclaimed enemies of constructivism would be willing to concede that linguistic facts are constructed. What makes people want to call themselves 'constructivists' is that they regard the scope of our constructive activities to be significantly greater than is generally supposed.

In order to describe the extant varieties of constructivism, I've found it necessary to distinguish the following classes of facts. I don't claim that all these distinctions are coherent. In fact, I'll eventually question the coherence of some of them myself . But these are the categories in terms of which the debate about constructivism is being carried on. There are, to begin with, *scientific facts* – those that are discovered or invented (at this stage in the proceedings, you can take your pick) by the institution of science. I include here only facts of the (putatively) natural sciences. The facts of the social sciences I call *social facts*. This distinction may or may not prove to be philosophically interesting. But in any case there are issues relating to constructivism that rely on it. Both scientific facts and social facts are to be distinguished from *everyday facts*. These are the facts whose discovery or invention takes place outside the institutional boundaries of science or any other professional epistemic enterprise. One of these facts is that there's a book on my desk (the indexicals are, of course, incidental). It won't be necessary to distinguish everyday physical facts from everyday social facts.

Suppose it were shown that all scientific, social and everyday facts are constructed. It still wouldn't follow that the world is constructed *in toto*.

For one thing, it would still be possible that there are independent facts which are epistemically accessible only by means of an enterprise other than natural science, social science and the 'common sense' that gives us our everyday facts. Maybe it's Biblical fundamentalism that yields the unconstructed truth, or the Azande chicken oracle, or some procedure that no human group has yet hit upon. I won't explore the consequences of this possibility here – but not because I think it's insane to suppose that there's a way to arrive at the truth that we don't yet possess. It's just that this additional possibility doesn't make any difference to the issues I'll be discussing. So far as my agenda goes, I can let 'scientific facts' stand for the non-social facts produced by any special epistemic enterprise that goes beyond the practice of common sense.

For the same reason, I will also ignore phenomenal facts about consciousness, or sense-data, or qualia (if there are such facts to be ignored). Relative to the issues of this book, phenomenal facts play the same role as the facts of physical science: they're just a funny kind of possibly unconstructed non-social fact. There's also a constructivist literature about necessary facts, like the laws of logic. These pose problems of their own, the consideration of which will be postponed until Chapter 14. Until then I take *reality*, or *the world*, to be the sum total of all contingent facts.

Finally, it's conceivable that there are facts about the world which are inaccessible by any method available to human beings (when I say that this is conceivable, I mean that there's no obviously compelling and widely known argument to the contrary). Let's call these *noumenal facts*. A proof that all the facts that we possess and can ever possess are constructed would not yet be a proof that *the world* is (in its entirety) constructed unless it's conjoined with an argument against the possibility of unconstructed noumenal facts. This brings up an interesting – and, as far as I know, hitherto unconsidered – question about noumenal facts: granted that there may be a noumenal world, is it possible that this world, or a part of it, is socially constructed? A constructed noumenal fact would be a fact about human activity which is inaccessible to human knowledge. Perhaps some variant of the psychoanalytic notion of the unconscious would fit the bill. At any rate, the idea doesn't strike me as obviously incoherent. This means, in turn, that an argument for the existence of noumena doesn't by itself establish that there is an independent world.

Various constructivist positions may be obtained by asserting or denying the constructed nature of different combinations of scientific, social, everyday and noumenal facts. *Strong constructivism* is the thesis that all the facts we can ever possess are constructed. *Very strong constructivism* is the stronger thesis that all facts are constructed – i.e., that there is no independent reality. Strong constructivists may take any view they like of noumenal facts, including no view at all. But very strong constructivists are committed either to the denial of the noumenal or to the adventurous thesis that the noumenal is also constructible. Devitt's (1991) 'fig-leaf realism' is the conjunction of strong constructivism with the thesis that there *are* unconstructed noumenal facts. Fig-leaf realists believe that there is an independent world, but that our knowledge is restricted to our own constructions.

Weaker constructivisms are obtained by allowing that there are or may be independent elements in various classes of facts other than the noumenal. *Scientific constructivism* is the thesis which asserts only that all scientific facts are constructed. There's an ambiguity in this formulation which will loom large in the analysis to come: do scientific constructivists believe merely that all the scientific facts in our possession are constructed, or do they believe that all the scientific facts that we might ever come to possess must be constructed? I'll use 'scientific constructivism' to refer to the stronger second thesis. When I want to talk about the weaker first thesis, I'll call it *weak scientific constructivism*.

The thesis of scientific constructivism leaves it open whether social or everyday facts are independent or constructed. Consider the belief that all scientific facts are constructed, but that some non-scientific, everyday facts are independent. My name for this thesis is *instrumental constructivism*, in recognition of its close kinship to traditional instrumentalist views of science. In its narrowest sense, instrumentalism is the view that our claims about the world can be divided into the observational and the theoretical, and that only the former are truth-valuable. On this account, theoretical claims are regarded as 'merely linguistic, uninterpreted tools for systematizing observations and making predictions' (Niiniluoto 1991: 145). However, there is a broader use of 'instrumentalism' which includes any view that regards theoretical claims as epistemically or metaphysically deficient in comparison with observational claims. The deficiency may be that theoretical statements have no truth-values, or that the truth-value of theoretical claims is epistemically inaccessible, or that theoretical claims can be dispensed with by translating them into observational language. The second of these is the sense in which van Fraassen's (1980) constructive empiricism, for instance, is often reckoned to be among the instrumentalisms. Like these classical instrumentalisms, instrumental constructivism makes a distinction between a privileged and an underprivileged class of claims. The instrumental-constructivist distinction may or may not be the same as the classical distinction. To be sure, everyday facts aren't perfectly co-extensive with observational facts. But there may be an overlap. For instance, one may regard facts couched in a theory-neutral observation language to be everyday facts. If this is so, then one and the same distinction might serve to formulate both the classical instrumentalist and the instrumental-constructivist theses. This is a good place to remind the reader that an observational/non-observational distinction that serves the purposes of classical instrumentalism has been hard to come by (Maxwell 1962; Kukla 1996). There's every reason to expect that it will prove just as difficult to distinguish between scientific facts and everyday facts. As far as I know, there's been no extended discussion of this distinction in the constructivist literature. If the distinction collapses, then the constructivist brand of instrumentalism would collapse into either strong constructivism or the position that I will call 'metaphysical socialism' below.

It's also unclear whether the nature of the privilege at stake is different in instrumental constructivism and constructive empiricism. Classical instrumentalist underprivilege consists in either lacking a truth-value, or being epistemically inaccessible, or being eliminable by translation. Underprivileged claims in instrumental constructivism are those whose truth-value is determined by our own actions, rather than by the properties of an independent reality. This new form of disadvantage is clearly different from two of the three classical forms: to be constructed is not the same thing as to lack a truth-value or to be epistemically inaccessible. On the other hand, being constructed out of something else sounds very much like being reducible to something else. So both the privileged–underprivileged distinction and the nature of the privilege might be the same in instrumental constructivism and the classical instrumentalisms. One might therefore suspect that the two doctrines would generate very much the same dialectic. That this is actually the case will be demonstrated in Chapter 9.

But is this type of instrumentalism really a live option among construc-tivists, or is it a straw-person position? Latour and Woolgar (1986) don't tell us explicitly whether the process of negotiation whereby scientific facts are constructed is peculiar to science, or whether similar processes among non-scientists constitute everyday facts as well. The tenor of their discussion suggests a strong-constructivist reading (this will be documented in Chapter 9). But it's my impression that, as time has gone by, Latour (but not Woolgar) has come to sound more and more like an instrumentalist. Consider the following passage:

> [I]n the first frame, nature and society are the *causes* that are used to explain the delicate content of scientific activity. It is the opposite in our frame, since the activity of scientists and engineers and of all their human and non-human allies is the cause, of which various states of nature and societies are the consequence … The definition of observ-ables is entirely different in the two frames. In the first one, social scien-tists were allowed to use a unobservable state of society and a definition of social relations to account for scientific work – or to alternate by using an equally unobservable state of nature. In the other frame the only observables are the traces left by objects, arguments, skills, and tokens circulating through the collective.
>
> (Callon and Latour 1992: 350–1)

Don't ask me what the 'traces left by objects' are, or what 'arguments, skills, and tokens circulating through the collective' look like when they're being observed. Whatever these things may be, it seems that Callon and Latour espouse the instrumentalist view that both scientific and social facts are constructed, but that there are some other facts – those, for instance, relating to 'the traces left by objects' – that are what they are independently of our constructive activity. If this is a correct reading, then the later Latour's philosophy of science must be considered a species of instrumentalist constructivism. Moreover, there can be little doubt that the distinction between 'traces left by objects' and 'states of nature' is going to be at least as problematic as the much-maligned classical distinction between the theoretical and the observational.

There's one more constructivist position that needs to be delineated – the one that maintains that the only independent facts are social facts. On this account, the non-social world, however conceived, is constructed out of social episodes. This view is explicitly repudiated in the passage by Callon and Latour quoted above. Yet the distinction between the social and the non-social which underlies this position doesn't seem as hopeless as the distinction between scientific facts and everyday facts. Moreover, the thesis in question has the virtue of relative novelty. Its contemplation tells us that materialism and phenomenalism don't exhaust the class of conceivable monisms (recall that I refer to a proposition as 'conceivable' if there is no compelling and well-known refutation of it). It's conceivable that the ultimate constituents of reality are social episodes such as negotiations and agreements, and that both the physical and mental worlds are constructions out of this primordial social material. The proper name for such a view – the etymological parallel to 'materialism' and 'idealism' – is obviously *socialism*. Since this term already enjoys a somewhat different usage, we may have to speak of the constructivist thesis as *metaphysical socialism*.

It's possible to make the same types of distinctions among metaphysical socialisms as those between strong constructivism, very strong constructivism and fig-leaf realism. Corresponding to strong constructivism would be the thesis that social facts are independent, and that all other facts that may come into our possession are constructed. The analogue to very strong constructivism would be the view that social facts are independent, and that all other facts are constructed, whether or not they are within our ken. Finally, the socialist counterpart to fig-leaf realism is the view that social facts are independent, that all other ascertainable facts are constructed, but that there are also unconstructed noumenal facts which may be non-social. These distinctions won't come up again.

It might be questioned whether metaphysical socialism really is a conceivable position. Aren't social facts the clearest example we have of constructed facts? For example, isn't a social convention constructed out of individual beliefs and intentions? Didn't I begin this very chapter with the claim that social conventions and the like are almost universally regarded as constructed out of individual beliefs and intentions? The claim stands; but it doesn't, by itself, entail that metaphysical socialism is false. It can be maintained – in fact, many people, constructivists and non-constructivists alike, *do* maintain – that supposedly individualistic facts about beliefs and intentions are themselves constructed out of more basic social facts. They reject the idea that all social events can be reduced to or otherwise constructed out of the events that comprise the subject matter of individual psychology, regardless of whether psychology is conceived to be behaviouristic or mentalistic. They claim, for instance, that it's incoherent to suppose that an individual human being could be said to have a belief or an intention outside the context of a social milieu. If this is right, then the construction of a social convention out of beliefs and intentions is merely a case of constructing one social fact out of other social facts. And that's why this construction doesn't make any problems for socialism.

The *locus classicus* for this line of thinking is Wittgenstein's (1953) *Philosophical Investigations*, wherein some social facts are regarded as unanalysable into anything else. Believing and intending are parts of our 'form of life', and there's no accounting for forms of life other than in their own terms. Explanations have to come to an end somewhere. Wittgenstein pointed to, though he did not explicitly endorse, the stance of metaphysical socialism. To be a socialist, one has to affirm not only the Wittgensteinian doctrine that there's no deeper non-social analysis of some social phenomena, but also that there *is* a deeper *social* analysis of all *non-social* phenomena.

Are there any socialists among contemporary social constructivists? Harry Collins comes close. According to Collins, the facts of natural science are social constructions, but the social world should be treated 'as real and as something about which we can have sound data' (1981: 217). Collins specifies, however, that this is a methodological rather than a metaphysical doctrine. He believes that the strong constructivist claim that *all* facts are constructed is incoherent. He also wants to maintain that the facts of physics are constructed. Finally, he doesn't want to say that the social world is really more real than the physical world. His solution is to say that, in order to avoid incoherence, we must *treat* the social world as unconstructed, even though it really is constructed. An unsympathetic critic might note that this manoeuvre provides us with a general recipe for resolving any and all conceptual problems without ever changing our opinions: if A conflicts with B and we don't want to reject either of them, just say the assumption of not-B is merely a methodological requirement!

Here's a simple argument to the effect that metaphysical socialism is incoherent. By definition, a fact is constructed (in the constitutive sense) if and only if it's constituted out of human actions. Metaphysical socialists want to say that some facts about human actions, conceived as social events, are unconstructed. But this is to say that some human actions aren't constituted by human actions. This is obviously impossible, because everything is trivially constituted by itself. Therefore socialism is incoherent.

This argument reveals an infelicity in the terminology; but it doesn't cut very deep. It may be trivially true that everything is constructed out of itself. But there's a big difference between constructing a chair by putting together the legs, seat and back, and constructing it by starting with a complete chair, performing the null action and coming up with a chair. One of several equally easy ways to take care of this problem is to stipulate that a 'construction' involves putting together at least two separate pieces into a new whole. This allows us to continue to say that socialism entails that some social events are unconstructed.

The fact that metaphysical socialism is a monistic alternative to materialism and phenomenalism is worthy of some elaboration. The history of the more familiar metaphysical theses tells us what we might expect to find if the pros and cons of socialism were seriously debated for a while. To begin with, we would expect to get the same range of doctrines as has been generated in the earlier debates. A socialist could claim

1   that physical facts can be *reduced* to social facts, or
2   that talk about the physical world comprises a *theory* about the social, or
3   that the relation between the physical and the social is one of several flavours of *supervenience* (with the physical supervening on the social).

My guess is that the course of these debates would recapitulate that of its predecessors: strong reductive theses are going to turn out to be untenable, and the other theses are going to encounter severe problems, but none so conclusive as to eradicate all hope for success among its proponents. The main lesson to be learned from this comparison isn't that socialism is likely to be beset by problems (though it will be), but that it will probably prove to be just as defensible as the more traditional metaphysical stances.

The contemplation of socialism sheds new light on the status of the traditional metaphysical positions. So long as the only candidates are materialism, phenomenalism and a dualism of the material and the phenomenal, it's easy to fall in with the assumption that the material–phenomenal distinction exhaustively dichotomizes the range of conceivable existents. After all, our conceptual world is replete with exhaustive dichotomies, such as good versus evil, darkness versus light, and so on. When we add the social as a *tertium quid*, however, the situation changes drastically. We're not so ready to presuppose that trichotomies are exhaustive. There's a Law of Two and Three that operates in our mental functioning. When a hypothesis posits two kinds of things, we're content to accept the posit. We're not prone to wonder whether there's a third category of moral evaluation besides good and evil. But when a hypothesis posits three kinds of things, we immediately want to know: why three? Why not four, or five, or seven? Why three dimensions of space, as opposed to four or seven? Certainly, the material, the phenomenal and the social don't strike us as capable of being generated by a small number of underlying dimensions. They seem rather to be drawn out of a much broader set of possibilities. When we finally meet up with extraterrestrials, it may turn out that what they take to be the furniture of the world is not material nor phenomenal nor yet social.

supervenience

metaphysical noumena —
grounded in sociological sensibility
— science a collective social activity.
Involving cooperation, negotiation, critique,
competition for resources

tertium quid

5 The empirical case for constructivism

How do constructivists argue for their position? Some of their writings explicitly contain philosophical arguments. The most important of these will be discussed in Chapter 6. But constructivists are (for the most part) sociologists, and sociology is an empirical science. It's not surprising that they often represent themselves as having been led to their global views by the outcome of their own empirical research. Constructivists are wont to claim that, when we look at scientific activity with an unprejudiced eye, constructivism is the hypothesis that best explains what we see. The strategy of this empirical argument is laid out by Nelson (1994):

> By emphasizing aspects of the actual processes of scientific decision making, aspects that are often inconspicuous in the reconstructions of philosophers, constructivists have attempted to make the alleged superiority of constructivism into a matter upon which a kind of empirical evidence can be brought to bear. In other words, they try not to understand the dispute as a purely philosophical one ... They think that the history itself, when accurately presented, supports the hypothesis of constructivism more strongly than the hypothesis of rationalism.
>
> (Nelson 1994: 537)

By 'constructivism', Nelson means the conjunction of the views that I've called metaphysical constructivism and epistemic relativism. By 'rationalism' he means realism and epistemic absolutism. Nelson continues:

> Constructivism and rationalism are to be treated in the manner of competing explanatory hypotheses. The historical episodes are to be treated as data or evidence on the basis of which philosophers, sociologists and other interested parties are to choose between the hypotheses. In short, we are to take seriously the idea that we are practicing the science of science ... constructivists are claiming that prevailing standards of scientific rationality ... favor the constructivist hypothesis.
>
> (537)

Before we examine this constructivist claim, it's necessary to lay down certain ground rules for the discussion. As Nelson's nomenclature suggests, most metaphysical constructivists are also relativists who deny that there are universally valid standards governing the use of scientific evidence. Obviously, this view is going to impinge on the dialectic engendered by the empirical argument. There are several directions in which constructivists-cum-relativists might move. If the empirical argument for constructivism should succeed, they might regard this success either as a direct confirmation of their constructivism or as a *reductio ad absurdum* of the realism-cum-absolutism of their opponents. If the empirical argument should fail, they might take refuge in their relativism, claiming that the argument's failure relative to currently accepted standards of scientific evaluation doesn't compel them to give up its conclusion. These issues are not at stake in this chapter. Whatever constructivists ultimately want to make of it, the claim is, as Nelson puts it, that 'prevailing standards of scientific rationality' support the constructivist hypothesis. For the purpose of evaluating the empirical argument, problems relating to relativism, reflexivity and the like are to be shelved, and we're to rely on the sorts of considerations that would be deemed appropriate in a normal controversy between opposing groups of contemporary scientists.

What are the data that supposedly warrant the constructivist thesis? Most of the relevant investigations rely on the document-centred methods of historical scholarship. Shapin (1982) provides a survey of this body of research. There's also a smaller group of studies that use the method of participant observation: the sociologist insinuates himself or herself into the community of scientists to be studied and directly observes their activity. One of the pioneering works in this genre is Latour and Woolgar's *Laboratory Life* (1979; I'll usually refer to the 1986 second edition). My main purpose in this chapter will be to point out some deficiencies in the *form* of the empirical argument. For this purpose, it isn't necessary to conduct an exhaustive review of the literature. In fact, I will soon be granting, for the sake of the argument, that the sociological data to which constructivists appeal are as good as they can possibly be. Nevertheless, it makes for more interesting reading if the general discussion is related to a concrete case study. I've chosen Latour and Woolgar's enormously influential study for a closer look.

Latour and Woolgar describe their undertaking as a project in the *anthropology* of a neglected culture – the culture of the laboratory scientist:

> Since the turn of the century, scores of men and women have penetrated deep forests, lived in hostile climates and weathered hostility, boredom, and disease in order to gather the remnants of so-called primitive societies. By contrast to the frequency of these anthropological excursions, relatively few attempts have been made to penetrate the intimacy of life

among tribes which are much nearer at hand. This is perhaps surprising in view of the reception and importance attached to their product in modern civilised societies: we refer, of course, to tribes of scientists and to their production of science. Whereas we now have fairly detailed knowledge of the myths and circumcision rituals of exotic tribes, we remain relatively ignorant of the details of equivalent activity among tribes of scientists

(1986: 17)

Latour and Woolgar portray themselves as radical empiricists who, eschewing all preconceptions about their subject matter, resolve to be instructed only by what they directly observe. In particular, they will not presuppose that their subjects are engaged in a rational pursuit:

we regard it as instructive to apprehend as strange those aspects of scientific activity which are readily taken for granted ... We take the apparent superiority of the members of our laboratory in technical matters to be insignificant ... This is similar to an anthropologist's refusal to bow before the knowledge of a primitive sorcerer. There are ... no a priori reasons for supposing that the scientist's practice is any more rational than that of outsiders.

(29–30)

As if to prove their lack of theoretical prejudices, they begin with a drastically unselected grab-bag of observations:

6 mins. 20 secs ... The staccato noise of typewriting can be heard from the lobby.
9 mins. Julius comes in eating an apple ...
9 mins. 30 secs ... They talk in John's office and laugh.

(1986: 15–16)

This extreme even-handedness is not maintained for long, however. Theoretical hypotheses are introduced early in the text, and observational reports are soon restricted to events that have a bearing on the authors' views. To proceed in this manner is entirely in accord with the 'prevailing standards of scientific rationality' which are presumed by the empirical argument. Like B.F. Skinner's, Latour and Woolgar's radical empiricism is only a pretence.

The scientific episode that Latour and Woolgar observed was Roger Guillemin's discovery (they will say: construction) of the chemical structure of thyrotropin releasing hormone (TRH). This substance, which is produced by the hypothalamus, triggers the production of thyrotropin, which in turn governs the activity of the thyroid gland. Guillemin's undertaking was made particularly difficult by the fact that the amounts of TRH secreted by the hypothalamus are extraordinarily minute (about 2×10^{-8} grams per hypothalamus). About 500 tons of pigs' brains were needed to extract a single milligram of 80-percent TRH. Even so, the amount was too small for the usual sorts of chemical analyses to be undertaken. Guillemin and his team had to proceed by indirection: they synthesized a substance whose properties matched those of their TRH sample and inferred that the structure of TRH was identical to the structure of the synthesized substance. Guillemin received the Nobel Prize (along with Andrew Schally) as much for the methodological novelty of analysis by synthesis as for their actual discovery.

Latour and Woolgar claim that what they observed in Guillemin's laboratory calls for a constructivist explanation. Both friends (Hacking 1988) and foes (Brown 1989) of *Laboratory Life* have alike laid particular stress on certain peculiarities relating to the initial sample of TRH. Latour and Woolgar argue that the technique of analysis by synthesis presupposes that we have an uncontested sample of the substance to be synthesized. Assuming that we all know that the initial sample is TRH, it's reasonable to infer that the structure of TRH is identical to the structure of a synthesized substance with the same chemical properties as the sample. But in fact there were no pre-existing criteria of identity for TRH. Different laboratories championed different bioassays. But if, in answer to the question 'What is the structure of TRH?', you get to choose the criterion for TRH-hood, then the answer is not ordained by an independent nature. It's rather like asking how long a metre is prior to the establishment of metric standards. There is an answer, but it's not dictated by nature. You don't *discover* the length of a metre; you *decide* on it. This is how Latour and Woolgar regard Guillemin's putative discovery.

Whatever we make of this argument, it's noteworthy that Latour and Woolgar's anthropological activities play no essential role in its formulation. The argument could have been conceived and advanced solely on the basis of the relevant journal publications. But still, does it achieve its purpose? Brown responds to it by denying that the selection of a bioassay was analogous to the selection of a metric standard. He concedes that there were no prior criteria of identity for TRH, but maintains that the choice of assay was nevertheless constrained by certain independent facts of nature:

> In the particular bioassay adopted, rats were used instead of mice because mice are thought to have more sensitive thyroids; males are used because it is thought the female reproductive cycle might interfere; the rats used are about 80 days old because it is thought that at that age the thyrotropin content of the pituitary is greatest; etc. ... Each feature of the bioassay seems to be getting some sort of justification. It may be a fallible justification, but it is there none the less.
>
> (Brown 1989: 85)

This controversy over the status of the bioassay is important. But it's irrelevant to the subject matter of my book. My aim is to assess the thesis that *all* facts, or at least all scientific facts, are constructed. Nobody denies that *some* facts are constructed. But there's no way to parlay the bioassay argument into any of the more general conclusions. For one thing, the bioassay anomaly is a highly specific configuration of circumstances that don't arise in the course of most scientific investigations. The argument simply doesn't apply to most research. Moreover, the argument doesn't show – or even purport to show – that Guillemin didn't discover *any* independent facts. For the sake of the argument, let's grant that the choice of bioassay was the result of a social negotiation in which nature played no part. Then the fact that the chosen sample was TRH could reasonably be described as a constructed fact. It's less clear whether, on the bioassay argument alone, the Nobel-Prize-winning fact that TRH has the structure pyroGlu-His-Pro-NH$_2$ is constructed. And it's undoubtedly an independent fact, so far as the bioassay argument goes, that there is a substance in pigs' brains which has the structure pyroGlu-His-Pro-NH$_2$. This discovery may not, by itself, be worth a Nobel Prize. But it's a scientific fact that eludes the reach of the bioassay argument.

In order to make an empirical case for constructivism, what's needed is the observation of certain features of scientific activity that warrant a constructivist interpretation *and that are arguably universally implicated in the epistemic decisions of scientists*. Latour and Woolgar report having observed such a feature. They begin with the unsurprising observation that scientists uniformly act so as to secure the reward of peer recognition. In this respect, scientists are pretty much like stage magicians, football-players and other groups of professionals. Just for that reason, however, approval-seeking fails to account for the *differences* between science and football. In particular, it doesn't explain what becomes a scientific fact. What does explain it, according to Latour and Woolgar, is the hypothesis that science is a form of commerce that trades in the commodity of *credibility*:

> it would be wrong to regard the receipt of reward as the ultimate objective of scientific activity. In fact, the receipt of reward is just one small portion of a large cycle of credibility investment. The essential feature of this cycle is the gain in credibility which enables reinvestment and the further gain of credibility. Consequently, there is no ultimate objective to scientific investment other than the continual redeployment of accumulated resources. It is in this sense that we liken scientists' credibility to a cycle of capital investment.
>
> (Latour and Woolgar 1986: 197–8)

On this account, a successful scientist is one who has accumulated large reserves of credibility. This doesn't mean that scientists are always and uniformly *motivated* to increase their credibility. There's nothing in Latour and Woolgar's hypothesis that rules out the possibility of a senior scientist making a magnanimous gift of credibility to a younger colleague without expectation of return. This would be akin to a capitalist engaging in genuine philanthropy. Nevertheless, the business of business is money, and the business of science is credibility. Scientific facts are constructed by investing large amounts of credibility in certain formulas. If virtually all the experts in a discipline endorse the same formula, it's invested with so much credibility that it becomes almost impossible to overthrow. This is what gives constructed scientific facts the 'out-there-ness', the resistance to negation, that we take to be the hallmark of the real.

What is the anthropological evidence for this account? It's the occurrence of dialogues like these:

L:	Look at these figures, it's not bad.
K:	Well, believe in my experience, when it's not much more above 100, it's not good, it's noise.
L:	The noise is pretty consistent though.
K:	It does not change much, but with this noise you can't convince people … I mean good people.

(Latour and Woolgar 1986: 200)

I bet you the peptide is going to do nothing … this is the confidence I have in my friend T. [C squeezed the syringe and enjoined the rat]: O.K., Charles T., tell us. [A few minutes passed.] See, nothing happened … if anything the rat is even stiffer [sigh]. Ah, my friend T … I went to his laboratory in New York and saw his records … which lead to publication … it made me feel uncomfortable.

(202)

Commenting on the first exchange, Latour and Woolgar remark:

From the perspective of some epistemologists, we would expect the reliability of data to be an issue quite distinctly separated from the evaluation of individuals in the field. Thus, the assessment of data should not be so obviously linked to the rhetorical operation of convincing others and should vary neither according to the individual who is doing the interpreting nor according to the audience to whom the results are addressed. Nevertheless, examples such as the above reveal that scientists frequently make connections between these superficially foreign issues. In fact, such issues are all part of one cycle of credibility.

(200)

Of the second passage, they write:

This incident underscores the common conflation of colleague and his substance: the credibility of the proposal and the proposer are identical.

(202)

Obviously, the fit between observation and theory is much looser here than in, say, physics. Given the information provided by authors, it's a judgment call whether there really is a common conflation between the credibility of the proposal and that of the proposer, or whether the conversants are merely engaged in idle chatter as they go about their work. (By 'idle chatter' I mean talk that doesn't affect the content of the ultimate research report.) Exponents of the prevailing standards of scientific rationality are also going to worry about a number of other points. They might wonder whether the authors have fallen prey to the temptation to suppress observations that didn't fit well with their theoretical predilections, or whether they simply failed to notice them. (Doesn't anyone in the lab ever appeal to an absolute methodological principle?) They might also question whether it's appropriate to take the inductive leap from these data to the view that *all* scientific activity is consistent with the credibility hypothesis. Maybe there's something peculiar and unrepresentative about Guillemin's crew, or about endocrinology, or about the biological sciences. But these are all secondary issues, potentially resolvable by more and better empirical research in SSK. Nelson (1994) discusses a more fundamental shortcoming of the empirical argument, to which I now turn.

It's Nelson's view that the data of SSK *are* uniformly amenable to a constructivist interpretation. He thinks that constructivism can explain everything that has happened in science, because it can explain anything that conceivably *could* happen in science – the thesis of social construction provides us with such enormous explanatory latitude that there's virtually no human activity that's inconsistent with it. But, according to Nelson, the same is true of the 'rationalists'' explanations:

> it is virtually impossible that there not be a retrospective account that renders scientific decisions uniquely rational.

> (1994: 546)

For instance, it's easy to imagine a rationalist account of Latour and Woolgar's observations: the perennial preoccupation with credibility is due to the fact that individual scientists have to rely on the reports of others for almost all their scientific information. An abiding concern for the reliability of their informants would therefore be expected – perhaps even predicted – by a rationalist view. Even the bartering in credibilities isn't obviously an irrational way to arrive at warranted opinions about an independent reality. This account of the matter (minus the last, but necessary, point about the trade in credibility) is in fact advanced by Brown (1989).

The counterpoint between Latour–Woolgar and Brown is echoed in countless debates in the field of science studies. For instance, there's the debate between Pickering, the constructivist, and Franklin, the rationalist, on the acceptance of the standard model of electroweak processes in the face of what appeared to be incompatible experimental evidence. Pickering

(1984, 1991) tells a social story about institutional divisions and status relations between the atomic physics and high-energy physics communities. Franklin (1990) tells a story about rational inferences to the best explanation. Or compare Shapin and Cantor on phrenology. Shapin (1975) shows how the rise and fall of phrenology can be understood as manifestations of a clash between social classes, and Cantor (1975) shows how it can be understood in rationalist terms. Et cetera.

The moral that Nelson draws from this state of affairs is that the issue between constructivists and rationalists isn't a scientific issue at all:

> insofar as there is real material for dispute between constructivists and rationalists, it does not concern the actual history. It is, instead, a philosophical dispute that can be settled only with purely philosophical arguments.
>
> (Nelson 1994: 546)

I have some reservations about Nelson's moral. The situation as Nelson depicts it is one that routinely surfaces in the history of normal science: if it's possible to devise both constructivist and rationalist explanations for every episode in scientific history, then constructivism and rationalism are *empirically equivalent theories*, like the standard Schrödinger–Heisenberg quantum mechanics and David Bohm's quantum theory. To be sure, one can't settle the conflict between empirically equivalent rivals by doing empirical research. What this situation precipitates is *theoretical debate* wherein the conceptual properties of theories – their simplicity, their prospects for unification with other favoured theories, etc. – are analysed and evaluated. Nelson is right to suppose that the means for resolving the constructivism–rationalism dispute have to be non-empirical. But to call them 'purely philosophical' is to suggest, misleadingly, that these means must transcend those that are routinely deployed in the conduct of everyday science. I take this to be a friendly amendment to Nelson's analysis. His main point stands: if both constructivism and rationalism can explain everything that happens in science, then constructivist case studies, however numerous, aren't going to clinch the point. Nor will rationalist tales, however numerous, add up to a victory for rationalism. The answer simply won't be found in the data of history or anthropology of science.

But is it true that constructivism and rationalism can each explain all the data? There have been claims to the contrary on both sides. In Chapter 8, I will consider several claims in the philosophical literature to the effect that there are features of scientific practice that elude the constructivists' explanatory net. In Chapter 11, I'll make some suggestions of my own along those lines. At the present juncture, however, I will discuss only the converse proposition that there are features of scientific practice that can't be explained rationalistically. Constructivists point to the plethora of unsolved problems that have been encountered in the course of trying to provide rational justification for scientific decisions. Fine (1996), for instance, reports (without endorsing) the polemical use by constructivists of the underdetermination of theories by data, the theory-ladenness of observation and the Duhem thesis, according to which falsification in science is necessarily inconclusive. The problem pointed to by each of these phenomena is that the rules of rationality have never been formulated precisely enough to single out the unique course which was actually taken in the history of science. Hence rationalism fails to explain the facts of scientific history; and hence the constructivist explanation has no rival:

> Ultimately the sociologist must broach sociological factors to explain why some beliefs in science are accepted by the actors and others rejected ... In other words, it must be shown how interpretative flexibility vanishes from scientific findings ... Given that epistemological/methodological canons do not conclusively settle this matter, the sociologist must offer some alternative to explain how agreement arises in science.
>
> (Pinch 1986: 21)

I call this the argument from *the underdetermination of theories by rational considerations*, or UTRC for short.

Here are three ways to criticize the UTRC argument. The first line of attack is Laudan's (1996). Laudan maintains that the rationality of scientific decisions doesn't necessarily depend on their being produced by the application of an explicit rule. For instance, there is no algorithm for measuring the generality or scope of a scientific theory; nevertheless, everybody agrees that Newtonian mechanics is a theory of broader scope than, say, Sheldon's theory of body types. I don't think that this counter-argument is very persuasive. For one thing, I doubt that that there is any proposition which commands universal (or even near-universal) assent, so long as the voting population includes schizophrenics, members of exotic non-Western cultures and extraterrestrials. Moreover, it isn't easy to see how we might disenfranchise these dissenting constituencies without begging the question against the relativists. But there are other, more telling criticisms of UTRC waiting in the wings.

The second criticism is that the UTRC argument, if sound, shows only that *some* scientific decisions can't be explained rationalistically. The underdetermination of theories by data, for instance, entails (let us agree) that the choice between two empirically equivalent theories isn't rationally founded. But it says nothing about the choice between two theories that make opposite predictions. Similarly, each of the other cited problems with rationalistic explanations has its own less-than-universal sphere of application. To show that *no* scientific choices can be explained rationalistically would require more than an enumeration of various categories of problematic decisions. One would also need an argument showing that all scientific decisions fall into one or another of the listed categories. Once again, a listing of problematic cases shows no more than that some (perhaps many) scientific decisions can't be explained rationalistically. But this is all the manoeuvring room that rationalists require. In order to be in the running, constructivists have to be able to explain any and all episodes in scientific history. But it isn't necessary for rationalists to match that feat; they can afford to admit that some facts, or even very many facts, are socially constructed. Their rationalism is safe so long as there are at least a few scientific decisions which are best explained rationalistically.

Finally, constructivism has another explanatory rival to contend with besides the alternative that Nelson calls 'rationalism'. In order to describe this rival, I need to unravel two conceptual knots that I've let ride in my discussion so far. The first is that I've been referring interchangeably to 'constructivist' and to 'social' explanations of scientific activity. These aren't necessarily the same thing. Recall from Chapter 2 that one can maintain that all scientific decisions are socially caused without thereby committing oneself either to metaphysical constructivism or to relativism. This conceptual option provides us with a third way of explaining the putative data of SSK which is intermediate between the constructivist and the rationalist theses. Nelson's 'rationalists' insist that the best explanation for (at least some of) the epistemic decisions of science makes no references to social factors. The constructivists insist that social factors are always involved in the best explanations for the epistemic decisions of science. But non-constructivist SSKists could very well say the same thing. Even if constructivists are right about the universal necessity of social explanation, it doesn't necessarily follow that their particular brand of social explanation – their thesis that the social activities of scientists *constitute* scientific facts – is indicated. The most favourable data that constructivists can hope to obtain for their thesis are one-to-one correlations between types of scientific decisions and the social circumstances in which the decisions are made. But such data will *always* be compatible with the non-constructivist view that the social circumstances *cause* the decision to be made as it is, but that the decision is nevertheless either correct or incorrect depending on the properties of an independent nature, and that it's either warranted or unwarranted on the basis of absolute epistemic standards. For instance, one can accept Latour and Woolgar's thesis that all scientific decisions are made on the basis of credibility negotiations without buying into the constructivist addendum that the scientific facts that the decisions are about are constituted by these negotiations.

By endorsing realism and absolutism, the non-constructivist social explanation qualifies as a 'rationalist' explanation in the sense of Nelson. But it's not the rationalist explanation that Nelson pits against constructivism. Here's the second conceptual knot that needs unravelling. In my discussion up to this point, I've sometimes equated rationalism with the conjunction of realism and absolutism, and sometimes with the aforementioned conjunction *plus* the view that the best explanation for (some) scientific decisions is one that adverts to absolutely rational principles and to properties of an independent reality. The hypothesis that scientific decisions are socially caused but that scientific facts aren't constructed is rationalistic in the first sense, but not in the second. The payoff for all our unravelling is this: the empirical equivalence between the constructivist and what Nelson calls the 'rationalist' explanation is conjectural at best; but the empirical equivalence between constructivism and a non-constructivist thesis of universal social determination is beyond doubt. There are no possible data relating to scientific activity that could favour one of these views over the other. This doesn't mean that constructivism can't win. But it does establish that it can't win by means of the empirical argument alone.

Now let's assume not only that every episode in the history of science has a constructivist (not just social) explanation, but also that the constructivist explanation is the best one available in every case. Then, by the current standards of scientific rationality, we should all accept the weak scientific constructivist thesis that all the facts of science are constructed. But these assumptions still fall drastically short of establishing what some constructivists are wont to insinuate: that we live in a constructed reality. This thesis – the one dubbed 'very strong constructivism' in Chapter 4 – entails that there are no unconstructed noumenal facts. But the existence or non-existence of noumenal facts obviously isn't an issue that can be settled by normal scientific work – i.e., empirical research and ordinary theoretical argumentation. At the very least, the case for very strong constructivism would have to include an argument against the existence of an unconstructed noumenal world. There are arguments of this sort around – verificationist arguments, for instance. But these are not the sorts of arguments that occur in the course of conducting normal science. Nelson's judgment applies here without qualification: very strong constructivism is 'a philosophical dispute that can be settled only with purely philosophical arguments'.

For that matter, the scientific study of scientific activity isn't, by itself, going to establish the thesis of merely strong (as opposed to very strong) constructivism either. This is the thesis which asserts that all the facts that can ever be ascertained are constructed, and which says nothing about the noumenal world. The scientific study of scientific behaviour can't establish this thesis because it's conceivable that scientists construct all their facts, but that the Azande don't. To investigate the thesis of strong constructivism, one would have to observe not only scientists' behaviour, but also that of all social groups that engage in epistemic enterprises – including the behaviour of lay persons engaged in the common-sense reasoning whereby everyday facts are certified. And even if we did that, and found that everybody had always constructed their facts, we still wouldn't have established strong constructivism. The problem *isn't* one of projecting these past observations into the future – it would be just as inappropriate to invoke philosophical problems about induction here as it would be in the midst of a normal-science debate in geology. Let's allow that our observations of human behaviour give us sufficient grounds to conclude that the facts possessed by human beings always have been and always *will* be constructed. Even so, it would still be possible that there exists an epistemic enterprise which never has been and never will be practised by human beings and which involves the independent properties of reality in an ineliminable way. Strong constructivists don't just want to claim that all the facts that we ever *will* possess are constructed; they want to say that all the facts that we could *possibly* possess are constructed. But such possibility claims are not within the purview of science. They're philosophical if anything is.

What about the thesis that I've dubbed 'scientific constructivism' – the claim that all possible scientific facts are constructed? This thesis falls short of *strong* constructivism by restricting its claim to scientific facts, as opposed to all non-noumenal facts. But it goes beyond the *weak* scientific constructivist claim that all scientific facts have been constructed, and even beyond the inductive generalization of this claim to the hypothesis that all past, present and future scientific facts are constructed. This last claim about scientists is compatible with the hypothesis that science provides a method for arriving at the truth about the independent properties of reality, but that scientists have been running – and will continue to run – a *racket*. They purport to do one thing but instead do another. Instead of tracking the independent properties of nature, they determine their facts by negotiation. The scientific study of how scientists behave doesn't, by itself, inform us of what scientists *might* do under more ideal circumstances. One couldn't ascertain what scientists ideally might do merely by conducting scientific investigations into the behaviour of actual scientists. One would have to study *science* as a system of ideas and precepts. That is to say, one would have to do philosophy of science. *Weak* scientific constructivism is, as its proponents rightly claim, a scientific hypothesis in the sociology of science. But scientific constructivism *tout court* isn't just a sociological hypothesis – it's a hypothesis in the philosophy of science.

To recapitulate: the sociological study of scientific behaviour leads at most to weak scientific constructivism. If the scientific case for this thesis were to be sound, it would expose a monumental scandal of several centuries' duration. It would be very big news. But this is the limit of what empirical studies in the sociology of science might be able to tell us about science. The stronger and more exotic claims about the construction of reality are not within the purview of sociology. This conclusion might have been expected from the start. It shouldn't come as a surprise that questions about the nature of the world and the status of science can't be settled just by looking at how people behave.

6 The *a priori* case for constructivism

Despite indulgences in the rhetoric of radical empiricism, Latour does present something like a philosophical argument for constructivism. In *Science in Action*, he lists seven 'rules of method', which describe 'what a priori decisions should be made in order to consider all of the empirical facts provided by the special disciplines as being part of the domain of "science, technology and society" ' (1987: 17). Among the *a priori* decisions is the following:

> *Rule 3*. Since the settlement of a controversy is the *cause* of Nature's representation, not its consequence, we can never use this consequence, Nature, to explain how and why a controversy has been settled.
>
> (1987: 258)

Which of our several grades of constructivism is this '*a priori* decision' intended to support? It arises in the context of a discussion of scientists' practices, which suggests that the thesis being supported is scientific constructivism. But the claim sounds as though it was intended to apply to any and all epistemic practices. Surely the settlement of a controversy in everyday life, or in Azande practice, is neither more nor less the cause of Nature's representation than it is in science. So perhaps it's an argument (or a 'decision') for strong constructivism. In any case, it's clearly not an argument for *very* strong constructivism, since there's no incompatibility between its conclusion and the hypothesis of an unconstructed noumenal world.

Despite its being referred to as a 'decision', Rule 3 sounds very much like an argument: the antecedent is a 'since'-clause, which suggests that it's supposed to motivate our acceptance of the consequent. As an argument, however, Rule 3 is a *non sequitur*. The fact that the settlement of a controversy is the cause of 'Nature's representation' may mean that *Nature's representation* can't be used to explain how a controversy is settled; but it doesn't mean that *Nature* can't be appealed to in this regard. To be sure, Latour believes that Nature's representation is *constitutive* of Nature itself. But that's supposed to be his *conclusion*. It's patently circular to appeal to the constitutive thesis in its own defence.

Another feature of this argument is that, if it's accepted, then it renders the empirical argument superfluous. Rule 3 amounts to no less than the claim that constructivism is true and that realism is false. To accept Rule 3 *is* to be a constructivist. The *a priori* decision we're being asked to accept is so strong that it obviates Latour's anthropological appeal to the facts about what scientists actually do. If Latour used Rule 3 as a guiding methodological precept in reporting his anthropological observations of science, then there's no possibility that these observations might *not* have supported constructivism. So far as the constructivist thesis is concerned, he might as well not have spent all those tedious months washing bottles in Guillemin's laboratory.

As far as I can tell, Rule 3 embodies the *only* philosophical argument for constructivism that's been formulated to date. To be sure, there are many other arguments to be found in the literature generated by self-styled 'constructivists'. But these belong to the following two classes. First there are arguments relating to the deficiencies of competing 'rationalistic' explanations of scientific decisions. Characteristic of this class is the argument from the underdetermination of theories by data. These arguments, even if successful, don't yet establish the constructivist thesis because there are explanations of scientific decisions which are both non-rationalistic and non-constructivist (see Chapter 5). Secondly, there are arguments having to do with relativism and semantic constructivism – doctrines which are at least *prima facie* independent of metaphysical constructivism (see Chapter 1). The only direct arguments for metaphysical constructivism that I discern in the constructivist literature are the empirical argument discussed in Chapter 5 and the *a priori* argument of Rule 3. The rest of the story to be told about strong and scientific constructivism concerns various defensive operations aimed at deflecting the refutations of realist critics. The positive case for constructivism is that thin. But we should recall that the positive case for most other strong metaphysical theses is also thin. There are no arguments for idealism or materialism that rationally compel assent from any of its opponents. There are only manoeuvres for blocking the rational imperative to give one's thesis up. Purveyors of metaphysical hypotheses aspire only to a strong defence against objections. If constructivists can do that much, they'll be doing as well as anybody else.

7 Three brief and inadequate objections to constructivism

There are three very simple objections to constructivism that are so widespread in realist circles as to belong to the public domain. Moreover, many realists regard these objections as decisive. In their view, everybody knows what's wrong with constructivism – the subject isn't worth pursuing any further. These realists are wrong. The objections are:

1   that constructivism is based on a confusion between facts and beliefs about facts,
2   that constructivism leads to the bizarre conclusion that there was no world before human beings existed, and
3   that constructivism is unable to explain the pragmatic successes of science.

Let's look at each of these in turn.

The first objection is a mirror image of Latour's Rule 3. Latour begs the question by presupposing that Nature and Nature's representation are one. The first objection is based on the opposite presupposition – namely, that Nature and its representation are two:

> The way to sort this out is just to make the obvious distinction between fact and what is believed to be a fact. Our beliefs are true when what is believed to be a fact is indeed a fact. It would seem to be an obvious distinction, hardly worth making. But Latour and Woolgar's study of TRF(H) rests on ignoring it.
>
> (Brown 1989: 83)

This passage is explicitly endorsed by Niiniluoto (1991). The same idea is indirectly alluded to in many other realist critiques. Wherever constructivism is accused of mixing up epistemological and metaphysical issues, there is the question begged. It's true that Latour may be accused of not providing adequate support for his thesis that Nature and its representation are one. But to claim, as Brown and Niiniluoto do, that his mistake is that he overlooks the fact that Nature and its representation are *not* one, is merely to presuppose that constructivism is false. If Latour is right, then there is no 'obvious distinction between fact and what is believed to be a fact'; therefore the distinction can't, without begging the question, be used to show that Latour is wrong.

The second objection is that there was a world before people existed:

> A second objection concerns the strange causal powers that constructivism seems to assign to the mind, allowing it to ontologically constitute a world that doubtless existed before there even were minds.
>
> (Trout 1994: 47)

The intended dilemma is clear: the events that occurred before there were human beings could not have been constituted by human activity; therefore the strong constructivist thesis that *all* facts are constituted by human activities must be false. Moreover, most of the facts about the pre-human world are *bona fide* scientific data (e.g., the facts of palaeontology). Therefore the second objection refutes scientific constructivism – even *weak* scientific constructivism – as well.

I agree that there are problems for constructivism lurking here. But the problems aren't connected in any essential way to the putative existence of a world prior to humanity. The social construction of events in the *recent* past already presents constructivists with all the conceptual dilemmas that they need to resolve. If they can handle facts about 1974, then they can handle facts about dinosaurs or the Big Bang. For example, consider the thesis that the Renaissance was constructed by Jakob Burckhardt in 1860. There are two serious problems associated with this claim. The first is, once again, the problem of reflexivity: if all historical events are constructed, then the construction of event X (e.g., Burckhardt's construction of the Renaissance) is in turn constructed, and we're off on an infinite regress. It remains to be seen how the several constructivisms are able to cope with this problem. (My treatment of reflexivity is to be found in Chapter 10.) It's immediately clear, however, that strong constructivists are going to have a harder time dealing with reflexivity than merely scientific constructivists.

The second problem associated with the construction of historical facts impinges on strong and scientific constructivism to the same degree. If we say that Burckhardt constructed the Renaissance in 1860, we're claiming that an event in 1860 constitutes an event in the sixteenth century. But if A constitutes B, then A *is* B. Therefore it's logically impossible for A and B to have different dates – or so it seems at first blush. Latour and Woolgar have a gloss that covers – or at least papers over – this difficulty. Speaking of the construction of TRH they concede that it's a fact that TRH existed before its construction in 1969. But they claim that it only became true in 1969 that TRH had existed prior to 1969. Isn't this merely double-talk? In a sympathetic review of *Laboratory Life*, Ian Hacking gives Latour and Woolgar a helping hand. He essentially admits that this kind of temporal talk doesn't make any sense, but suggests that the senselessness is necessitated by the fact that 'the grammar of our language prevents us' from speaking the truth in this case (Hacking 1988: 282) . According to Hacking, the strictly nonsensical formulation serves to point up the fact that 'what logicians would call the modality and tense structure of assertions of fact is misunderstood' by our ordinary ways of speaking (281).

Of course, it's one thing to claim that we need a new logic, and it's quite another thing to *have* a new logic to present to the world. The former without the latter is altogether too facile a mode of extricating oneself from any and all philosophical difficulties. I will assess the prospects for Latour's incipient treatment of time in Chapter 13. My present point is rather limited – it's that there's no *special* problem for constructivism due to the existence of events before people. All the problems are already present in the claim that a fact about 1974 was constructed in 1975. Latour and Woolgar tell us that we should say that it became true in 1975 that the fact obtained in 1974. If this gloss is vindicated, then it will serve just as well to make sense of the construction of dinosaurs and quarks. If the gloss is exposed as arrant nonsense, then their case is as lost as it possibly can be. There's no *extra* problem attaching to the existence of a world before humanity.

The third objection to constructivism is that it's unable to account for the success of science in achieving technological goals:

> The problem of accounting for success is one that has been repeatedly raised in the context of looking at sociology of science. It has been raised so often that it has almost ceased to have force as a problem that has to be dealt with. I want to try to reinstate a little of its earlier force. 'Success' here is referring not to a global property of science, but to local, goal-oriented achievements. So it need not be tied up with eulogies: science can be locally successful without necessarily being globally successful, or being a positive force in society. In fact, some of the most notable and obvious successes of science have been linked to military projects that many people do not see as desirable parts of our societies. When presented with a military goal, scientists, usually physicists, have at times behaved remarkably well with respect to achieving that goal. It is this ability which is hard to understand from the 'knowledge is nothing but negotiation' view.
>
> (Sismondo 1993a: 542)

In other words, since scientists are able to destroy cities on demand, they must have knowledge of an independent reality.

As is usually the case in the constructivist literature, Sismondo doesn't tell us which variety of constructivism is supposed to be discomfited by the problem that he poses. The success of science certainly makes no difficulties for the *strong* constructivist thesis that all facts are constructed. The strong constructivist response to the argument is clear: if all facts are socially constructed, then the fact that science is successful is also socially constructed. And then there's nothing left over that strong constructivism can't explain: the success of science is a fact because we've agreed to consider science successful. To be sure, strong constructivism may be heir to insuperable problems relating to reflexivity. But that's a different argument. If strong constructivists *can* coherently maintain that every fact is socially constructed, then the (socially constructed) fact that science is successful makes no problem for them. And if it turns out that strong constructivism *can't* coherently maintain that every fact is socially constructed, then it loses to realism on *that* account, and not because science is successful. In fact, since the existence of *any* independent fact would show strong constructivism to be false, the case for realism would be exactly the same if it were an independent fact that science is a dismal *failure*. What matters is not whether science succeeds or fails, but whether the facts about science, whatever they may be, can coherently be regarded as constructed.

There's an interesting moral issue relating to constructivism that I'd like to indicate briefly. Our moral sensibilities are outraged by the suggestion that the destruction of Hiroshima is not an event that takes place in an independently existing realm of phenomena. This reaction suggests in turn that we implicitly subscribe to the doctrine that independent events are morally weightier than constructed events. It's not immediately clear why this should be so. The view that it *is* so is reminiscent of the popular claim that physical suffering is weightier than mental suffering – that we belittle an affliction by relegating it to the realm of the mental. In the past, we've attempted (unsuccessfully) to comfort neurotics by assuring them that their problems were 'just in their minds'. As sociological thinking becomes more deeply entrenched, will the conventional reassurance be changed to 'it's just a social construction'?

What's the import of the success-of-science argument on *scientific* constructivism – the thesis which asserts only that scientific facts are constructed? Well, it could be argued that the efficacy of scientists is an everyday fact *about* science rather than a proper 'scientific fact'. Thus the view that scientific facts are constructed doesn't entail that the success of science is constructed. But then, how can the scientific constructivist explain the (independent) success of science? The realist explanation is that scientists have twigged some independent truths about the universe. What explanation can scientific constructivists offer?

Scientific constructivists have at least two replies available. The first is to claim that the success of science *is* constructed after all. To be sure, their scientific constructivism doesn't compel them to regard all everyday facts as constructed. But neither does it *forbid* them to regard any particular everyday fact as constructed. They can take the view that some everyday facts are independent and some are constructed, and that the success of science happens to belong to the constructed category. Perhaps this is labouring the obvious. After all, there's no chance that the success-of-science argument could have worked against scientific constructivism if it failed to work against strong constructivism. Strong constructivism *entails* scientific constructivism; therefore any refutation of the latter would also constitute a refutation of the former. It's impossible for there to be an escape hatch that's available to strong constructivists but closed to scientific constructivists.

Scientific constructivists can also accept the success of science as an independent fact without giving up the view that scientific facts are constituted by their own activities. All they have to do is provide an alternative, non-realist explanation for scientific success. These are easily come by. One of them is that there are no independent scientific facts, but that immersion in the culture of science improves one's ability to *guess right* about what happens next. We can distinguish two versions of this thesis – the general and the specific. According to the general version, it doesn't matter what scientific theory you accept. It's non-theory-specific aspects of the scientific enterprise – the mental discipline, the hard work, or whatever – that hones our ability to guess right. A *prima facie* objection to this view is that it fails to account for the fact that proponents of some theories are often more successful than proponents of other theories. This could be accounted for by the hypothesis that immersion in some theories has a particularly beneficial effect on our capacity to guess correctly. On this account, the 'right' theory isn't the one that more accurately describes independent truths about the world – it's the one that provides you with the most beneficial spiel. I call this the *abracadabra* theory of scientific success. According to the abracadabra theory, the success of science is reduced to the success of scientists, and the latter is given a causal explanation.

Is the abracadabra theory too implausible to carry any weight? I don't think it's implausible at all. The view that scientists' predictive success is due to a tacit understanding that goes beyond anything which is explicitly delineated by their formal theories has a respectable philosophical ancestry: see Polanyi (1958). At the very least, realists should find it to be no less plausible than the constructivist thesis itself. If they agree with this assessment, then they can't very well take on the dialectical burden of refuting constructivism while dismissing the abracadabra theory on the grounds of implausibility. They could just as well dismiss constructivism itself.

In sum, the success-of-science argument doesn't come close to refuting constructivism.

8 The problem of misrepresentation

Recent critics of constructivism have mounted a cluster of related objections having to do, in one way or another, with the constructivist treatment of misrepresentations. The target of these critical attacks is scientific constructivism. Needless to say, the success of these attacks would also constitute a refutation of the stronger thesis of strong constructivism. Here is Robert Nola's objection:

> I have a further related objection to make ... It is that our theories, or our representations if you like, can be false, yet what the theory says exists is true. The theory can be right about what exists, but have a wrong account of how things are related, or employ false laws, or whatever. For example, the early Bohr theory of the atom was right about the existence of electrons and a nucleus for atoms but the theory was wrong about all sorts of things, including the laws that Bohr later improved upon in his Quantum Theory. What puzzles me is how a theory that is right about what exists but false about many other matters can be used to construct what exists – or construct the objects of the theory, as constructivists are wont to say ... I cannot see what answer could possibly be given.
>
> (Nola 1995: 706)

Nola isn't speaking in his own voice in this passage. His article has the form of a dialogue, and the quoted portion is delivered by a realistically inclined Hamlet to a constructivist Polonius. It's clear, however, that Nola's sympathies lie with the Prince.

Now Hamlet isn't as explicit as he might be about the nature of the difficulty. Here's what I take his point to be. The constructivist thesis is that scientific objects are constituted by the negotiated *victory* of the theory which posits them. But then the objects posited by *defeated* theories should *not* exist. Yet scientists routinely do believe in the theoretical entities posited by defunct theories. Thus the constructivist account fails to explain actual scientific practice. And thus scientific constructivism (*a fortiori* strong constructivism) is false.

Trout (1994) gives a fuller version of essentially the same objection. He begins, like Nola, with the observation that scientists frequently accept the ontologies of rejected theories. In addition, he demonstrates that this acceptance figures ineliminably in the rationale for essential scientific practices. According to Trout, it's this ontological commitment that underwrites the use of old evidence to confirm current theories. Trout cites the example of the use of 'archaic' reports of comet sightings in contemporary calculations of cometary orbits. Some of these reports were made by scientists who subscribed to radically different theories about the nature of comets. Until the 1500s, for instance, comets were widely believed to be meteorological rather than astronomical phenomena. Nevertheless, these and other archaic reports are routinely regarded as providing information about currently accepted scientific objects. In some cases, the archaic reports are *essential* to contemporary calculations of cometary orbits: without them, modern science would have to diminish its knowledge claims by a substantial degree.

But if, as constructivists claim, theories constitute their objects, then presumably different theories must constitute different objects:

> it is a consequence of the constructivist account of evidence that the object observed by the archaic scientist is a *different* object from the one currently observed, since it has different associated features. This is not an artifact of attributing to the constructivist a description theory of reference, but rather of the constructivist's own account of the *theoretical constitution of ontology*.
>
> (Trout 1994: 53)

Moreover, if our modern comets are not the same objects as the ancients' comets, then the practice of confirming current theories by citing archaic evidence becomes incomprehensible. Therefore constructivism fails to account for a common scientific practice.

In the passage quoted above, Trout talks about the constitution of objects by theories. This is not an entirely accurate representation of the constructivist thesis. According to constructivists, theories don't constitute their objects by themselves. If I make up a theory, refrain from telling anyone about it and then forget it, the theory is not going to do any constituting. The 'constitution of ontology' is effected by a *social process* in which the theory is merely one of the elements. No doubt Trout is simply availing himself of a verbal shortcut here. I did the same thing myself in Chapter 6, when I described constructivism as the thesis that objects and their representation are one. In the present context, however, this abbreviated mode of speech covers up a lacuna in the argument. Trout's analysis doesn't rule out the following constructivist account of the use of archaic data. The main precondition for the success of the account that I'm about to suggest is that the archaic lore should have *entailments* that can be expressed in terms of the successor ontology. This condition is easily satisfied. Take the cometary example. It's true that the ancients couched their observational reports in terms that have no referents on the modern view: when they said that comet X at time t was in position p on the celestial sphere, they were referring to a meteorological phenomenon. We now believe that this observational report was false – there was no meteorological phenomenon at (t,p). But there are *generic* concepts which subsume both our modern concept and the archaic concept of a comet. One of these is the concept of an object with luminous tail which appears in the sky. Let's call any such object a 'protocomet'. Both archaic and modern scientists have a much more detailed story to tell about the objects they call 'comets'. But neither of them should have any objection to accepting the protocometary implications of their beliefs. Archaic scientists who reported a comet at (t,p) would no doubt have acceded to the weaker claim that there was a protocomet at (t,p). It's fair to say that this weaker claim is a part of archaic cometary lore. Moreover, the weaker claim doesn't violate the modern scientist's ontology.

Of course, the fact that a claim stays within the bounds of modern scientists' ontology doesn't mean that modern scientists have to accept it. But if they *do* accept it, constructivism has a ready account. Let's introduce the notion of a *constitutive scenario*: for any putative fact x, the constitutive scenario Sx of x is the social circumstance the occurrence of which would constitute x. Scientific constructivism is the thesis that there's an Sx for every scientific fact x. We also need the concept of a *subscenario*. Sy is a subscenario of Sx if the occurrence of Sx logically entails the occurrence of Sy. The agreement among scientists that TRH has been synthesized is a subscenario of the scenario wherein it's universally agreed, by scientists and non-scientists alike, that TRH has been synthesized.

Now if constructivists observe modern scientists accepting an archaic datum, this is how they may explain it. Let x be the archaic claim in full. In Trout's example, x might be the archaic claim that a 'comet' – i.e., a meteorological phenomenon of a certain type – was observed at (t,p). Let y be the weak subclaim which is compatible with the modern ontology, and which modern scientists accept – e.g., that a protocomet was observed at (t,p). From a constructivist point of view, the fact that scientists accept y simply indicates :

1   that the constitutive scenario Sy is a subscenario of Sx, and
2   that, though Sx no longer obtains, Sy still obtains.

In other words, the constitution of ancient reality was effected by a social scenario, Sx, which now no longer obtains. Thus the ancient reality x is no longer our reality. But there is a subscenario Sy of that defunct social scenario which has survived, and which continues to constitute some elements of the ancient reality.

This analysis provides a remedy for both Nola's and Trout's qualms. Nola thought that all the entities constituted by a scenario Sx would have to be deconstituted when Sx fell apart. But to suppose this is simply to assume, without argument, that constitutive scenarios *don't* have subscenarios that can survive the dissolution. As for Trout's worry about the use of archaic data, it's easy to see how the surviving aspects of the constitutive scenario may sustain some archaic data that have confirmatory consequences on modern theories: when the old facts about protocomets are conjoined with the more recently constituted fact that protocomets are all *comets* (in the modern sense of the word), we generate additional information about comets.

This constructivist explanation relies on the principle that to every contemporary use of archaic data, there corresponds a constitutive scenario which

1   is a subscenario of the scenario that constituted the archaic lore *in toto*, and which
2   has survived intact to the present day.

There is, of course, no possibility of establishing this existential claim in the absence of a detailed specification of the principles whereby scenarios constitute facts. But neither have Nola or Trout given us any reason to suppose that the existential claim fails. Without an argument to that effect, they can't be said to have contrived a dilemma for constructivism. They've merely pointed out, once again, that constructivists need to get more specific.

Moreover, there are compelling reasons to suppose that the conditions for the use of *some* archaic data are satisfiable. This supposition amounts to the very weak claim that some facts are *socially independent* of some other facts. To say that fact x is socially independent of fact y is to say that the constitutive scenarios of x and y, Sx and Sy, can occur either alone or together – that Sx and Sy, Sx and $-Sy$ and $-Sx$ and Sy are all realizable states of affairs. Even if constructivism is true, there are bound to be socially independent pairs of facts. Let a be the fact that TRH has been synthesized, and let b be the fact that Bangkok is the capital of Thailand. There's presumably a constitutive scenario Sab whose occurrence constitutes the conjunctive fact that TRH has been synthesized and that Bangkok is the capital of Thailand. But no doubt this scenario has a subscenario Sa that would survive some dissolutions of Sab. That is, there are some possible social upheavals as a result of which it would no longer be the case that TRH has been synthesized, although Bangkok would still be the capital of Thailand. There's nothing in the general description of the constructivist point of view that would lead one to conclude that the social scenario which constitutes archaic cometary lore can't be like Sab in this regard.

Trout also expresses the opinion that constructivists will find it difficult to explain how theories get rejected:

The first challenge to constructivism occurs in the attempt to explain why scientists are ever forced to abandon a theory if, as constructivists hold, theories define the very world they were introduced to explain.

(Trout 1994: 46)

The problem is this: since accepted theories are *ipso facto* true, there can be no grounds for rejecting a theory once it's been accepted. To mount such an objection is to suggest that there's a special problem about rejecting accepted theories which constructivists don't face when they try to account for how new theories are accepted in the first place. But acceptance and rejection pose equivalent explanatory challenges. Suppose we grant that constructivists have an adequate account of theory acceptance. Then they would be able to explain how it comes about that events develop in the following sequence. First a new theory is proposed that goes counter to prevailing views. Secondly, because it goes counter to prevailing views, it's rejected as false; this is not yet the rejection of a *previously accepted* theory that Trout regards as problematic – it's the initial rejection of a never-before-accepted theory on account of its conflict with already accepted views. Note that at this stage, the rejecters are *right*: if constructivism is correct, then the prevailing view is *ipso facto* true, which entails that its competitors are false. Third, as a result of a process of social negotiation, the prevailing views are abandoned and the new theory is accepted, whereupon it constitutes a new truth. Trout singles out the process whereby the prevailing views are abandoned as especially problematic. But the repudiation of the old theory and the adoption of the new theory are in the same boat. Indeed, it's entirely a conventional matter that one of these processes is described as an acceptance and the other as a rejection. The rejection of the old theory X can just as well be described as the acceptance of its negation, −X; and the acceptance of the new theory Y is the same thing as the rejection of −Y. If we allow that social negotiation can explain one of these processes, then we can't claim that the other is problematic.

Perhaps Trout's point is that it's the process of *theory change* that's problematic for constructivists. On this reading, his discussion doesn't focus on theory rejection because the rejection of a superseded theory is more problematic than the acceptance of the superseding theory – he focuses on rejection because theory change (which involves rejection of the old) is more problematic than the acceptance of the *initial* theory of some domain (which doesn't involve rejection). Even if it's admitted that constructivism is able to explain the phenomenon of initial acceptance, constructivism still falters on the fact that scientists frequently change their minds – or so Trout arguably maintains. The presumed problem is that accepted theories can't be abandoned, because their acceptance ensures their truth, and new, rival theories can't be accepted, because they conflict with the old theories, which are true.

The impression that there's a special difficulty here stems from the importation of an individualistic mindset into the *social*-constructivist world view. One imagines a community of individual researchers, each of whom is unable to find evidence contrary to prevailing views, because the phenomena are constituted by those very views. But what an individual researcher perceives or believes need have nothing to do with the social construction of reality. The ontology of a theory is not constituted by the vindication of its observable consequences in the private sensoria of researchers in the field. It's constituted by the public victory of those who negotiate on its behalf. The constitutive effect is entirely compatible with the possibility that indefinitely many individual scientists have serious personal reservations about the theory which, for political reasons, they refrain from expressing. But then the political situation might change, whereupon private reservations are made public, the balance of epistemic power shifts, and a new reality is negotiated.

This kind of shift happens routinely in the case of social realities whose social construction is uncontroversial. Laws and customs change, currencies become worthless, the meanings of words drift. The very existence of these phenomena already stands as a refutation of the argument that constructivism can't explain theory change. Maybe there's something fundamentally wrong with the idea that physical reality is socially constructed. But if we grant that the idea is coherent, then it can't be objected that constructed realities can't change, for we know, from the uncontroversial cases of socially constructed realities, that they do change.

There's really no question that constructed realities can change. There is another potential problem for constructivists, however. It could be argued that those who perpetrate the change are either making a mistake or acting unethically. In order to mount an attack on received views, you have to take exception to views which are in fact *true*. Now either you believe that the received views are false, or you promulgate the new view without believing it. In the first case, you embrace a factual error; in the second case, you're guilty of insincerity. Thus it seems that only defenders of the status quo are blameless. This problem has been raised by Sismondo (1993b: 567). One constructivist reply can be that the acceptance of a constructivist world view brings in its train a re-evaluation of traditional notions of epistemic ethics. The idea that we should only promulgate beliefs that we ourselves hold to be true loses much of its sway if we think that false promulgations may re-create the truth. In any case, it can't simply be assumed that right epistemic conduct in an independent world is the same as right epistemic conduct in a world that's constituted by that very conduct.

There's an entirely different and rather more interesting avenue for dealing with Sismondo's problem. Constructivists and their realist critics alike have presumed that constructivist theses are necessarily tied to consensual effects: it's some sort of acceptance that makes a theory true. It isn't necessary for constructivists to adopt a strictly consensual theory of truth. In fact, most of them represent the constitution of facts as involving something more than a democratic vote. But it's always assumed that facts are constituted by some people in some circumstances adopting some sort of affirmative stance toward the putative fact. My point is that this generic assumption isn't required by the constructivist thesis. To say that human actions constitute a phenomenon is not yet to be committed to the view that anybody has any sort of affirmative attitude toward the phenomenon in any circumstance. The idea that our collective fears and anxieties constitute their objects is also a constructivist thesis. Relative to *this* thesis, however, Sismondo's problem simply doesn't arise. Suppose that what we collectively fear becomes the truth, and that we collectively fear the consequences of theory T. Then T is true. Moreover, this truth is constructed by our own activities. Yet it needn't be the case that any of us believe or agree to this truth. In fact, our actual opinions and pronouncements could be incompatible with the socially constructed truth of T. Conversely, the fact that everyone agrees that T is true doesn't yet entail that T *is* true, even if constructivism is true. Therefore scientific rebels may be able to disagree with the status quo without espousing false doctrines, even if they live in a constructed reality. It all depends on the principles of construction.

How plausible is the supposition that there are non-consensual constructions of reality? Here again, the world of uncontroversially constructed social phenomena provides a source of examples. In Chapter 4, I cited social conventions as an example of a socially constructed reality: for everyone to agree that a social convention is in place *is* for that convention to be in place. In this situation, an isolated individual who denied the existence of the convention would simply be wrong. If the construction of scientific reality follows this model, we get Sismondo's problem: an isolated scientist who denied the truth of a currently accepted theory would be wrong. But there indubitably exist other social constructions that don't have this consequence. Suppose, for example, that everybody thinks that the name of Willard V. Quine is undeservedly unknown to the general population. Then, by virtue of everybody having this thought, the name of Willard V. Quine would be known to everyone. Moreover, this fact about Quine's name is clearly a socially constructed fact – it's made true by human activity. But everyone would have got this socially constructed fact wrong! In this case, an isolated individual who disagrees with the status-quo opinion about a socially constructed fact could be the only one who gets it right.

The foregoing remarks serve to shield constructivism from Sismondo's problem. But they also stand as a criticism of current constructivist thinking from within the constructivist enterprise. Constructivists take the uncontroversial construction of social reality as a model for the construction of scientific reality. They also universally assume that scientific realities are always based on self-validating claims: it's some kind of affirmative stance toward a theory that makes it true. But the uncontroversial construction of social reality involves other types of constructive processes as well. Sometimes it even involves self-*defeating* claims, wherein it's everybody's *denying* a fact that makes the fact true. Granting that scientific facts are constructed, why should we suppose that they're always constructed along self-validating lines?

9 Constructive empiricism and social constructivism

Readers of this book who are familiar with the philosophy of science literature of the past decade or two may be experiencing a queasy sense of *déjà-vu*. Surely they've seen these arguments, these strategic parries and counter-parries, before. The aim of this chapter is to reassure them that they're not hallucinating. Most of the points being made in the 1990s about social constructivism, both pro and con, went through the philosophical mill in the 1980s. The first time around, however, the subject of analysis was the philosophy of constructive empiricism as expounded in van Fraassen's *Scientific Image*.

The reason for this parallelism is not hard to locate. It's that constructive empiricism is a species of constructivism. More precisely, the relationship between social constructivism and constructive empiricism is akin to that between an out-of-focus photograph and a sharper image that's consistent with all of its blurred features. The latter is van Fraassen's Scientific Image; the former is the social constructivists' Blurry Image. To be sure, no self-proclaimed social constructivist would be willing to endorse van Fraassen's views *in toto*. Moreover, I'm sure that van Fraassen has significant points of disagreement with Latour, Knorr-Cetina and probably every other student of science who sails under the flag of constructivism. But the philosophical differences between van Fraassen and some social constructivists are not greater than the differences between different constructivists. In fact, it's arguable that the differences between van Fraassen and Latour in some of his moods are not greater than the differences between Latour in some of his moods and Latour in others of his moods. If this comparative thesis is correct – if constructive empiricism is a precisification of constructivism – it follows that all the arguments and counter-arguments relevant to the evaluation of constructive empiricism are also relevant to the evaluation of constructivism. Because of the blurrier nature of the second target, however, the same philosophical points take on a different coloration, which imbues them with a deceptive appearance of novelty. This is why the debate is being recycled.

The bulk of the discussion in this chapter falls into two parts. First, I'll elaborate on the relation between the substantive doctrines of constructivism and constructive empiricism. By 'constructive empiricism', by the way, I mean the philosophy of science expounded in *The Scientific Image*; van Fraassen's later (1989) writings present some significant departures from the classical 1980 statement. Secondly, I'll display some of the striking parallels in the dialectical exchanges that each thesis has engendered. I'll show that to every important strategic move in the critique or defence of constructive empiricism, there corresponds a homologous – often, an identical – move in the controversy about constructivism. I'll end with a brief reflection on the prospects for a future bifurcation of the two debates.

Here's a brief comparative sketch of constructive empiricism and social constructivism. To begin with, van Fraassen divides our claims about the world into two categories – those that posit observable properties of observable objects, and those that posit properties of unobservable objects. Moreover, the former are granted certain epistemic privileges – never mind which – that are to be withheld from the latter. At first blush, this might already seem to constitute a major difference with constructivism. For don't constructivists want to treat both observational and non-observational claims in the same way? The answer in the Blurry Image is both 'yes' and 'no'. There's no doubt that the constructivist rhetoric about living in a world of our own devising strongly suggests an even-handed treatment of all factual claims. This is the view that I've been calling strong constructivism. But it's also easy to find passages – often by the same author – that seem to endorse a distinction between a more privileged and a less privileged type of claim. We've already seen a pair of quotes from Latour that exemplify both tendencies. Recall Latour's Rule 3:

> Since the settlement of a controversy is the *cause* of Nature's representation, not its consequence, we can never use this consequence, Nature, to explain how and why a controversy has been settled.
>
> (Latour 1987: 258)

I'll have occasion to remind the reader of the demerits of Rule 3 shortly. Whatever merits or demerits it may possess, however, it presumably applies equally to any claims about Nature that are subject to controversy. Since any sort of claim whatever may elicit controversy, it would seem that Rule 3 entails that *all* the facts about Nature are constructed. That is to say, Latour sounds a lot like a strong constructivist in this passage.

But we've also read a passage in which Latour endorses something like an observational–non-observational distinction. In an article with Callon, he notes that in his 'frame', as opposed to the realist's, 'the only observables are the traces left by objects, arguments, skills, and tokens circulating through the collective' (Callon and Latour 1992: 350–1). This characterization of the realm of observables is not as translucent as one might hope. Whatever a trace left by an object may be, it seems that the Blurry Image is able to accommodate an observable–unobservable distinction. The importation of such a distinction into a constructivist framework results in the doctrine that I called *instrumental constructivism* in Chapter 4. The strategic retreat from strong to instrumental constructivism may provide an exit from the logical problems of reflexivity that are likely to plague strong constructivism. But it does so at the cost of a substantial reduction in the novelty quotient of the thesis. For, if all that Latour is saying is that putative facts about unobservables are constructed, then it's been said before. Van Fraassen:

> I use the adjective 'constructive' to indicate my view that scientific activity is one of construction rather than discovery: construction of models that must be adequate to the phenomena, and not discovery of truth concerning the unobservable.
>
> (van Fraassen 1980: 5)

To be sure, it sounds as though Latour wants to cut the realm of observables closer to some unnamed philosophical bone than van Fraassen does. But this is a difference in detail that can be settled amicably between philosophical allies.

The most obvious difference between van Fraassen and those who call themselves constructivists is that the latter emphasize the *social* construction of scientific facts: what gets accepted into science is determined by a social process of negotiation. When van Fraassen talks about construction, he talks about it in cognitive rather than social terms. This difference is not very significant, however, for two reasons. First, there's nothing in constructive empiricism that's *inimical* to social construction. Van Fraassen could concede that the acceptance of scientific theories over their empirically equivalent rivals is determined entirely by a social process of negotiation, without having to alter any of the views that are central to *The Scientific Image*. Secondly, some constructivists themselves have been de-emphasizing the role of the social in constructive processes. A striking manifestation of this trend is Latour and Woolgar's famous change in the subtitle of their book, from *The Social Construction of Scientific Facts* in the first edition to *The Construction of Scientific Facts* in the second.

The most substantial difference between the two constructive philosophies concerns the epistemic status of the constructed artifacts. According to van Fraassen, the constructed theoretical claims may be true or false, but we can never have adequate warrant for believing that they're true. Constructivists, on the other hand, usually maintain that the constructive activities *constitute* the fact. Having constructed quarks, it's not irrational to believe that quarks exist; but to say that quarks exist is to say no more than that a certain kind of constructive activity has taken place. This is more reminiscent of old-time logical positivism, with its 'reduction' of the theoretical to the observational, than of van Fraassen's position. The difference between constructivism and classical reductionism seems to be in the nature of the materials out of which the constructions are fashioned. The positivists constructed theoretical entities out of observations; constructivists make them out of social episodes. But, as the previous quotation from Callon and Latour indicates, constructivists may also use 'traces left by objects' in their constructions. If Latour had explained to a logical positivist what a trace left by an object was, the positivist might have been willing to accept it as raw material for the construction of theoretical entities. In any case, it will be seen in Chapter 12 that this difference between constructive empiricism and most social constructivisms makes the latter susceptible to a new argument to which the former is immune.

In sum, one can't simply equate constructivism with constructive empiricism, or with positivism, or with any of the other classical anti-realisms. But that doesn't mean that it's a new position in the philosophy of science. *Strong* constructivism is new. But, while constructivists are given to frequent outbursts of strong-constructivist rhetoric, almost everything that's probative in what they have to say demands, or is at least compatible with, a blander instrumental-constructivist reading. For the most part, modern constructivism can be understood as a *blurrification* of the traditional anti-realisms. If this is so, one would expect the current dispute about constructivism to recapitulate the earlier history of anti-realism. In the next section, I'll demonstrate the remarkable extent to which both constructivists and their realist critics have been repeating philosophical history. Perhaps I should reiterate that I'm talking about constructivism as a philosophy of science, and not the social studies of science conducted by constructivists. The latter are interesting, informative, and indeed represent something new in the intellectual world. It's the philosophical gloss that routinely accompanies these empirical studies that tends toward the stale.

Now let's trace some of the parallels between the two lines of argumentation. (In the ensuing discussion, the term 'anti-realist' includes both constructive empiricists and social constructivists, while 'realists' are people who deny both constructive empiricism and constructivism.) On the anti-realist side, both constructive empiricists and constructivists rely primarily on an argument from scientific practice. This is a sort of empirical argument according to which scientists' behaviour is best explained by the anti-realist philosophy. Among constructivists, for instance, Latour and Woolgar present their study as a contribution to the 'anthropology of science': observing the laboratory antics of scientists without preconceived notions leads to a corpus of data for which a constructivist hypothesis is the best explanation. As noted in Chapter 5, the argument from scientific practice is very nearly the only argument there is for constructivism.

Similarly, on the constructive empiricist side, van Fraassen has famously argued that his philosophical hypothesis provides the best account of scientific practice. By my reckoning, the scientific-practice argument is the *only* new argument for anti-realism to be found in *The Scientific Image*. Thus arguments from scientific practice hold a central position in both anti-realisms. The sorts of practices that van Fraassen has in mind are rather different from those discussed by Latour and Woolgar. The practices that van Fraassen talks about are *cognitive* practices of the sort that normative accounts of science have traditionally regarded as essential to scientific rationality. For instance, van Fraassen is concerned to defuse Putnam's (1975b) 'conjunction' argument for realism. Putnam maintains that anti-realism is incapable of explaining the fact that scientists routinely believe in the empirical consequences of the *conjunction* of theories that they accept. Van Fraassen's well-known rebuttal is that the history of science does not show that the conjunction of two accepted theories is itself accepted 'without a second thought' (van Fraassen 1980: 85). In fact, there 'can be no phenomenon of the scientific life of which this simple account draws a faithful picture' (85). And what follows from *this* observation in turn is that the actual scientific practice is adequately accounted for by constructive empiricism.

Both constructive empiricists and social constructivists are evidently concerned to account for the 'phenomena of the scientific life'. To be sure, the two anti-realisms focus on different aspects of the scientific life. But the next move in the game – in both games – causes this difference to recede into insignificance. We find that *critics* of the respective anti-realisms are willing to concede that the anti-realisms possess so much interpretative latitude that they're able to account for *any conceivable scientific practice*. The constructive empiricist version of this claim is argued for at length by Fine (1984). The constructivist version, discussed in Chapter 5, is due to Nelson (1994). The difference between the dates of these two articles is a rough measure of the amount of time by which the constructivist recapitulation lags behind the history of constructive empiricism.

The fact that the anti-realisms can explain any scientific practice doesn't, of course, mean that anti-realism wins – for there may be a competing *realist* explanation for every scientific practice as well. Anti-realists, as well as realists, need to do more than allude to the data on scientists' behaviour to make their case. They need to engage in a comparative evaluation of the two explanatory proposals. It isn't entirely clear whether the founders, Latour and van Fraassen, fully acknowledge this necessity (recall that I'm talking about the van Fraassen of 1980). Latour, in particular, often sounds like a radical empiricist. He suggests that just looking at 'laboratory life' with an unprejudiced eye is enough to turn one into a constructivist. Van Fraassen acknowledges that a comparison between realist and anti-realist accounts of scientific practice is needed. He says that the realist account is inferior by virtue of its 'inflationary' nature. But, at least in 1980, he forgets to tell us why inflationary accounts are deemed to be inferior. There are passages in Latour, and in the later van Fraassen, that can be construed as providing the missing argument for the superiority of the anti-realist explanation. But both sets of considerations suffer from the same pair of conceptual maladies. First, supposing that the arguments are sound, they would render superfluous the scientific practice arguments that they're supposed to be underwriting. Secondly, the arguments beg the question against their realist opponents. We saw (in Chapter 6) that this is so on the constructivist side. The closest thing to an *a priori* argument for constructivism that can be found in Latour's writings is the one that's obliquely expressed in Rule 3. But Rule 3 merely presupposes the truth of constructivism. Moreover, if Rule 3 were to be accepted, it would render Latour's anthropological investigations superfluous.

Now let's see how the same drama unfolds in the history of constructive empiricism. In 1980, van Fraassen claims that his view of science can account for all the facts about scientific practice. But, of course, this claim, even if it's true, is not by itself sufficient to underwrite his philosophical conclusion. Van Fraassen also needs to show that his account is superior to rival realist accounts. At this juncture, van Fraassen appeals to the virtues of ontological parsimony: the constructive empiricist account does the same job as the realist account, and it does it 'without inflationary metaphysics' (1980: 73). The realist account refers to theoretical entities as well as to observable phenomena, while the equally adequate constructive empiricist account refers only to observable phenomena. But who says that ontological parsimony is an overriding virtue? Let's grant that constructive empiricism accounts for all scientific practices, and that it does so with less metaphysical baggage than the realist account. The van Fraassen of 1980 seems to think that these admissions are enough to conclude in favour of constructive empiricism. Evidently, he presupposes that if two hypotheses account for the same data, we should give greater credence to the one which makes the fewer metaphysical posits. What this presupposition *rules out* is the possibility that we may prefer a metaphysically richer theory on the non-empirical grounds that its explanations of the data are simpler or more elegant. But to presuppose this is to presuppose constructive empiricism itself! For let T* be the hypothesis which asserts that the observable consequences of T are true, but which says nothing about the theoretical entities posited by T. By definition, T* and T are empirically equivalent – they account for all the same data. But T makes metaphysical posits that T* avoids. Therefore, by van Fraassen's presupposition, we should choose to believe T* rather than T. But to do this for every T *is* to be a constructive empiricist. Therefore, if we grant the presupposition of van Fraassen's scientific-practice argument, we can skip the scientific-practice argument: the presupposition already gives us the result. By the same token, it's not to be expected that a realist is going to grant van Fraassen the presupposition that he needs. To grant it would be to grant that realism is false.

The parallelism to Latour's anthropological argument is evident. Like van Fraassen, Latour claims that his view accounts for all scientific practices. Like van Fraassen, he needs to supplement this claim with an argument to the effect that the anti-realist account is superior to any available realist account. Van Fraassen appeals to a principle of parsimony. Latour appeals to Rule 3, which stipulates that it's illegitimate to refer to Nature in our explanations of scientific practice. Both appeals beg the question that's at issue. Moreover, the respective presuppositions are so strong that, if they were to be accepted, their proponents would no longer need to ascertain the facts about scientific practice – the presupposition alone would already give them the victory. Therefore neither van Fraassen nor Latour has a scientific-practice argument.

Now let's look at arguments for realism. Here again, we find striking parallels between the constructive empiricist and the social constructivist literatures – in this case, between the realist arguments that have been mounted *against* these positions. I begin by mentioning a relatively unsurprising parallel: realists have tried to refute both types of anti-realism by describing scientific practices that the anti-realists can't explain. The most famous critical attack of this type on constructive empiricism has already been mentioned – it's Putnam's (1975b) conjunction objection. Van Fraassen's equally famous rejoinder is that there's 'no phenomenon of the scientific life' in which scientists simply derive empirical consequences from conjoined theories. This counter-claim of van Fraassen's has itself been called into question by Trout (1992), who points to specific phenomena of the scientific life in which theories seem to be straightforwardly conjoined. According to Trout, a straightforward and unmodified conjunction of theories takes place every time scientists use a theory as an auxiliary hypothesis in deriving empirical consequences from the theory they're working on. Contrary to van Fraassen's claim, this 'mercenary' use of theoretical auxiliaries doesn't involve any corrections of the auxiliary theory. Indeed, the user is typically inexpert in the field that the auxiliary comes from, and is thus unqualified to suggest theoretical revisions. Trout's paper thus constitutes a scientific-practice argument against constructive empiricism. In another place, I've argued that, while Trout is right in his claim that scientists conjoin theories, this observation doesn't make any serious problems for constructive empiricism (Kukla 1994). The argument, in a nutshell, is that believing in the empirical consequences of conjoined theories doesn't logically commit one to believing in the theories themselves.

In a more recent article, Trout (1994) advances another scientific-practice argument – this time, against social constructivism. According to Trout, constructivists are unable to explain the fact that scientists frequently make use of old evidence, formulated in terms of the ontology of rejected theories, to confirm or disconfirm current theories. Like Trout's earlier argument, this one has also been defused by showing that the practice at issue is compatible with the brand of anti-realism under scrutiny. The perpetrator of this critique of Trout is, once again, me (see the previous chapter). Evidently, the correspondences between the histories of constructive empiricism and social constructivism even extend to the identities of the personnel.

The main dialectical weapon wielded by realists against both types of anti-realism has been an argument from the success of science. The success-of-science argument for constructivism was examined in Chapter 7. The upshot of that examination was that the argument suffers from the same sorts of failings as the scientific-practice arguments for anti-realism. To begin with, it begs the question against constructivism by assuming that the success of science is an independent, unconstructed fact. Moreover, if the degree of scientific success were an unconstructed fact, then it wouldn't matter whether that degree is great or small. The independent fact that science is a *failure* refutes strong constructivism as surely as the independent fact that science is a success. Thus, the argument from the success of science suffers from this additional infelicity – that if the argument is sound, then it's superfluous. No matter how you slice it, allusions to the success of science don't strengthen the case against constructivism.

There's an entirely symmetric story to be told on the constructive-empiricist side. In the case of constructive empiricism, the argument from the success of science is primarily due (once again) to Putnam (1975a), whose version of it goes by the name of the 'miracle argument'. Putnam argues that the only explanation for the predictive success of our theories is the hypothesis that those theories are true (Putnam 1975a). More liberal versions of the argument make the weaker claim that theoretical truth is the *best* explanation for scientific success. Laudan (1984) and Fine (1984) independently noted some time ago that this argument begs the question against the constructive empiricists. In fact, it begs the same question as van Fraassen did in his scientific-practice argument – it just begs it the other way. For suppose that the realists are right in their claim that theoretical truth is the best explanation for predictive success. To suppose further that this state of affairs constitutes rational grounds for realism is to assume that the explanatory virtues of a hypothesis count toward its belief-worthiness. But, as we've seen, this is just what constructive empiricists deny. Moreover, if realists *could* avail themselves of the assumption that explanatory goodness counts toward belief-worthiness, then they wouldn't need the success-of-science argument – they could just move directly from an observed fact to belief in its best theoretical explanation. Once again, allusions to the success of science don't advance the scientific realist's position.

The extensive parallelism between the two literatures isn't surprising in light of the conceptual relationship between the two target doctrines. If constructive empiricism is a precisification of constructivism, then every consideration that's relevant to the former is also going to have a bearing on the latter. What about the converse of this proposition? Is there anything new to be said about constructivism that doesn't have a constructive empiricist counterpart? I think there is. There are, after all, other potential precisifications of the Blurry Image besides constructive empiricism. It's understandable that the analysis of constructivism would have begun with a recapitulation of the earlier exchange. The ideas were already in the air. But after the considerations bearing on constructive empiricism are exhausted (a point in time which is very close at hand), there will still be things to say about other versions of constructivism. Relative inexhaustibility is the main virtue of blurry doctrines. The remaining chapters of this book will deal with issues that have no parallel in the constructive empiricist literature. Almost all of these, not surprisingly, have to do with strong constructivism.

10 The infinite regress of constructions

In the previous chapters, I systematically evaded every threatened encounter with the problems of reflexivity. But the time of reckoning is at hand. The statement that all facts are constructed, by virtue of its universality, obviously falls under its own scope: if it's indeed a fact that all facts are constructed, then that metafact must itself be constructed. Moreover, the metametafact that the metafact is constructed must also be constructed, and so on. It appears that the thesis of strong constructivism leads to an infinite regress. Several philosophers have claimed that this regress (or one of its conceptual cousins) renders strong constructivism untenable. Their arguments will be evaluated in this chapter. But first, we need to discuss an influential attempt from the sociologists' camp to deny that there could possibly *be* an argument from reflexivity that compels them to abandon constructivism.

Malcolm Ashmore (1989) presents an argument which, he claims, robs 'the tu quoque' of its putative power to disallow certain forms of discourse. Criticizing his argument is a delicate operation, however, because he also lets it be known that he doesn't take logical argumentation entirely seriously. For instance, he cites the reflexive dilemma produced by the positivists' verifiability criterion of meaning: if unverifiable statements are meaningless, then the claim that unverifiable statements are meaningless is itself meaningless by virtue of its unverifiability. Does this mean that the verifiability criterion of meaning is untenable? Here's what Ashmore says:

> Now, I have no intention of *arguing* with this wonderful piece of irony – for those who live by logic, to die by logic is an eminently satisfying state of affairs ...
>
> (Ashmore 1989: 88)

This pronouncement of course suggests that the author is not among those who live by logic, and that he's thereby impervious to its force. Nevertheless, there are arguments in Ashmore's text, and they have the appearance of having been crafted with as much care for coherence as the author can muster. This places the would-be critic in a classical double bind. In the original double-bind theory of schizophrenia, the schizophrenogenic mother proclaims her love for her child, but embeds her proclamation in cues that it's to be taken ironically. If the child responds to the love, she's a pathetic literalist who misses the irony; if she responds to the irony, she's an ungrateful wretch for not acknowledging the overt proclamation of love. By the same token, if critics take Ashmore to be having a bit of fun, they lay themselves open to the taunt that Ashmore's conclusions stand unrefuted; but if they offer a refutation, they merely reveal themselves to be of the stodgy company of those who live by logic. After all, Ashmore himself puckishly tells us that his analysis of reflexivity 'is a failure' (110) – so what possible point could there be to subjecting it to criticism?

This critical dilemma has been encountered before. In Chapter 5, I noted that most of those who promulgate the empirical argument for constructivism are also relativists. This puts them in a position to play schizophrenogenic games: if the empirical argument succeeds, they can lay claim to victory, and if it fails, they can deny the significance of the failure by adverting to their relativism. My strategy for dealing with this dialectical situation was to treat the empirical argument and the relativism separately. In Chapter 5 I tried to assess whether the empirical argument succeeds *according to prevailing standards of scientific rationality*. The issue of relativism itself has been deferred until we get to Chapter 15. I admit that the failure of the empirical argument doesn't, by itself, spell the defeat of constructivism-cum-relativism. But it does rob relativistic constructivists of a stick that they're wont to bash absolutistic realists with. I propose to deal with Ashmore's double bind in the same manner. In this chapter, I will try to assess the merits of Ashmore's argument on the basis of prevailing standards of logical coherence. Once again, the failure of Ashmore's argument doesn't by itself spell his defeat. But it does take away his stick. Questions relating to the status of logic itself in the constructivist enterprise are relegated to Chapter 14.

Actually, I discern two arguments in Ashmore's discussion of the tu quoque, though only one of them is developed. The undeveloped one is based on the idea that

> both the tu quoque and its counter share a logician's prejudice against paradox grounded in a magical belief in its evil power.
>
> (88)

The evil power is the power to induce paralysis (89): the 'logician' supposedly believes that a demonstration of incoherence makes it impossible for the recipient of the argument to continue to think or speak in the same way. But obviously logical arguments don't have that power. The incoherence of the verifiability criterion of meaning didn't have the result that 'logical positivism … ceased to exist' (88). If the tu quoque had the power to paralyse, 'the book you are reading would not exist' (110). Despite the tu quoque, 'here I am, still speaking' (100). Therefore, Ashmore concludes, the enterprise of constructivism has nothing to fear from the tu quoque. Now it's true that the logically inclined often talk about logic as 'compelling' us to say or to refrain from saying certain things. Evidently, Ashmore has interpreted this compulsion as actual rather than normative. But who ever thought that logic could make anybody shut up? A gun is a much more effective instrument for that purpose. There is no doubt a sense in which it may be said that logical arguments have no 'force'. But this sense doesn't in any way challenge the absolutist view that logic prescribes limits to what *should* be said. Whether and in what sense logic can be said to have this kind of normative force is the topic that's to be dealt with in later chapters. Whatever the outcome of these investigations may be, it doesn't count as a defence against an argument that, having heard it, one is physically able to keep on talking in the same way.

Ashmore's main argument is that the infinite regress produced by the tu quoque is merely a 'theoretical' problem that admits of a 'pragmatic' solution. On Ashmore's view, wielders of infinite-regress arguments think that the regress counts against a project because it tells us that once we embark on the first step, we're doomed to a life of never-ending toil:

> Infinity represents a phenomenon which cannot be experienced or known or reached. It is a purely 'theoretical' term and does not name any-thing. So why is it so frequently treated as a threat? Why so much talk of the spectre and the abyss? Presumably, if the image of the abyss is anything to go by, such talk expresses the fear that once you start you cannot stop because there is no bottom because the abyss is infinite: a fear of eternal death or a dream of Hell.
>
> (104)

Ashmore undertakes to exorcise the fear of damnation by the following reflection: we don't have to worry about theoretically infinitary tasks, because in practice everything comes to an end. He cites Naess's (1972) tu quoque against Kuhn (1962) as an example. Kuhn regards modern science and old science as on an epistemic par: each one is justified relative to its own paradigm, and neither is justified absolutely. Naess makes the point that, applying the Kuhnian theory to Kuhnian historiography itself, we obtain the result that Kuhnian historiography and its predecessor historiographies are on an epistemic par. Kuhn's many pronouncements to the effect that his historical analysis of science is closer to the truth than his predecessors' is therefore seen to be unwarranted on the basis of his own theory. What his theory requires is a treatment of Kuhnian historiography and its rivals which represents them as being on an epistemic par. This would constitute what Naess calls a Kuhnian historiology – a doctrine concerning the proper writing of history. But of course, if the Kuhnian analysis is right, then Kuhnian historiology is only one of many competing historiologies, all of which have to be treated as on an epistemic par. Infinite regress. Does this mean that the Kuhnian is condemned to engage in a never-ending ascent of metainquiries upon metametainquiries? Well, maybe this is so 'theoretically'. But, like all processes in the real world, this one can't help but peter out. In this particular case, it peters out because

> there is always a comparative paucity of paradigmatic environments (in the Kuhnian sense) within which to undertake such inquiry. This is because metainquiry is parasitic upon its objects: it requires, for its existence, the prior development of the lower level(s) ... in practice there is always a level at which metainquiry stops ...
>
> (105)

More generally, the pragmatic solution is that, even if a task is theoretically infinite, we can't help but run out of things to do. The same pragmatic limitation is seen in conceptually infinite processes in the physical world:

> An example is the effect produced in a mirror when it reflects the image of another mirror which reflects the image of the first mirror ... repeatedly with no theoretical end point to the process. However, the images do get smaller all the time, and if you count them, you will stop quite soon. The *theoretically* infinite has a *practical* end. The point is brought out even more clearly with the cornflakes packet example. On your breakfast table is your packet of cornflakes, and on your packet is a picture of the smiling Kellogg family at breakfast, and on their table is a picture of your packet which has a picture of the smiling Kellogg family, and so on (you know the one I mean). If you count how many packets there are the number will probably not be greater than the number accounted for in the last sentence, that is, four. Ah! you say, that is merely due to the limitations of the printing technology. And this, of course, is precisely my point.
>
> (104)

There are at least three things wrong with this therapy for tu quoque anxiety. To begin with, not all reflexive arguments have their effect by generating an infinite regress. Consider the statement 'All statements are false'. Suppose that this statement is true. Then, by applying it to itself, it follows that the statement is false. Therefore the statement is false. Here, tu quoque reasoning has its critical effect without the invocation of an infinite regress. If a tu quoque having this structure is wielded against a thesis, proponents of the thesis will obtain no comfort from the reflection that theoretically infinite tasks always have a practical end. Now Ashmore himself cites a non-infinitary argument of this type as an example of a tu quoque: the argument against the verifiability criterion of meaning that was discussed above. So perhaps he meant his pragmatic reflection to apply only to tu quoques that *do* generate an infinite regress. As will be seen, the main arguments against constructivism and relativism do involve infinite regresses. Thus Ashmore's first infelicity doesn't render his argument irrelevant to the point at hand. But he is guilty of a stylistic *faux pas*: his pragmatic reflection should not have been so consistently represented as a remedy for the ills of 'the' tu quoque. The pragmatic reflection is really an attempt to de-fang infinite-regress arguments. It doesn't apply to non-infinitary reflexive arguments like the verifiability argument.

The second infelicity is that Ashmore wrongly presumes that all infinite regresses present the same problems and are amenable (or not) to the same solutions. This is simply wrong: there are infinite regresses, and then there are infinite regresses. Some regresses are so benign that they don't even need a palliative. An example is the regress generated by the reflexivity principle of Bloor's strong programme (see Chapter 2). Bloor boldly asserts that the social causation of belief reflexively entails that the belief in social causation must itself be socially caused. Far from seeking for a remedy for this situation, Bloor regards it as one of the strengths of the strong programme that reflexivity is explicitly accommodated. Moreover, Laudan, the harshest critic of the strong programme, doesn't even try to make an issue of the reflexivity thesis. Yet the thesis clearly entails an infinite regress: if all beliefs are socially caused, then the belief in P is socially caused, as is the belief that the belief in P is socially caused, and so on. There's no problem here, however, because this particular infinite regress doesn't entail that anybody has to do an infinite amount of work. The fact that every belief is socially caused entails that there is always an additional SSK project to work on *if one is looking for work*. But this no more precipitates us into the abyss of Hell than the fact that there we can always count more numbers. In both cases, there's no end to the amount of work that *can* be done, but there's no reason in the world why we should have to do it all.

If that were the end of the story, we would conclude that Ashmore's remedy is superfluous, but that Ashmore is right in not fearing the consequences of a regress. But there are vicious regresses as well as benign ones. The Kuhnian regress discussed by Ashmore is one of the vicious ones, though I won't back up this assertion until we get to the chapter on relativism. What makes a regress vicious is, just as Ashmore supposes, that it *requires* us to do an infinite amount of work (more generally, a vicious regress requires that an infinite number of things must happen). In such a case, however, the undoubted fact that we can't do an infinite amount of work doesn't constitute a pragmatic solution to the problem – it *is* the problem. The dilemma posed by a vicious regress isn't that it threatens to rob us of our rest and recreation. It's that if a task *does* require an infinite amount of work, then, of course, *it won't get done*; therefore, if it *does* get done, then the thesis which entails that it requires endless labours must be false. There are no tricky logical steps or exotic metaphysical claims about the infinite involved. It's really a very down-to-earth dilemma. Suppose, for instance, that someone claims that he has always rung a bell before performing any action. If this were true, then he would have had to ring a bell before imparting this information to us. Moreover, since the ringing of the bell was itself an action, he would have had to ring a bell before the last ring, and so on. Obviously, if what he told us were true, he would have had to ring the bell infinitely many times, by which I mean that no number of bell ringings would prove to be sufficient. What does Ashmore's palliative do for us here? To be sure, our agent couldn't, for 'practical' reasons, have rung the bell infinitely many times. But, far from constituting an escape from his dilemma, this is the mundane fact that establishes that what he told us can't have been the truth: he didn't ring the bell infinitely many times; therefore it's not the case that he has rung a bell before performing any action.

At least on the face of it, the tu quoque against strong constructivism has the same structure as the bell-ringing example: if every fact is constructed, then the fact F' that fact F was constructed must itself have been constructed, the fact F'' that F' was constructed must have been constructed, and so on. The previously discussed regress of social causations made available infinitely many SSK projects, but it didn't require us to engage in any of them. The regress of constructions is different. It seems that we *must* construct infinitely many facts in order for any single fact to be constructed. Ashmore's reminding us of the practical truth that we can't do infinitely many things, rather than being reassuring, leads to the false conclusion that nothing has ever been constructed. In reality, the dialectical situation is more complicated than I've just presented it. The fact that a thesis entails that infinitely many things must happen doesn't automatically invalidate the thesis – for it's sometimes the case that infinitely many things *do* happen, even in finite time. These niceties will be explored below. Whatever the ultimate disposition of the infinite-regress argument against constructivism may be, however, enough has been said to establish that Ashmore's remedy doesn't address the problem.

Now let's take it from the top.

I will examine two versions of the infinite-regress argument against constructivism. Here is Niiniluoto's:

> Note first that some radical forms of relativism are inconsistent or imply a vicious infinite regress. Let us imitate Plato's argument ... by applying it to the claim that facts cannot exist unless constructed in a laboratory. Thus, a fact F exists if:

> (2) there is a laboratory B where F has been constructed.

> Now (2) expresses a fact, F' say, and it exists if:

(3) there is a laboratory B' where F' has been constructed,

etc. Continuing in this way, either we admit at some stage that some fact exists without construction or else we are involved in an infinite regress of an endless sequence of labs B, B', B'', ...

(Niiniluoto 1991: 151)

The reference to laboratories in this passage confuses things a little. It might be reasonable to attribute to Latour and other constructivists the view that all *scientific* facts are constructed in laboratories. But nobody would ever want to suggest that *all* facts, even the non-scientific ones, emanate from laboratories. For example, no laboratory was involved in the construction of the fact that Richard Nixon was a President of the United States, even if, as seems quite likely, this fact has been constructed. There are two ways to repair this deficiency in Niiniluoto's statement of the premises.

One course is to restrict the claim under examination to scientific facts. If we do this, however, then it's possible to block the regress by denying that the social construction of a scientific fact is itself a scientific fact. More generally, constructivists can avoid the regress by taking refuge in a retrenched position which claims only that certain classes of facts are constructed. The exemption may be granted either on the basis that the social construction of scientific fact F is an everyday fact, or on the ground that it's a *social*-scientific fact. People who take the first course are instrumental constructivists; those who take the second are (metaphysical) socialists. Instrumentalists and socialists have their share of problems. But the infinite-regress argument isn't one of them.

Alternatively, one might drop the reference to laboratories. The premise of this amended argument is the strong constructivist thesis that all facts are constructed (never mind where), and the dilemma is that this commits us to an infinite regress of constructive events. This more general conclusion promises to be just as unsettling to constructivists as Niiniluoto's infinite sequence of labs. It should be noted that Niiniluoto doesn't spell out exactly why the infinite regress is a problem for constructivists. His discussion of the problem ends with the presentation of the regress. Presumably, what he has in mind is the fact that even Latour is committed to the finitude of laboratories. When the missing finale is added, Niiniluoto's original argument looks like this:

1   Suppose that (strong) constructivism is true.
2   Then there must be an infinite sequence of laboratories B, B', B'', ...
3   There are only finitely many laboratories.
4   Therefore, constructivism is false.

The premise of the amended argument – that there have been only finitely many human constructions of any type – is, of course, just as compelling as the thesis that there are finitely many labs. If this is what the problem is, then the substitution of generic constructions for laboratory constructions would certainly not weaken the argument. Here's what the generic argument looks like after a few additional details have been inserted:

1　Suppose that (strong) constructivism is true.
2　Then for any fact F, there's another fact F' – namely the fact that F is constructed.
3　Therefore, if anything is a fact, there must be infinitely many constructive events.
4　There are facts.
5　Therefore, there are infinitely many constructive events.
6　But there can only be finitely many constructive events.
7　Therefore constructivism is false.

Finn Collin gives an infinite-regress argument that's at least superficially different from the one I've derived from Niiniluoto. Collin begins by explicitly exempting metaphysical socialism – the view that 'social facts are somehow autonomous and ontologically prior to natural facts' (Collin 1993: 25) – from the scope of the argument. His target is the 'broad symmetry thesis' that 'we should conceive both natural fact and social fact as constructed' (26):

> The phenomenon under examination is the *social* construction of fact; that is, the constructing agent is society. The new, broad symmetry thesis makes it clear how this social construction is to be understood in concrete terms: social fact must be conceived as being constructed by the research activities of social scientists and by the way their results are adopted by larger social groups, building those results into various artifacts, technologies and procedures. But these activities are themselves social phenomena, which, by the same reasoning, must be taken to be themselves constructed by yet other social activities, and so on *ad infinitum*.
>
> (26)

Unlike Niiniluoto's truncated presentation, Collin's goes on to specify why this is a problem for constructivism. Here is where the superficial difference arises. According to Collin, the infinite-regress argument reveals 'a radical indeterminacy of social fact and, as a consequence, natural fact as well' (26):

> The indeterminacy comes about as follows. For any putative social fact, it follows on constructivist assumptions that its status as a fact is due to certain social activities through which it is constructed. Prominent among these activities are scientific research efforts that have the

constructed facts as their subject matter. We now go looking for these social activities. Either we find none, which renders the putative fact indeterminate right away, or some can be found. In the latter case, we may repeat the procedure, investigating the activities through which those certifying facts are themselves certified. Since the number of social science projects is necessarily finite, we will sooner or later arrive at some putative social fact that is not certified by such a research effort (that is, it is not constructed by some meta-fact). We must conclude that this uncertified fact is radically indeterminate, since the conditions that would render it determinate are missing. No sentence S expressing the fact may be asserted, nor may the contradictory sentence non-S. From this point, the indeterminacy spreads backward through the chain of (putative) facts that certify other (putative) facts …, finally reaching the fact at which the regress started. Both social and natural reality end up being radically indeterminate.

(26)

Collin concedes that those who draw a distinction between scientific facts and everyday facts – in our terms, instrumental constructivists – may be exempt from this *reductio* (though he's not entirely sure). Strong constructivism, however, is deemed to have been definitively refuted: 'social constructivists must retrench' (44).

So which is the problem for constructivism? Is it that it entails an infinitude of constructive events, or that it entails a radical indeterminacy? The two charges come to the same thing. Collin's argument merely permutes the deductive steps of Niiniluoto's. His argument can be represented as follows:

1   Suppose that (strong) constructivism is true.
2   Then for any fact F, there's another fact F' – namely the fact that F is constructed.
3   Therefore, if anything is a fact, there must be infinitely many constructive events.
4   There can only be finitely many constructive events.
5   Therefore there are no facts (this is what 'radical indeterminism' seems to come to).
6   But there are facts.
7   Therefore strong constructivism is false.

Obviously, this argument works if, and only if, the previous argument works. They both arrive at the same conclusion from the same premises – that constructivism is true, that there can only be finitely many constructive events, and that there are facts. The only difference is that the first argument derives the infinitude of constructive events from the premise that there are facts, while Collin's argument derives the absence of facts from the finitude of constructive events. I'll direct my subsequent remarks to the earlier argument, since it strikes me as more straightforward.

Let me start with a criticism of the original laboratory-based version of the argument that Niiniluoto gives us. If we take Niiniluoto's words literally (to an unreasonable degree), there's an obvious gap in the argument. Niiniluoto tells us that for any fact F, there is a laboratory B where F has been constructed, and that therefore there must be a laboratory B' where 'F is constructed' is constructed, and so on. The dilemma, according to Niiniluoto, is that constructivists seem to be committed to the existence of 'an endless sequence of labs' (151). One weakness in this formulation, already noted, is that not even the strongest of strong constructivists would want to claim that every fact is constructed in a laboratory. But set that problem aside. Niiniluoto's argument won't go through even if we suppose that constructivists are committed to the laboratory-based construction of all facts. The assumptions (1) that every fact is constructed in a laboratory, and (2) that there are infinitely many facts aren't strong enough to yield the conclusion that there must exist infinitely many laboratories. It's true that there has to be an infinite sequence of laboratories B, B', B'', ... corresponding to the infinitude of constructed facts. But the premises don't dictate that all these Bs need to be *distinct*. For all that the premises tell us, the fact F, the fact that F is constructed, the fact that the fact that F is constructed is constructed, and so on *ad infinitum*, can all be constructed in a single lab.

This is, of course, a pedantic objection. The root problem obviously resides in the infinitude of *constructive events* that seems to be entailed by constructivism. Even if a single lab provided adequate facilities for the construction of the entire infinite sequence of facts beginning with F, the (undoubtedly finite) personnel of the lab still wouldn't have enough *time* to construct them all. No doubt Niiniluoto's talk about an endless sequence of labs was a loose way of referring to the endless sequence of constructions. It doesn't matter that the infinitude of constructions doesn't entail an infinitude of laboratories. The infinitude of constructive events is itself as much of an impossibility as the existence of infinitely many labs. The latter is ruled out by lack of adequate space; the former is impossible on account of limitations of time.

This corrected version of the argument still has some important gaps, however. For one thing, it suffers from the same lacuna as the original argument about laboratories. The infinite-regress argument establishes that there has to be an infinite sequence of constructive events; but it doesn't yet show that all these events have to be distinct. I don't claim that they *aren't* all distinct. I merely point out that realists who want to refute strong constructivism with the infinite-regress argument have to do more work than either Niiniluoto or Collin have done. Actually, this isn't the problem that I want to press. My guess is that realists can provide *this* missing piece of the argument (though I don't think it will be trivially easy). I bring up the issue only as a means of introducing a more general problem for the infinite-regress argument.

Let's grant that each of the facts in the infinite sequence 'F', 'F is constructed', and so on, is distinct from all the others. Then constructivism is committed to the view that we need to construct infinitely many facts in order to constitute any single fact. The dilemma is supposed to be that we can't have accomplished this feat in the finite amount of time that's been available to us. But the derivation of this dilemma is based on another tacit assumption – namely that *the construction of each fact in the infinite sequence fills a different non-zero interval of time*. This assumption may be true; but it isn't obviously true. It's certainly possible to decompose temporally finite events into infinitely many distinct parts. This is what at least some of Zeno's paradoxes are about. Presumably, the general answer to problems like those posed by Zeno is that decompositions of events don't necessarily result in parts that correspond to real-time stages of the event. That being the case, how can we be sure that the infinite sequence 'F', 'F is constructed', … isn't such an infinitary decomposition of a finite event? Perhaps there are temporally finite constructive operations that have the effect of constituting infinitely many facts at once.

Here's an analogy that makes this possibility more salient. It's a sort of social version of an Eleatic paradox. Suppose two agents, A and B, find themselves in a prisoner's-dilemma situation. If they both perform action x, they receive 10 utiles each; if they both perform action y, they both *lose* ten utiles; if one of them does x and the other does y, the first loses 100 utiles and the second gains 100 utiles. In this game, y is the dominant move, and it results in a loss of 10 utiles by both players. When placed in such a situation, however, people often arrive at an understanding whereby each one makes the non-dominant move x, which results in a *gain* of 10 utiles by both players. This kind of understanding may very well be the prototype for a social convention. But how is such an understanding possible? Player A will make the non-dominant move x only if she believes that B will also do x. But B will do x only if he believes that A will do x. Moreover, A knows this. Therefore, A will do x only if A believes that B believes that A will do x. But of course, B will believe that A will do x only if B believes that A believes that B will do x – and so on *ad infinitum*. The social understanding between A and B is dependent on their each having a prior belief, which in turn depends on a still prior belief, and so on. Evidently, the players have to establish infinitely many conditions for their understanding to be in place. But then, since the game takes only a finite amount of time, how can such an understanding ever be established? The answer, once again, can only be that the infinitely many parts into which the understanding is decomposed must not correspond to real-time steps. We're willing to say this even before we understand exactly how the parts of the understanding are put in place. Why can't constructivists say the same about the infinitely many facts that have to be constructed in order to constitute any single fact? This is not a rhetorical question. There may be a good answer to it; but realists haven't given it yet.

I don't wish to suggest that the infinite-regress objection counts for nothing. It points to a conceptual problem that constructivists need to address. But the objection isn't as decisive as Niiniluoto and Collin take it to be. There may be ways of addressing it, just as there are ways of addressing the formally very similar Eleatic paradoxes.

11   The Duhemian asymmetry

Each of the next three chapters is devoted to a new argument against strong constructivism. Featured in this chapter is a scientific-practice argument with the same structure as Trout's (see Chapter 8): a practice is cited, the occurrence of which is presumably conceded by constructivists, but which can't be explained by the constructivist thesis. Trout maintained that the scientific use of archaic data was such a practice. I argued that this practice doesn't pose any insurmountable problems for constructivism. But there's another practice that's going to be harder for constructivists to rationalize.

The history of science is replete with episodes wherein a theory in good standing generates observational expectations that are not borne out by empirical research. On some obsolete views of science, such occurrences already provide us with sufficient grounds to reject constructivism – for by delivering the datum not-X when the scientific community's belief in theory T leads it to expect X, isn't the world speaking against the belief in T with its own independent voice? We all know by now that matters aren't quite so simple. For one thing, Lakatos (1978) and Duhem (1951) before him have taught us that proponents of T may routinely shield their theory from the accusation of having been truly disconfirmed by attributing the *apparent* disconfirmation to faults in the auxiliary hypotheses. Let's call this defensive move the *Duhemian manoeuvre*. The availability of Duhemian manoeuvres opens the door for a constructivist account of apparent disconfirmations – at least temporarily. If, as seems to be admitted all round, an apparent disconfirmation of T may or may not be regarded as an actual disconfirmation, then it's open to constructivists to argue that T's fate is determined by negotiation. Indeed, given the eternal availability of Duhemian manoeuvres, it's at least arguable that the voice of Nature cancels itself out and has *no* bearing on the fate of T. So it seems that the phenomenon of apparent disconfirmation doesn't, by itself, make a serious problem for constructivism.

Let's grant, for the sake of the argument, that the voice of Nature has no bearing on the disposition of apparent disconfirmations. Still, what about the occurrence of the apparent disconfirmation itself? To grant that the voice of Nature has no effect on the outcome of a scientific decision is not yet to grant that Nature hasn't *spoken*. One might claim that Nature speaks, but that Science ignores her. This would not be strong constructivism. Strong constructivists are not only committed to the view that the disposition of apparent disconfirmations is a matter of negotiations; they also have to regard it as negotiable whether the apparent disconfirmation occurs in the first place. But, if this is so, then why would partisans of the theory T ever admit, without a struggle, that the apparent disconfirmation of T *has* taken place? Why would they ever take on the burden of engaging in Duhemian manoeuvres? This is the scientific practice that needs explaining – the fact that, in scientific disputes, it typically happens that one side spontaneously takes on the burden of saving a favoured hypothesis by means of Duhemian manoeuvres, while the other side doesn't. Let's call this phenomenon the *Duhemian asymmetry*.

A pair of historical examples will help to bring the issue into focus. The first episode is discussed by Laudan:

> The Newtonian theory predicted that the rotation of the earth on its axis would cause a radial protrusion along the equator and a constriction at the poles – such that the earth's actual shape would be that of an oblate spheroid, rather than (as natural philosophers from Aristotle through Descartes had maintained) that of a uniform sphere, or a sphere elongated along the polar axis. By the early 18th century, there were well-established geodesic techniques for ascertaining the shape and size of the earth (to which all parties agreed) ... Advocates of the two major cosmogonies of the day, the Cartesian and the Newtonian, looked to such measurements as providing decisive evidence for choosing between the systems of Descartes and Newton. At great expense, the Paris Académie des Sciences organized a series of elaborate expeditions to Peru and Lapland to collect the appropriate data. The evidence was assembled by scientists generally sympathetic to the Cartesian/Cassini hypothesis. Nonetheless, it was *their* interpretation, as well as everyone else's, that the evidence indicated that the diameter of the earth at its equator was significantly larger than along its polar axis. This result, in turn, was regarded as decisive evidence showing the superiority of Newtonian over Cartesian celestial mechanics.
>
> (Laudan 1996: 48)

In this case, the vanquished Cartesians didn't even try to defuse the apparent disconfirmation. They capitulated on the spot. This capitulation is unmysterious from a realist perspective: Nature spoke, and Science listened. From a constructivist point of view, however, the behaviour of the Cartesians must appear exceedingly bizarre. If it's all a matter of negotiation, then, by simply conceding that the data had disconfirmed their hypothesis, the Cartesians gave away one of their strongest bargaining chips. But the dilemma for constructivism doesn't depend on this type of immediate capitulation in the face of contrary evidence. The Cartesians *could* have engaged in Duhemian manoeuvres to explain the anomalous data without giving up their mechanical hypothesis. They might have argued that the earth is a special case, its anomalous shape having been imparted to it directly by the hand of God. But this alternative scenario would have been just as problematic for constructivism as the actual one. For, by engaging in these Duhemian manoeuvres, the Cartesians would still have tacitly accepted that the measurements of the earth's shape were correct. Once again, this concession doesn't make good bargaining sense.

Laudan makes the point that the Cartesians could also have engaged in Duhemian manoeuvres at a lower level by denying that the apparent disconfirmation had occurred in the first place:

> It would have been *logically possible* for the defenders of Cartesian physics to find some way post hoc for challenging the data ...
>
> (49)

Well, if constructivism is true, then the fact that denying the data was a *logical* possibility would have been licence enough (perhaps more than enough!) to engage in that denial. Moreover, the explanatory challenge to constructivism would have been the same even if the defenders of Cartesian physics *had* tried to defuse the data by Duhemian operations such as claiming that the phenomena had been misobserved or misrecorded. For, once again, to engage in these defensive operations is tacitly to concede that there's something that needs to be defended against. By denying that the data were as reported, the Cartesians would have admitted at least that the data that were *reported* made a problem for their physics. In this scenario, they would have denied that their theory was disconfirmed – they would even have denied that their theory was *apparently* disconfirmed. But they would have conceded that there was an apparent disconfirmation of their belief that Cartesian physics was not apparently disconfirmed. Once again, this concession is just as troublesome for constructivism as the immediate capitulation that actually took place. The problem for constructivism is to explain why either side in a dispute *ever* has to adopt a defensive stance, at *any* level. Why not simply maintain that there's nothing to defend against?

The second example is drawn from a discussion by constructivists Collins and Pinch (1993). The authors review the findings of the famous Eddington expedition which supposedly confirmed Einstein's theory of general relativity. Einstein had predicted that starlight passing close to the sun would be displaced by an amount substantially greater than was predicted by Newtonian theory. A solar eclipse in 1918 provided Eddington and his team with an opportunity to measure the displacement. As is well known, Eddington proclaimed the results to be a triumph for general relativity. Collins and Pinch note that this conclusion was far from ordained on the basis of the data. Some of the photographic plates did produce measurements of displacement that were roughly in accord with Einstein's prediction. But there were also plates that produced measurements in conformity to the Newtonian theory. Nevertheless, 'on 6 November 1919, the Astronomer Royal announced that the observations had confirmed Einstein's theory' (Collins and Pinch 1993: 50). The data from the Newtonian plates were explained as the result of 'systematic error', although Eddington was unable to provide any convincing evidence that this was indeed the case.

In contrast to the Cartesians' capitulation in the face of apparently disconfirming data, the Einsteinians proclaimed a *victory* in the face of apparently disconfirming data. Collins and Pinch tell us this story because they think it will incline us toward a constructivist and away from a realist reading of scientific history:

> We have no reason to think that relativity is anything but the truth –
> and a very beautiful, delightful and astonishing truth it is – but it is a
> truth which came into being as a result of decisions about how we
> should live our scientific lives and how we should license our scientific
> observations; it was a truth brought about by agreement to agree about
> new things. It was not a truth forced on us by the inexorable logic of a
> set of crucial experiments.
>
> (Collins and Pinch 1993: 54)

Certainly Eddington's Duhemian manoeuvre is unsurprising from a constructivist perspective. At least it's unsurprising *given* the existence of the apparently disconfirming data from the 'Newtonian' plates. But where did these data come from? Who negotiated that there would be Newtonian data, and why did they negotiate it? Once again, the very need to engage in Duhemian manoeuvres has no ready explanation in the constructivist paradigm.

What can constructivists say about the Duhemian asymmetry? Well, they could take refuge in instrumental constructivism or some other thesis which claims less than the strong-constructivist hypothesis that all facts are constructed. They could claim that scientific hypotheses have a bearing on everyday facts, and that some everyday facts are independent. Even the most arcane of quantum-mechanical hypotheses eventually issues in expectations that some middle-sized objects are going to have some pedestrian properties – e.g., that the needle on a particular dial is going to swing to the right. If this is so, then apparent disconfirmations of our expectations about everyday facts may be given to us by Nature. In brief, the Duhemian asymmetry makes no problems for the weaker constructivisms. In light of the discussion of Chapter 9, however, this is a boring conclusion. We're no longer talking about the weaker forms of constructivism.

If you're a strong constructivist, you have to say that there's no independent fact of the matter whether a theory has been disconfirmed. If a favoured theory is apparently disconfirmed, one can always engage in Duhemian manoeuvres to preserve it. But for constructivists, there's also no independent fact of the matter whether an *apparent* disconfirmation has occurred. At least on the face of it, there's no reason why a theory should ever fall on such hard times that it needs to be defended against an apparent disconfirmation. Proponents of the theory can instead deny that the apparent disconfirmation has taken place. They can explain the *apparent* occurrence of an apparent disconfirmation by Duhemian manoeuvres at a lower level. At this level, the claim is that the putative data which constitute the apparent disconfirmation of the theory are not data at all – that events were misrecorded, that the records were misread, etc. Moreover, there's no independent fact of the matter at this lower level either. The claim that a record was (or wasn't) misread is in turn open to negotiation. And so on. For strong constructivists, there's no end to the sequence of evidential claims that can be negotiated.

Here's a more precise description of the problematic scenario. Let $X0$ be a contested claim (empirical or theoretical – it makes no difference) about the natural world, and for all $i > 0$, let Xi be the claim that there's a fact which apparently confirms $X(i-1)$. Now suppose that two scientists A and B disagree about $X2$, namely, the claim that $X1$ is apparently confirmed. Then they will begin to negotiate the truth-value of $X2$. If the pro side wins – if it's established by negotiations that $X2$ is true – then opponents of $X0$ still have two more chances to avert the undesirable conclusion that $X0$ is truly confirmed. Having been forced to concede that $X1$ is apparently confirmed, they can try to establish by negotiation that the apparent confirmation of $X1$ isn't an actual confirmation – i.e., that $X0$ isn't really apparently confirmed. And, if they fail in that endeavour, they can try to negotiate the result that, while $X0$ really is apparently confirmed, it isn't really confirmed. In general, *the higher up in the sequence the negotiations begin, the more negotiations have to be gone through before one side has to concede defeat.*

Now suppose that negotiations begin at Xn. This means that opponents of $X0$ concede that $X(n+1)$ is true (equivalently, that Xn is apparently confirmed), and that they take on the Duhemian burden of arguing that the apparent confirmation of Xn isn't a real confirmation (equivalently, that $X(n-1)$ isn't apparently confirmed). They get n strikes, and then they're out. But if they refused to concede $X(n+1)$ – if they started negotiations at the $(n+1)$th level – they would have $(n+1)$ strikes before they're out. Therefore, it would be more rational for them to start bargaining at $(n+1)$ than at n. But this is true for any n. Therefore the indicated course is not to concede that there's a problem at *any* level. If you want to establish that $X0$ is false, then you should always deny that it's even apparently confirmed, and that there's any apparent confirmation for the notion that it's apparently confirmed, and so on. In sum, your position should be that there's no problem at all. But if there's no problem, then why does anyone ever shoulder the Duhemian burden?

The broad outlines of the indicated strong constructivist reply are clear. Shouldering the Duhemian burden makes the task of winning the current round of negotiations more difficult. But for strong constructivists, negotiations are everything in the game of science. Therefore, the only reason we might have for taking on the Duhemian burden in the course of some negotiation is that this liability is compensated by the fact that it will facilitate *other* negotiations that we're also engaged in, or that we anticipate that we might be engaged in. Now there are circumstances in which, so far as I can tell, an analysis along these lines might work. But I'm sure that there are also circumstances where it won't work. It might work when the requisite denial of some putative fact is inconsistent with a vast network of already-negotiated facts. For instance, suppose it's claimed that X apparently disconfirms T, and suppose also that the denial of X entails that the earth is flat. If strong constructivism is true, then the sphericity of the earth is just another negotiated construction. But that doesn't necessarily mean that it's easy to dislodge. Dislodging it would require that we renegotiate an enormous array of already-negotiated facts about the nature of the universe we live in. If your main interest is in promulgating T, you may very well have an easier task of negotiation if you accepted both X and the sphericity of the Earth, and engaged in Duhemian manoeuvres to avoid the conclusion that X truly disconfirms T. According to Latour and Woolgar, every scientific hypothesis is situated in an 'agonistic field' of supportive and conflicting hypotheses, and the reality that the hypothesis describes (which is nothing more than the difficulty of negotiating its negation) is constituted by its location in the field. The explanation of the Duhemian asymmetry just proffered is that it's resorted to when an outright denial of the problematic statement is unnegotiable on account of the statement's strong position in the agonistic field.

So far as it goes, I think this explanation works (more precisely, I think it would work if strong constructivism weren't plagued by the conceptual problems to be discussed in the next two chapters). In fact, I want to defend it against a potential realist objection. In effect, the constructivist claim is that the Duhemian asymmetry can be accounted for by the different locations of the thesis and its contradictory in the agonistic field. But, realists might object, if you're a strong constructivist, there's no independent fact of the matter about where a particular hypothesis is located in the agonistic field. In that case, why would anyone ever admit that their favoured position has a weak place in the field? Isn't such a concession just a variant of the Duhemian asymmetry itself? It is – but I've just conceded that there are explicable cases of the Duhemian asymmetry. The constructivist answer to why anyone would ever agree that their favoured position has a weak place in the agonistic field is that it's sometimes the case that it's been negotiated that this thesis shall have a weak place in the field. And if it's asked why anyone should agree that such a fact has indeed been negotiated, the answer can be that it's been negotiated that this fact has been negotiated. These are, of course, the first two steps of the infinite series generated by Niiniluoto and Collin. If Niiniluoto and Collin are right in supposing that the traversal of this infinite series is a temporally infinite task, then strong constructivism is incoherent, and there's no need for the argument that I'm in the midst of developing. But it's my view that the Niiniluoto–Collin arguments are inconclusive (see Chapter 10). If this is right, then it hasn't yet been demonstrated that people can't arrive at infinitely many negotiated agreements in finite time. And if people *can* negotiate infinitely many facts, then there's no reason why everyone shouldn't agree about the structure of the agonistic field. Moreover, if everyone agrees about the structure of the agonistic field, then it's not surprising that one party to a scientific dispute sometimes takes on the Duhemian burden. They do so when the hypothesis that there is nothing to defend against has a weak position in the field.

I grant that these cases make no new problems for strong constructivism. But there are other scenarios which aren't susceptible to this type of explanation. Sometimes the conflicting hypotheses of different scientists are located in *equipotent* places in the field, and yet one side shoulders the Duhemian burden. Suppose that one of two equally well-regarded theories makes the untested prediction X, that the other makes the prediction not-X, and that X and not-X are agonistically equipotent – i.e., that the negotiation of X is neither more nor less difficult than the negotiation of not-X. Then the experiment is done. I claim that in virtually every case, when the experiment is done, one side or the other either immediately capitulates and gives up their theory, or (much more often) takes a defensive posture and begins Duhemian manoeuvres to save their theoretical hypothesis. Laudan's example of the Cartesian versus Newtonian predictions about the shape of the earth is a case in point. Prior to the measurements by the Académie des Sciences, the two theories and their resultant hypotheses about the earth were agonistically more or less equipotent. After the measurements, the Cartesians conceded defeat. This instance of asymmetry can't be explained by the agonistic inequality of the contenders.

There's a temptation here to suppose that the Cartesians (and the Einsteinians of our second example) couldn't have denied the validity of the troublesome measurements without making further problems for themselves down the line. Let's liberate the example under consideration from extraneous historical detail. Suppose that scientist A's hypothesis is that a needle swings to the left (under certain conditions), and that B's agonistically equipotent hypothesis is that it swings to the right. Then, after the experiment is done, isn't one or the other of them going to have to deny a host of solidly negotiated facts about optics, the psychology and neurophysiology of perception, the physical construction of the instrument, etc.?

The answer is: not if they're agonistically equipotent and strong constructivism is true. The suspicion that one of them is going to get into more trouble than the other is due to a surreptitious *realist* assumption that there's an independent fact of the matter about what they observe – that they're both going to *see* the needle swinging to one side or the other, and that either A or B is going to have to deny the testimony of their senses. But, of course, if strong constructivism is true, then whether A sees the needle swinging to the left or to the right is also a product of negotiation. And if it's true, as was assumed, that A and B are agonistically equipotent prior to the experiment, then either account of the result of the experiment is as negotiable as the other. To suppose that either side is going to have a harder time negotiating its case is to suppose that there's something outside the agonistic field that affects how difficult it is to negotiate some results. And that's to concede the victory to the realists.

So the dilemma for strong constructivists remains: agonistic considerations don't help to explain the Duhemian asymmetry in cases where the contending hypotheses are agonistically equipotent. What could possibly impel a scientist to shoulder the Duhemian burden when his prospects for winning the point are just as good as his opponent's? The existence of independent facts that intrude on our negotiations provides a ready explanation. If not realism, then what? The strong constructivist has, I think, only three minor cards left to play, and none of them looks very promising. The first is to explain the Duhemian asymmetry by the ineptitude of some negotiators. This desperation move won't do, for it won't be able to explain the co-ordination that obtains between scientific opponents. After the crucial observation is made, it's inevitably the case that the proponents of one side either capitulate or take on the Duhemian burden, and that proponents of the other side don't. If the Duhemian asymmetry were due to intellectual deficiencies of the personnel, it would happen just as frequently that both sides claim victory, or that both sides spontaneously start to engage in defensive operations. (There's no reason to suppose that better bargainers would systematically favour either one of two agonistically equipotent hypotheses.) But scientific adversaries are always able to find some level of phenomena where they both agree about who needs to go on the defensive.

The second gambit is to deny that the Duhemian asymmetry is a fact that needs explaining. After all, it's not as if the Duhemian asymmetry were itself an independent fact that's forced on the constructivist. It, too, is a negotiated outcome. The situation is superficially similar to that which obtains with the success-of-science argument (see Chapter 7). In the latter argument, the realist claims that the success of science can't be explained by constructivism. The constructivist replies that the success of science is itself constructed, and so poses no explanatory problem. In the Duhemian argument, I claim the constructivists can't explain the Duhemian asymmetry. Can't constructivists, here too, reply that the phenomenon in question is merely constructed? They can. In fact, to be consistent, this is what they *must* say. But there's an important difference between the consequences of this reply in the two arguments. What drives the success-of-science argument is the suspicion that if everything is constructed, then there would be no way to account for the success of science. This suspicion is exorcised by realizing that it's founded on the tacit assumption that the success of science is an independent fact. When we recall that the success of science is itself constructed (if strong constructivism is true), there's no longer any mystery about it that requires a realist explanation. We can easily imagine how a certain confluence of interests and advantages might have led to such a negotiated result. The claim that the success of science is constructed *undercuts* the realist's demand for an explanation. It's only the *independent* success of science that calls for a realist explanation.

But not everything ceases to be mysterious on the hypothesis that it's constructed. Suppose that, all at once, everybody in the world came to subscribe to the view that an event had taken place which goes counter to countless opinions which are universally held and deeply cherished by all of humanity. Such an event would be exceedingly mysterious from a strong constructivist point of view. To be sure, strong constructivists would say that the fact that this event had taken place was itself constructed. But that wouldn't diminish the mystery at all. If it were to be established that such an event had taken place, the hypothesis that the fact was discovered would have to be considered more explanatory than the hypothesis that it was invented – for who would have invented such a fact, and why? Similarly, the hypothesis that the Duhemian asymmetry is constructed doesn't explain why the Duhemian asymmetry is a fact. If strong constructivism is true, the putative fact that the Duhemian asymmetry takes place should have a very lowly position in the agonistic field. Recall the co-ordination that's required for the Duhemian asymmetry to take place: one party to the dispute inevitably initiates defensive manoeuvres, and the other party doesn't. It never happens that both start to defend, or that neither starts to defend. How is this co-ordination effected? There's no mystery about it on the realist assumption that Nature has had her say. But if Nature plays no role in the proceedings, then how is the mutual determination made that one side and not the other shall begin to defend? On our view of how things work in this universe, such a feat would be nomologically impossible. To be sure, this view of how things work in the universe, like the Duhemian asymmetry itself, is a constructed fact. But the first of these constructed facts is *antagonistic* to the second. Given that we've negotiated the view of the universe that we have, there's no accounting for how the incompatible fact of the Duhemian asymmetry has also managed to get itself negotiated. On the other hand, there is an entirely adequate realist explanation for the Duhemian asymmetry: the disputants are cued by a signal emanating from an independent realm. This explanatory advantage is a reason for realism.

Do constructivists have to recognize explanatory goodness as a desideratum for an account of the world? I'll examine the constructivist attitude toward *a priori* principles like inference to the best explanation in Chapter 14. But here's a preliminary reply the persuasiveness of which even a constructivist will have to recognize: there's no *market* for non-explanatory systems of the world. Theories that *don't* explain the data can be generated *ad lib*. Adding one more to the pile isn't any kind of accomplishment.

Finally, constructivists may avail themselves of the observation, made in Chapter 8, that the constructivist thesis isn't logically restricted to consensual effects. In actual practice, constructivists have promulgated only a minute subset of logically possible constructivisms. All of these have been elaborations on the theme that the majority wins. Perhaps a vast majority is required, or a majority of experts. In any case, it's clear that all the extant constructivisms are committed to the view that if *everybody* subscribes to X, then X is a fact. In Chapter 8, I noted that not all social constructions are of this consensual type. There are even facts which are *anti*consensual: they become true if everybody disavows them. So there's a logical space for a position that says that natural facts are constructed by non-consensual social processes. Even the apocalyptic vision of a revelation that nobody wants or expects but everybody accepts is, at least *prima facie*, compatible with such a non-consensual constructivism. The Duhemian asymmetry can only be easier to accommodate. Suppose that putative facts X and not-X are equipotent in *consensual* processes – i.e., that it's neither more nor less difficult to get people to agree to X than it is to get them to repudiate it. Then a constructivism that postulates only consensual processes would be unable to explain the fact that one side spontaneously adopts a defensive stance. But the asymmetry can be explained by postulating the appropriate non-consensual processes. Here's one that will do the job: subscribing to X constitutes X, and subscribing to not-X also constitutes X. If this is how the facts about X are constructed, then the occurrence of a debate between proponents and opponents of X is already sufficient to construct X – i.e., to ensure the victory of the proponents. In these circumstances the opponents of any thesis T which implies not-X have no choice but to take on the burden of protecting T from its apparent disconfirmation by Duhemian manoeuvres. This is one way in which the Duhemian asymmetry may arise in a socially constructed world.

It might be objected that my sample principle of construction, according to which both avowal and disavowal of X constitute X, is indistinguishable from the hypothesis that X is an independent fact. I agree that the distinction isn't easy to make. But it's premature to say that it's impossible. Maybe the fact that X isn't true if nobody has any opinion about it at all would incline us to a constructivist view of X. More persuasively, it can be shown that there are facts which are clearly socially constructed, but whose principle of construction is just the one I used to explain the Duhemian asymmetry. Here is one: everybody's subscribing to the view that some individual P is widely known constitutes P's being widely known, and everyone's subscribing to the view that P is *not* widely known also constitutes P's being widely known. Moreover, P's renown will be constituted by any mix of the two opinions. Nevertheless, renown is a socially constructed property if anything is: P is not going to be renowned if nobody ever thinks about her at all. *Ab esse, ad posse*.

Doesn't this mean that strong constructivism is saved from refutation? Well, it's an avenue for salvation that warrants exploring. But nobody has explored it yet. The Duhemian argument isn't defused simply by noting the logical possibility that there might be constructive processes that lead to a Duhemian asymmetry. Once non-consensual processes are brought into play, it's possible to devise a *post hoc* constructivist explanation for *any* constellation of putative facts. But the same is true of an endless number of uninteresting hypotheses about the world, such as that everything happens according to God's will, that life is but a dream, that we are brains in a vat, and so on. What's required to give constructivism a measure of persuasive appeal is a prior specification of the conditions under which various constructive principles come into play. (The same type of repair job could produce interesting versions of any of the other cosmologies cited – the view that everything happens according to God's will becomes significant if one is able to give a prior account of God's cognitive processes from which certain intentions follow and others don't.) Without such a prior specification, the constructivist account is explanatorily empty. It has to be admitted that strong constructivism may one day be saved from the Duhemian objection by a theory about non-consensual processes. But this isn't much of an admission, since no coherent hypothesis can ever be so discredited as to be beyond all conceivable hope of resuscitation.

12   The problem of the two societies

Suppose that society S1 constructs a world in which the planets and stars are enormous spheres located at unimaginably great distances from us, and that society S2 constructs a world in which the heavenly bodies are immaterial lights in the sky placed directly overhead for our convenience by a solicitous deity. Then, if constructivists are right, there will be propositions X such that X is true on account of certain facts having been constructed by S1, and not-X is true on account of certain contrary facts having been constructed by S2. Is this a serious problem for constructivism?

My scenario has superficial similarities to Barnes and Bloor's (1982) classic example of the two tribes, each of which judges the other's beliefs to be peculiar by its own standards (see Chapter 2). Barnes and Bloor didn't think that this state of affairs made any problems for them. In fact, they brought it up because they thought that its contemplation would incline the reader to their view. But the view in question wasn't (metaphysical) constructivism. It was epistemic relativism. In Barnes and Bloor's scenario, the two tribes don't construct incompatible facts – they merely adopt incompatible beliefs. Barnes and Bloor's recommendation that we describe each of the beliefs as warranted relative to the 'methods and assumptions' of the respective tribe will be evaluated in Chapter 15. Whatever the outcome of that evaluation may be, it's clear that the mere existence of societies with conflicting belief systems doesn't make a problem for epistemic relativism. There's no contradiction in saying that belief in X is warranted relative to the methods and assumptions of S1, and that belief in not-X is warranted relative to the methods and assumptions of S2. But (metaphysical) constructivism isn't merely an epistemic thesis. Latour, Woolgar, Collins, Pinch, Knorr-Cetina, Ashmore, Pickering, etc., don't regard the social negotiations relating to a scientific hypothesis as merely providing epistemic warrants for certain beliefs. *The negotiations supposedly turn the hypothesis (or its negation) into a fact.* But then the problem of the two societies needs an answer. We can't simply say that negotiations in S1 turn X into a fact and that negotiations in S2 turn not-X into a fact, and leave it at that – for how can X and not-X both be facts?

   This dilemma lies so close to the surface that one might have expected that it would be addressed in the earliest rounds of the debate about constructivism. Yet the only relevant discussion that I'm familiar with occurs in Nelson Goodman's (1978) *Ways of Worldmaking*. Goodman's views will be discussed below. As the title of his book indicates, Goodman puts forward an unequivocally constructivist thesis. However, his philosophical ancestry is quite different from that of the sociologists of science whose philosophical pronouncements comprise the main target of my analysis. As far as I know, the problem of the two societies has not been discussed in the sociologically inspired constructivist literature.

   The analysis of the two-societies dilemma turns on whether or not constructivism is combined with *ontological* relativism. Latour and Woolgar try to manage without any relativism at all (1986: 180). Evidently, their view is that facts are constructed, but that once they've been constructed, they are realities, or have 'out-there-ness', for everyone. This view leads directly to the dilemma – for how can X and not-X both be realities for everyone? Since Latour and Woolgar don't address the problem, we'll have to work out for ourselves what can be said in defence of their ontologically absolutistic constructivism. Goodman, on the other hand, deals with the two-societies problem at considerable length. He reasons as follows: if S1 constructs a world in which the stars are enormous and distant, and S2 constructs a world where the stars are small and close, then S1 and S2 must live in different worlds. This is the thesis that I call ontological relativism – it's the view that incompatible facts may both be true if they are facts about different worlds. We'll look at Latour and Woolgar's absolutistic constructivism first and then turn to Goodman's relativistic solution.

Can there be a constructivism without (ontological) relativism? In light of the two-societies scenario, there's only one way to avoid the derivation of a contradiction without invoking relativism: deny that the scenario can ever take place. It has to be shown that S1's construction of X precludes S2's construction of not-X, for all X and for all S1 and S2. One strategy might be to deny that any and all hypotheses are constructible. If it's true that some hypotheses are unconstructible, then constructivists may be able to defuse putative instances of the two-societies dilemma by claiming either that X or its negation cannot be constructed. The problem for *strong* constructivists is that to make this move is to admit that there are independent facts about the world. For suppose that X cannot be constructed. This doesn't yet rule out the possibility that X is true. Scientific realists don't think that electrons can be constructed; but this doesn't preclude their believing that electrons exist. Now every fact is either a constructed fact or an independent fact – constructivists and realists agree that construction and independence are the only two paths to facticity. Thus if X can't be constructed, and X is true, then X must be an independent fact – in which case strong constructivism is false. So the assumption that X can't be constructed forces the constructivist to admit that X is false. But this is to say that not-X is a fact. Now we may or may not be able to claim coherently that not-X is constructible in these circumstances. But, even if it makes sense to say that not-X is constructible, there could be no opportunity for anyone to perform the construction, since the truth of not-X follows deductively from the assumptions that X can't be constructed and that X isn't an independent fact. No matter how you slice it, the assumption that some hypotheses can't be constructed leads to the conclusion that there are independent facts.

The situation for constructivism is even more hopeless than the foregoing argument suggests. In order to avoid contradiction by this route, constructivists have to claim more than that some facts can't be constructed. The contradiction is derivable unless it's claimed that for *every* proposition X, either X or not-X is unconstructible. But we've just seen that if X is unconstructible, then either X or not-X is an independent fact. Evidently, this manner of avoiding contradiction requires us to postulate not only that independent facts exist, but that *all* facts are independent. So it's not just strong constructivists who are unable to avail themselves of this gambit. The appeal to unconstructible facts doesn't resolve the two-societies dilemma for constructivists of *any* stripe.

An alternative strategy for dealing with the two-societies problem is to concede that any hypothesis is constructible, but also to claim that the principles of construction are such that the conditions for the construction of X and the conditions for the construction of not-X can never simultaneously be satisfied. Would this fact about the laws of construction already constitute an independent fact about the world which belies the strong constructivist thesis? I'm not sure. It seems *prima facie* possible for constructivists to defend themselves against this charge by claiming that the laws of construction are *logical* truths, and that the constructivist thesis applies only to contingent propositions about the world. In any case, this is not an objection that I feel capable of driving home. But constructivists are going to have problems enough without it. For any particular X, whether or not the construction of X precludes the construction of not-X, is going to depend on what the laws of construction are. If the world were constructed by a simple majority rule (the thesis that has the most supporters wins), then the two-societies problem wouldn't arise. The more numerous society would win. (We would also need to postulate a rule to cover the possibility of a tie.) But no constructivist has ever championed such a rule. In fact, I know of nothing that's been said about constructive processes that would allow us to conclude that the construction of X precludes the construction of not-X, for any X. For Latour and Woolgar, for instance, a hypothesis is constructed by rising to a position of potency in the *agonistic field*. Let's place their description of the agonistic field before us:

An agonistic field is in many ways similar to any other political field of contention. Papers are launched which transform statement types. But the many positions which already make up the field influence the likelihood that a given argument will have an effect. An operation may or may not be successful depending on the number of people in the field, the unexpectedness of the point, the personality and institutional attachment of the authors, the stakes, and the style of the paper.

(237)

There is nothing in this characterization which would rule out there being *two* agonistic fields (just as there can be multiple 'political fields of contention') such that the personnel manning the positions that comprise either one have little or no influence on the personnel of the other, and such that X occupies a potent position in one field, while not-X occupies a potent position in the other. In fact, it surely is the case that there are conflicting fields of this kind. Compare the position of the astronomical hypothesis that the stars and planets are immense and far away in the agonistic field of the scientific community with its position in the agonistic field of Moslem fundamentalists. Latour and Woolgar's account of the principles of construction, together with their repudiation of relativism, leads ineluctably to a contradiction.

Of course, to refute Latour and Woolgar is not yet to refute non-relativistic constructivism itself. Perhaps there's another brand of constructivism with rules of construction that don't allow for the constitution of both X and not-X. However, any rules of construction possessing this property are also going to display certain other features that even a constructivist might baulk at. Consider the simple majority rule: what gets accepted by the greatest number wins. This rule would indeed enable constructivists to avoid the contradiction of the two-societies dilemma. But it would also have the consequence that a socially constructed reality has the property of 'out-there-ness' for individuals who have no connection to the players in the agonistic field. The fact that constructed realities impinge on those who play no role in the *negotiations* isn't a problem (I don't recall being consulted about the grammar of English). But it is curious to suppose that socially constructed realities impinge on *communities who haven't even heard about the negotiated results*. If the majority rule is to be understood in a way that defuses the two-societies problems, it has to be admitted that *our* reality might be constituted by a galactic consensus that we know nothing about.

Constructivists might say: so much the worse for the majority rule. But the galactic conspiracy is one horn of a dilemma which afflicts any rule of construction that avoids the two-societies problem. For suppose that the laws of construction preclude the possibility of constructing both X and not-X. These laws may or may not allow one society's constructions to be binding on another society with which it has no interaction. If they do allow it, then we get the galactic problem described above. If they don't allow it, then it follows that *nothing can be constructed unless all existing societies are in a state of interaction.* For if constructions are real (and if relativism is abjured), they must have out-there-ness for everybody. To admit that electrons don't have out-there-ness for Martians is to concede either that electrons are not real, or that reality is relative. But then the existence of any extraterrestrial community would render our own parochial agonistic activity powerless to construct realities. Moreover, the very possibility that such a community might exist already entails that we can't presently *know* that our constructions are real. In fact, we will never know it. For even if we discover one extraterrestrial community and merge our agonistic field with theirs, it still remains possible that there's another, undiscovered extraterrestrial community whose non-participation in our agonistic affairs cancels out the reality-producing effect of the new, expanded field.

Does this mean that nobody can construct any fact? Not at all. There's a special case where the conclusion of the galactic conspiracy argument is entirely acceptable. It costs us nothing to admit that there is a society on the other side of the galaxy that constructs facts which are binding on us, so long as those facts are *about their own society.* More generally, we don't get into trouble with the hypothesis that each society can only construct facts about itself: S1 can only construct facts about S1, and S2 can only construct facts about S2. (To be sure, S1 may be able to construct the fact that S2 has certain properties *according to S1* – that's still a fact about S1. What it can't construct is the fact that S2 really does have those properties.) Let's call the hypothesis that this is so by the name of *reasonable constructivism.*

There may be other constructivist theses for which the conclusion of the galactic conspiracy argument is acceptable, though I can't think of any. Be that as it may, it *isn't* acceptable for the general run of scientific facts about the physical world to be constructed. In order to avoid the contradiction which results from one society constructing one set of elementary particles for the universe and another society constructing an incompatible set, we must say that one society's construction precludes all others'. But then it must be supposed that this constructed physical reality is imposed on all other societies, regardless of whether they have any connection to the constructing society. Either our constructed quarks are imposed on the unsuspecting denizens of the other side of the galaxy, or vice versa. So the galactic conspiracy argument militates not only against strong constructivism but also against the substantially weaker thesis of scientific constructivism, i.e., the hypothesis which says only that scientific facts are constructed but leaves it open that there may be a class of unconstructed 'everyday' facts.

It's worth emphasizing that the two-societies argument is the only argument against less-than-strong constructivism in existence which doesn't pair up with a homologous argument against constructive empiricism. Constructive empiricists, like social constructivists, say that some scientific hypotheses are 'constructed'. But constructive empiricists don't regard this construction as a procedure which constitutes the truth of the hypothesis.

This is why they don't get into trouble with the two-societies scenario. When they say that S1 constructs X, and S2 constructs not-X, they mean it in a sense which doesn't imply that both X and not-X are true. On the contrary, van Fraassen makes it very clear that either S1 or S2 will have constructed a false hypothesis. It's just that neither S1 nor S2 may ever be in a position to know who made the mistake.

Briefly stated, it's been shown that if scientific constructivists abjure relativism, then they have to admit either that our scientific facts may be constructed by a galactic consensus that we know nothing about, or that we can never know whether our own constructions are real. It's clear that Latour, Knorr-Cetina and other social constructivists can't live with the second horn of this dilemma. I also doubt that they would be willing to accept the first. But who knows? It would greatly help to pin down the constructivist thesis to know whether constructed realities are supposed to have out-there-ness for individuals who are totally isolated from the players in the agonistic field. Until I hear otherwise, I'm going to assume that the galactic conspiracy argument forces scientific constructivists (*a fortiori* strong constructivists) to look to relativism for philosophical assistance.

Which brings us to Nelson Goodman (1978). Goodman would agree with Latour that we construct the world we live in. Unlike Latour, however, he explicitly adopts an ontological form of relativism: different people or groups may – and frequently do – construct and inhabit different worlds. This move seems to nip the problem of the two societies in the bud. If society S1 constructs X, and S2 constructs not-X, then S1 and S2 simply live in different worlds. S1 lives in a world where X is true, and S2 lives in a world where X *isn't* true. As Goodman says, 'contradiction is avoided by segregation' (Goodman 1996b: 152). The problem of the galactic conspiracy is avoided too. It can be admitted that extraterrestrials may construct a reality that we know nothing about, for that reality would merely be *their* reality. The fact that Goodman's ontological relativism avoids the two-societies problem without generating the dilemma of the galactic conspiracy is a strong argument in its favour. If you're going to be a strong or scientific constructivist, Goodman's way seems to provide the only hope for avoiding a rendezvous with disaster.

Goodman expends a lot of effort trying to persuade us to become onto-logical relativists. Given his philosophical agenda, however, this isn't really necessary. For he doesn't want to promulgate relativism by itself. He's selling a package of ontological relativism *and* constructivism. In fact, he's selling ontological relativism and *strong* constructivism. Now, establishing the truth of ontological relativism wouldn't yet give him strong or even scientific constructivism – for it's possible to maintain that there are many worlds with conflicting properties, but that all of them are independent. Maybe that's just the way the Creator set things up. So, even if Goodman had a good case for ontological relativism, he would still need an additional argument for his constructivism. But we saw, in the earlier discussion of Latour's views, that (strong or) scientific constructivism *without* ontological relativism is untenable. That is to say, scientific constructivism *entails* ontological relativism. Thus Goodman's philosophical success or failure doesn't depend on whether he can come up with a good argument for relativism. If he has a good argument for relativism but lacks one for constructivism, he fails anyway; and if he lacks a special argument for relativism but has one for constructivism, he succeeds because the ontological relativism comes free.

Of course, there's a flip side to this story: if constructivism entails ontological relativism, then a *refutation* of relativism would bring down the constructivism by *modus tollens*. So, while it's true that Goodman doesn't *need* to have an independent argument for relativism, such an argument would provide him with a measure of protection against an indirect attack on his relativistic flank. In the absence of a good argument for relativism, the presentation of a good argument *against* relativism results in Goodman's philosophical failure. But if he *has* a good argument for relativism, then a good argument against relativism merely produces a dilemma in which nobody loses and nobody wins.

How well-protected is the relativistic flank? By my reckoning, Goodman presents two major arguments in support of ontological relativism. The first is that there are conflicting truths that can't be accommodated in a single world:

> Some truths conflict. The earth stands still, revolves about the sun, and runs many other courses all at the same time. Yet nothing moves while at rest.
>
> (1996b: 151)

One-worldists may try to maintain that this apparent conflict can be resolved by interpreting 'The earth moves' and 'The earth is at rest' as ellipses (no pun intended) for mutually consistent claims, such as 'The earth moves according to the heliocentric system' and 'The earth is at rest according to the geocentric system'. Goodman argues that such interpretations are not available:

> Usually we seek refuge in simple-minded relativization: according to a geocentric system the earth stands still, while according to a heliocentric system it moves. But there is no solid comfort here. Merely that a given version says something does not make what it says true; after all, some versions say the earth is flat or that it rests on the back of a tortoise. *That the earth is at rest according to one system and moves according to another says nothing about how the earth behaves but only something about what these versions say.* What must be added is that these versions are true. But then the contradiction reappears, and our escape is blocked.
>
> (151, emphasis added)

Goodman also considers other one-worldist interpretations; but after some analysis he concludes that these alternatives lead back to one form or another of the 'simple-minded relativization' repudiated above (152). So the fundamental difficulty is that, when we try to avoid the contradiction by relativizing to a system, we end up with statements about the system which 'say nothing' about the world. This seems so plainly wrong to me that I worry about having missed the point. It's obvious (I would have thought) that among statements which are relativized to a system, there are some that merely describe a feature of the system and others whose truth-value isn't determined by the system alone. That the earth is at rest in the geocentric system is admittedly an instance of the first type. Goodman is right in claiming that it tells us nothing about the behaviour of the earth. But that the earth moves in the heliocentric system *does* tell us something about the behaviour of the earth. It's not a requirement of the heliocentric system that the earth be in motion. For all that the heliocentric system has to tell us, the relative positions of the sun and the earth might have been fixed.

Of course, one can *define* 'heliocentric system' in such a way that it's a fact about the system that the earth moves relative to it. Let H be such a system. If (in the system of contemporary astronomy) the position of the earth were fixed relative to the sun, then it would be an absolute truth about the one world that we all live in that, according to system H, our measuring instruments function with a systematic variability reminiscent of the Lorentz–Fitzgerald contraction. So even if H is what Goodman had in mind by 'heliocentric', it still wouldn't be right to say that any statement which is relativized to H tells us only about the system. As for the one-worldist interpretation of 'The earth moves', I suggest that the appropriate relativization isn't that the earth moves according to system H – this formulation does indeed tell us nothing about the behaviour of the earth – it's that the earth moves according to the system whose only postulate about motion is that the sun is at rest.

There are, to be sure, systems relative to which one can express nothing but truths about the system. Goodman uses some of these to good effect in the course of illustrating his thesis. For instance, he likens the relativization of the statements about the earth's motion and non-motion to the relativization of the conflicting claims

1   The kings of Sparta had two votes
2   The kings of Sparta had only one vote

to

3   According to Herodotus, the kings of Sparta had two votes
4   According to Thucydides, the kings of Sparta had only one vote.

Clearly, 3 and 4 tell us nothing about the kings of Sparta. They tell us only about what Herodotus and Thucydides said. In fact, the systems used for these relativizations – what Herodotus said and what Thucydides said – don't have the resources for generating anything but self-descriptions. But this is a special feature of these particular systems. These systems are, after all, nothing more than finite lists of permissible assertions which aren't even closed under logical operations (the fact 'X' and 'Y' are in the Herodotus system doesn't mean that 'X and Y' is). These systems are very bad analogies to the geocentric and heliocentric systems.

By the way, defenders of Goodman can't complain that this critique relies on a distinction between facts about a system which are merely conventional and facts about the world which transcend the conventional. It's true that Goodman frequently criticizes this distinction. But this counts for nothing when the object of critical analysis is his claim 'that the earth is at rest according to one system and moves according to another says nothing about how the earth behaves but only something about what these versions say' (1996b: 151).

So the argument against the availability of one-worldist interpretations of conflicting truths is not persuasive. Moreover, even if it were persuasive, one-worldists would still have other escape routes that Goodman doesn't even try to block. For one thing, they could maintain that one or the other or both of the putative conflicting truths aren't true at all. They could maintain this even if they couldn't tell us *which* of the conflicting claims aren't true. Alternatively, they could deny that there's a conflict by claiming that the same words don't have the same meanings in the two apparently conflicting sentences. This is, I think, the best way to handle another of Goodman's dilemmas – the fact that in some mathematical systems points are constructed out of lines, while in others points are *not* made out of lines or anything else. In this case, there seems to be nothing wrong with saying that the word 'point' is ambiguous – that the points that are made out of lines are simply different entities from the points that aren't made out of lines.

Goodman's second argument for ontological relativism is, surprisingly enough, an argument from parsimony. One might have thought that considerations of parsimony would count *against* the many-worlds hypothesis, here as in quantum mechanics. But that isn't how Goodman sees it. According to Goodman, the world of the one-worldists is a theoretical construct that can be eliminated without suffering any important consequences. This world is useless because it has no properties:

> Shouldn't we now return to sanity from all this mad proliferation of worlds? Shouldn't we stop speaking of right versions as if each were, or had, its own world, and recognize all as versions of one and the same neutral and underlying world? The world thus regained ... is a world

without kinds or order or motion or rest or pattern – a world not fighting for or against.

(1978: 20)

At this juncture, it would be nice to get clear what Goodman has to say about the relation between worlds and versions. But this is no easy matter. Scheffler has tried to pin Goodman down to one account or another for years (Scheffler 1980, 1986, 1996). Without clarity on this point, I find myself unable to decide whether the claim that a world without properties is 'well lost' carries any more liability for one-worldism than for Goodman's many-worldism. I also find myself disinclined to do the tedious spadework that would be required to achieve the requisite clarity. Luckily, there's no need to do it. It isn't necessary to figure out whether Goodman's claim supports his ontology simply because he hasn't secured the claim.

The claim is that the world is well lost because it has no properties. There are two potential one-worldist replies. The first is to deny that the world has no properties. Goodman relies here on the broad philosophical consensus against what Putnam calls 'metaphysical realism'. According to metaphysical realists, there is a uniquely correct description – or version – of reality. If this were so, then the one and only world would have a plethora of properties – namely, those ascribed to it by the one and only correct version. But metaphysical realists are hard to find these days. Even Goodman's most persistent critics, such as Scheffler and Putnam, are willing to grant that there are multiple versions of reality that have equal epistemic credentials. But to admit this is not yet to concede that the world has no properties. It may just be that the properties of the world have a rather more intricate structure than we first thought. Let X and Y be two versions of the world such that F(X) is a fact about the world according to X and F(Y) is a fact about the world according to Y. F(X) and F(Y) may even be incompatible facts. If metaphysical realism is rejected, it's true that we can't assert either that F(X) is a truth about the world or that F(Y) is a truth about the world. But we're still not restricted to a mute mysticism. We can say that the world has these definite and elaborate properties – that it reveals the face F(X) when interrogated with the concepts and assumptions of X, and that it reveals the quite different face F(Y) when interrogated from the standpoint of Y – more simply, that F(X) is true according to X, and that F(Y) is true according to Y.

The second counter to Goodman's claim is that, even if the world were utterly bereft of properties, it wouldn't automatically follow that the concept of the world is theoretically useless. To be sure, there are concepts that are of no use whatever in our epistemic activities. Consider the concept of a *doppelelectron* – an elementary particle that invariably accompanies regular electrons, but that enters into no interactions with any other particles in the universe. Where conventional particle physicists say that there's a stream of electrons, doppelelectron theorists say that there's a stream of electrons *and* doppelelectrons, but that only the electrons have any detectable effect on our instruments. In this case, it's easy to see that doppelelectron theory will never provide us with any explanatory advantage over conventional particle physics. Maybe the world is as useless as a doppelelectron. But it's by no means equally obvious that it's useless. The concept of a doppelelectron is, after all, an artificially contrived idea whose conceptual connections are exhaustively delineated in a few words. In contrast, the concept of the world is situated in an intricate web of ideas which are as old as speculative thought itself. We know for sure what happens to our system of ideas if we eliminate doppelelectrons from our conceptual scheme – nothing at all. But it's not nearly so clear what happens if we pull the concept of the world out of its web. Certainly one can't assume that the world's not having any specifiable properties is sufficient grounds for its elimination. It's possible that the world has no specifiable properties, but that eliminating it altogether from our conceptual repertoire so rends the web that massive incoherencies crop up all over the place. If this were to be the case, there might be grounds for one-worldism even if it's true that we can say nothing about the world beyond the fact that it exists.

Here's another way to express the same thought: the only reason that Goodman gives us for eliminating the world is that it has no ascertainable properties. If that were obviously sufficient grounds for elimination, then the Kantian concept of a noumenal world would be a non-starter. Kant would be guilty of the colossal stupidity of overlooking the fact that the noumenal world has no ascertainable properties. Kant may have been wrong about the noumenal world. But he wasn't wrong by virtue of a trivial oversight. Therefore Goodman's argument is inadequate.

So Goodman's relativistic flank is wide open to attack. Are there any offensive forces in the field? Sure there are. Anti-relativists from Plato to Putnam have charged that the thesis of relativism is self-defeating. For the most part, these arguments apply equally to any and all forms of total relativism, Goodman's included. If these critiques are on track, then constructivism must be abandoned along with relativism, because constructivism without relativism has no solution to the problem of the two societies. However, this is not the best place in the book to take up these entirely general anti-relativistic arguments. In Chapter 14, we'll see that the status of another, non-ontological form of relativism is implicated in the analysis of *logical constructivism*, the view that even the principles of logic are constructed. The same arguments apply to this non-ontological relativism as well as to Goodman's relativism. I've therefore relegated my consideration of these arguments to Chapter 15. In the meantime, I want to discuss a problem which is specific to Goodman's ontological brand of relativism. I call it *the problem of the interparadigmatic lunch*.

Whether or not we agree with the multiple-worlds hypothesis, it's easy to imagine that we understand what it claims. I suspect that this aura of coherence is due largely to our interpreting the thesis in terms of an undoubtedly coherent model of the universe: that of multiple continua between which there are no spatio-temporal relations. The following passage suggests that Goodman also relies on this model to guide his thinking:

> But where are these many actual worlds? How are they related to one another? Are there many earths all going along different routes at the same time and risking collision? Of course not; in any world there is only one Earth; and the several worlds are not distributed in any space-time. Space-time is an ordering within a world; the space-times of different worlds are not embraced within some greater space-time.
>
> (1996b: 152)

Whatever its other shortcomings may be, I see no reason to expect that we're going to get into logical trouble by using such a model. The problem, however, is that there are features of ontological relativism, not discussed by Goodman, which render this unproblematic interpretation inadequate. These are mentioned in passing by Hempel:

> If adherents of different paradigms did inhabit totally separate worlds, I feel tempted to ask, how can they ever have lunch together and discuss each other's views? Surely, there is a passageway connecting their worlds; indeed it seems that their worlds overlap to a considerable extent.
>
> (Hempel 1996: 129–30)

The passage continues:

> The fact that proponents of such conflicting paradigms as Newtonian and relativistic physics pit their theories against each other in an effort to explain certain phenomena shows that they agree on the relevant features of those phenomena ...
>
> (130)

This continuation makes it clear that Hempel's focus is on the fact that adherents of different paradigms who have lunch together are able to engage in fruitful discussions. My focus is on the even more remarkable fact *that they can have lunch together*. Regardless of how strained and unproductive their conversation might be, how does it happen that there's a common *venue* in which it can take place? Aren't the conversers supposed to be living in different worlds? Obviously, denying that they *can* have lunch together isn't an option. It's a feature of my world that it contains adherents of different paradigms or versions, and it's a feature of at least some of these adherents' worlds that they contain *me*. So, if adhering to different versions results in our inhabiting different worlds, there's no avoiding the conclusion that the different worlds overlap. But then the model of two unconnected continua won't do: if a point x is in both world W1 and world W2, then it's possible to traverse the space between x and any other point in W1 (because W1 is a continuum), and it's also possible to travel from x to any other point in W2 (because W2 is a continuum). But then it must be possible to travel from any point in W1 to any point in W2. On this account, it would be possible for us to *visit* the worlds constructed by adherents of different paradigms without changing our beliefs. All this is, of course, absurd.

But if Goodman's worlds aren't disconnected continua, then what are they? Maybe there's a coherent model that will capture what Goodman wants to say about the many worlds. But maybe there isn't. The point is that Goodman hasn't said nearly enough about his ontology to persuade us that it has a coherent description. What does this criticism accomplish? It falls somewhat short of the *coup de grâce* that would be delivered by an explicit demonstration that Goodman's thesis is incoherent. But it does show that the coherence of the thesis can't be taken for granted. I've noted that the most straightforward way of understanding his thesis (the multiple-continua model) simply doesn't work. This falls short of being a decisive refutation only because of the vagueness of the target hypothesis – because, for one thing, Goodman doesn't *tell* us how he would describe what happens when inhabitants of different realities have lunch together. If your tolerance for vagueness is great enough, it's algorithmically certain that you can escape from any putative demonstration of incoherence: when the incoherence is displayed, simply claim that the critical argument fails to capture the intended interpretation of the target hypothesis. A defender of Goodman's thesis, for instance, would undoubtedly respond to my argument by saying that the multiple-continua model is not what Goodman had in mind. So long as you don't have to specify what you *do* have in mind, this move is always available. Demonstrations of incoherence (or of coherence) are not to be expected when it comes to radically incomplete proposals like Goodman's. The most damaging critique that's available against such a proposal is that there's no coherent completion of the hypothesis on the table. This is the current status of the many-worlds hypothesis.

Goodman offers his multiple-worlds hypothesis as an escape from the contradiction of the two-societies problem. But it was seen earlier on that the contradiction can be avoided within the confines of a single world: we need only say that the sets of constructible facts for any two societies have empty intersections. The trouble, however, is that this renders us liable to the galactic conspiracy argument. So Goodman's ontological relativism is really a solution to the galactic conspiracy problem. Instead of saying that the elementary particles constructed by Andromedan scientists may be binding on us, he would have us say that our scientists and theirs live in different worlds. If this solution worked, it would vindicate strong constructivism as well as scientific constructivism (assuming that these doctrines encounter no other objections). But the fact that it doesn't work means that scientific as well as strong constructivism continues to be jeopardized by the galactic conspiracy objection.

13 Constructivism and time

According to constructivists, the process of constructing facts about the natural world is to be understood on the model of the construction of social facts, such as the value of money, social conventions, the meanings of words, and so on. There is, however, a glaring disanalogy between the constructions of money and the putative construction of TRH. In the former case, the constructandum and the constructans are temporally conterminous. Money didn't exist before the social activity that constituted it, and if we should ever cease to sustain the monetary system with the appropriate social activity, money would cease to exist forthwith. The same is true of social conventions and the meanings of words. When it comes to the construction of TRH, however, Latour and Woolgar don't want to say that a new substance began to exist in the hypothalamus (which had previously been constructed) some time in 1969. What became true in 1969 is the fact that TRH had existed for at least as long as hypothalami. In this case, the constructandum and constructans have different dates. This phenomenon does not occur in paradigmatic and relatively well-understood cases of the construction of social facts.

Can it coherently be supposed that we construct events located in our distant past? As with the problem of the two societies (see Chapter 12), one searches in vain through the sociological literature for an extensive discussion of this issue. As with the problem of the two societies, the sociologists' slack is taken up by Nelson Goodman. At one point, Goodman assures us that the construction of temporally antecedent events 'raises no special difficulty' (1996a: 213). However, this assurance is preceded by an admission that his previous attempt to explain the nature of time in a constructivist universe was 'tangled enough to confuse many a reader' (208). Goodman pleads extenuating circumstances: he was trying to 'deal with two matters at once' (208). Be that as it may, he takes the rare step of absolutely disowning his previous discussion of the topic: 'The best course now is to consider section 12.3 eliminated' (208). Moreover, he doesn't provide us with a new account to replace the eliminated section right away. He postpones the new treatment until the last page of his last article on constructivism. These do not seem like the actions of a philosopher making an unproblematic point. They're reminiscent of the story about the mathematician who tells his class that the proof of a particular theorem is obvious. A student asks a question about the proof that the mathematician doesn't immediately have an answer to. The mathematician goes home, works on it all through the night and into the next day. Then, when his class reconvenes, he announces that his first opinion was right: the proof is obvious.

Here's Goodman's last word on time:

> The question I have postponed so often will now be pressed again: 'How can a version make something that existed only long before the version itself?' Often declaimed as if it were plainly unanswerable and devastating, the question raises no special difficulty. Notice first that parallel questions such as 'How can a version make something far away from it?' seem to give us no concern, and so also for simpler common-places such as a flat version of a solid object, a black-and-white version of a multicolored object; we do not insist that a version of a green lawn be green, or that a drawing of a moving hockey player must move. *No principle requires that features imputed to a world be features of the version.* Why be disturbed, then, by a present version imputing a past temporal location to an event?
>
> (213, emphasis added)

The crucial claim is the one I've italicized. Let's call the principle that Goodman denies the *imputation principle*. The *prima facie* opinion that constructandum and constructans must have the same dates does seem to be based on something like the imputation principle. Goodman's disproof of the principle by example, however, is altogether inadequate. Most of his counter-examples can be defused by the observation that the physical objects used as representations (a black-and-white picture of a green lawn) and the objects represented (a green lawn) are not instances of constructandum and constructans in the constructivist paradigm. Physical objects like black-and-white photographs don't produce worlds. By themselves, photographs are just pieces of paper. What does the constructing is human *activity* in which the physical objects are implicated, and what get constructed are *facts* – or so a critic of constructivism responding to Goodman could say: but activities and facts have no colours, nor are they flat or three-dimensional. Thus Goodman's examples don't count as counter-examples to the imputation principle. Activities and facts can, however, be said to have temporal addresses. So the imputation principle had better be false, or else the constructivist story unravels completely.

I don't think that the falsehood of the imputation principle is at all obvious. Still, I admit that I haven't been able to come up with a persuasive argument *for* the imputation principle either. I won't burden the reader with my inconclusive ruminations on the subject. I concede to Goodman that there is no case for the principle. But Goodman is wrong if he supposes that this means that constructivists have 'no special problem' with time. Here's a temporal problem that has nothing to do with the imputation principle. Suppose that at time t1, we construct the fact X0 that X occurs at an earlier time t0; then, at a later time t2, we construct the fact −X0 that X *doesn't* occur at t0. Then it seems to follow that X0 is true (because that fact was constructed at t1) and that −X0 is true (because *that* fact was constructed at t2). What do constructivists have to say about that?

Whatever they may say, it's noteworthy that this temporal dilemma is different from the one that Goodman discusses. The question that Goodman addresses is how it can happen that we can construct events in the past. Goodman's reply is that the supposition that it can't happen is based on an imputation principle which there's no reason to adopt. Assume he's right. Assume that the imputation principle is false. Then the fact that constructandum and constructans have different dates is not *ipso facto* an argument against constructivism. Assume, in fact, that we *can* reconstruct the past. Then what happens when, on two different occasions, we construct a fact and its negation? The contradiction that's apparently obtained in this case is not alleviated in the least by the rejection of the imputation principle. Perhaps constructivism has an answer to this dilemma. But it isn't to be found in Goodman's writings, or in the writings of any other constructivists.

The new dilemma is, of course, a temporal analogue of the problem of the two societies discussed in the previous chapter. It's the problem of the two *eras*. In the two-societies problem, we have society S1 constructing X and society S2 constructing −X. The temporal version has one and the same society constructing X at one time and −X at another time. In both cases, the problem is how to avoid the contradictory conclusion that both X and −X are true. Goodman's putative solution to the two-societies problems is to segregate X and −X in different worlds. He doesn't discuss the two-eras problem. If he were asked about it, perhaps he would maintain that the temporal dilemma introduces no new problems that haven't already been encountered in the geographical dilemma – that the two-eras problem is a *special case* of the two-societies problem. In the two-societies problem, we avoid the contradiction by saying that the worlds created by S1 and S2 are different worlds. In the two-eras problem, we avoid the contradiction by saying that the worlds created by us at t1 and at t2 are different worlds. In Chapter 12, I argued that Goodman's solution to the two-societies problem doesn't tell us how to account for the possibility of interparadigmatic luncheon dates. Now this particular difficulty doesn't arise in the corresponding solution to the two-eras problem: we can't have lunch with our past selves. But there is a kindred difficulty in the temporal case. Let X0 be the fact that X occurs at time t0, and −X0 be the fact that X doesn't occur at t0. Also let C1(X0) be the fact that X0 is constructed at t1, and let C2(−X0) be the fact that −X0 is constructed at t2. Now the world at t1 has a past that contains the event X0, and the world at t2 has a past that contains the event −X0. But *pastness is transitive*: if event X is in the past relative to event Y, and event Y is past relative to event Z, then X is past relative to Z. Moreover X0 is in the past relative to C1(X0), and C1(X0) is in the past relative to C2(−X0). Therefore, by transitivity, X0 is in the past relative to C2(−X0). That is to say, the world that we construct at t2 has in its past the fact X0 that was constructed at t1. But it also has the fact −X0 that was constructed at t2. Therefore the attempt at segregating the contradictories fails in the temporal case as well as in the geographical.

The story to be told about the two eras exactly parallels the story about the two societies. In both cases, a *prima facie* contradiction is supposedly resolved by segregating the contradictories in different worlds. In both cases, the multiple-worlds model provides us with no way of adequately representing certain features of the worlds. In the case of the two societies, the model fails to represent the fact that each society can literally be contained in the world of the other society. In the case of the two eras, the model fails because the past of our past is our past. In both these cases, to say that the models give us no way of adequately representing certain states of affairs is a polite way of saying that the models are incoherent. To be sure, it's possible that the incoherence can be finessed by a more elaborate model. But, as I noted in the previous chapter, one can *always* say this when confronted with an argument that one's conceptual scheme is incoherent.

Some apologists for constructivism have conceded that constructivist talk about time is, strictly speaking, incoherent, but they've maintained that, in this case, the charge of incoherence is glib and superficial. It's correct as far as it goes, but it overlooks the possibility that we sometimes have good reasons for making statements that are, 'strictly speaking', incoherent. Sometimes the reasons are even epistemic. For instance, we may find ourselves compelled to utter incoherencies in the course of introducing a new conceptual system. A specific example will help to focus the discussion.

When Freud began to write about unconscious mental processes, he considered the objection that there could be no such processes simply because consciousness is one of the defining characteristics of the mental. He conceded that

> we are in the habit of identifying what is psychical with what is conscious. We look upon consciousness as nothing more nor less than the *defining* characteristic of the psychical, and psychology as the study of the contents of consciousness. Indeed, it seems to us so much a matter of course to equate them in this way that any contradiction of the idea strikes us as obvious nonsense. Yet psychoanalysis cannot avoid raising this contradiction ...

> (Freud 1917/1973a: 46)

In this passage, Freud admits that the central thesis of psychoanalysis was analytically false: according to the prevailing linguistic conventions, unconscious mental processes were akin to married bachelors. But of course Freud was not merely using the received language of psychology to make a new empirical claim. He was trying to reform the language. That Freud saw himself as a conceptual repair man comes through clearly in many passages. At one point, he straightforwardly describes his major contribution as a move 'to extend the concept of "psychical"' (Freud 1917/1973a: 363); and in a discussion of his 'conception of ... the basic instincts of mental life', he writes:

> I have a particular reason for using the word 'conception' here. These are the most difficult problems that are set to us, but their difficulty does not lie in any insufficiency of observations; what present us with these riddles are actually the commonest and most familiar of phenomena. Nor does the difficulty lie in the recondite nature of the speculations to which they give rise; speculative consideration plays little part in this sphere. But it is truly a matter of conceptions – that is to say, of introducing the right abstract ideas, whose application to the raw material of observation will produce order and clarity in it.
>
> (Freud 1933/1973b: 113)

An unconscious mental process was indeed a contradiction in terms – in the old way of talking that Freud wanted to supplant. Freud believed that there existed processes that were functionally identical to conscious processes in every way except that the agent was unaware of them; and he thought that the least disruptive way to accommodate this observation would be to draw a distinction between consciousness and mentality.

Can Latour's and Goodman's temporal incoherence be understood in the same way as Freud's? Hacking thinks so:

> There seems to be an air of trivial paradox here. Has not the hypothalamus of the higher vertebrates been secreting this substance ever since the animals came into being? Has it not always been a fact that this substance has a certain structure, a structure that became known in the laboratories of Texas and Louisiana? Latour and Woolgar do not say that something in the hypothalamus changed in 1969. But they think that what logicians would call the modality and tense structure of assertions of fact is misunderstood. Let *F* be a relatively timeless fact, say the fact that TRH has such and such a chemical structure. The official view would be: before 1969 one was not entitled to assert, categorically, that *F* is a fact, nor that *F* has always been a fact. But since then we know enough to be justified in asserting that *F* is a fact and has always been so. Latour and Woolgar say no: Only after 1969 and a particular series of laboratory events, exchanges and negotiations did *F*

> become a fact, and only after 1969 did it become true that *F* was always a fact. The grammar of our language prevents us from saying this. Our very grammar has conditioned us towards the timeless view of facts.
>
> (Hacking 1988: 281–2)

According to this diagnosis of the 'trivial paradox', the situation is essentially the same as the one confronted by Freud. In both cases, the authors' contradictory assertions are to be understood, not as manifestations of a deep confusion, but as an understandable by-product of the attempt to change the way we talk.

I find this diagnosis to be persuasive in the Freudian case, but I'm not so sure about Latour and Woolgar. There are huge differences between the two cases that must give us pause. In the case of psychoanalysis, it's easy to tell which statements are going to be considered meaningful in the new conceptual scheme and which are going to be rejected as nonsense. For instance, it's clear that unconscious mental processes are acceptable in the new scheme, but that conscious non-mental processes aren't. Moreover, it's obvious that Freud's scheme is consistent if the scheme that it altered is consistent: if the original way of talking is free of incoherence, then getting rid of consciousness as a precondition for mentality and leaving everything else the same isn't going to produce any new logical problems. None of this is true of Latour and Woolgar's conceptual revision. In contrast to the Freudian case, it's not at all clear what the new 'modality and tense structure of assertions of fact' would lead us to say about many temporal scenarios. To be told that mental processes needn't be conscious is already enough to understand the full scope of Freud's conceptual revision. But to be told that a natural fact at time t1 can be constructed at a different time t2 leaves an endless number of temporal questions unresolved. For instance, there's nothing in Latour and Woolgar's or Goodman's sparse and cryptic remarks – or in Hacking's indulgent gloss – that provides us with guidelines for what to say about the problem of the two eras. It's one thing to claim that we need an alternative grammar; it's another thing to present an alternative grammar.

Let's see what's involved in actually trying to develop a coherent way to talk about the case of the two eras within a constructivist framework. Suppose once again that C1(X0) and C2(−X0) obtain – i.e., that 'X occurs at time t0' is constructed at time t1, and that at a later time t2, 'X occurs at t0' is deconstructed. At one time, the world had phlogistic events in its past; now we want to say that phlogiston never existed. There's no way to accommodate both these observations within a single dimension of time. We need a branching structure in which each constructive event is associated with its own distinctive past – the one that contains all the past events that are constituted by the new construction, or that were constituted by previous constructions and which are not undone by the new construction. The relationships between C1(X0), C2(−X0), X0 and −X0 may be depicted as shown in Figure 1.

Evidently, the resultant structure is going to be of the same order of complexity as the structure posited by the many-worlds interpretation of quantum mechanics. So far as the analysis has taken us, the main difference between the two is that the time lines of the many-worlds interpretation branch into the future, while the lines of our incipient constructivist model branch into the past. But, of course, if constructivists are right, we construct the future as well as the past. There are quarks in our future now, though there didn't used to be. Therefore every constructive event has to be associated with a complete world history. Moreover, each of these world histories will itself contain constructive events which are in turn associated with different world histories: it's a fact about our current world that quarks were once not in our future. So the model requires us to posit worlds within worlds within worlds, to indefinitely many levels of recursion. Moreover, we're just talking about the temporal structure of a *single* Goodmanian world: the alternative pasts and futures are created by the history of constructive and deconstructive activities which *we* recognize as having occurred in our past (or in one of the pasts of our past, etc.). Other societies, or 'versions', may have entirely different constructive histories; and these will generate worlds that have totally different branches. It's easy to lose one's grip on these conceptual requirements. Indeed, it's a non-trivial mathematical task to ascertain whether an appropriate structure is available. One thing is certain, however: if an appropriate structure is available, it's going to be several orders of magnitude more complex than the structure of the quantum-mechanical many-worlds model, to say nothing of Ptolemaic astronomy. If the same theoretical job can be accomplished by positing that different generations and different contemporaneous societies simply have different perspectives on one and the same independent world, why would anybody want to be a constructivist?

Even worse, there are reasons to believe that this entire approach is doomed to failure. Look at the diagram of the relationships among C1(X0), C2(−X0), X0 and −X0. This diagram is presumably going to be a small

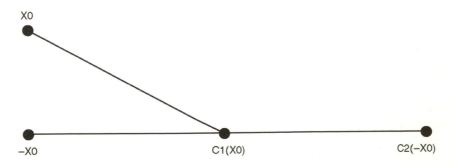

Figure 1

piece of the total backward- and forward-branching structure of the universe at t2. According to this diagram, the event X0 is deconstructed at time t2, but the earlier constructive event C1(X0) is *not* deconstructed at t2. If constructivists are right, the world once had phlogiston in its past, and now it doesn't. But our current world still has the phlogiston-constructing activities of past scientists in its past. Constructivists will want to allow that even constructive events can be deconstructed: in the future, we *may* reconstruct the past in such a way that phlogiston *theorists* never existed. But this is surely not mandatory. We have to allow for the possibility of deconstructing previously constructed events, while leaving the previous construct*ive* events intact. This is the possibility depicted in the diagram: the horizontal line containing −X0, C1(X0) and C2(−X0) tells us that both −X0 and C1(X0) are in the unidimensional past of t2. Looking at just the portion of this line from −X0 to C1(X0), we see that, in the unidimensional past of t2, the constructive event C1(X0) has the event −X0 in its past. Now look at the *oblique* line connecting X0 and C1(X0). This is a piece of the unidimensional world history that obtained at t1. In *this* history, C1(X0) has X0 in its past. So there's a history where C1(X0) has X0 in its past (the oblique line), and another history where C1(X0) has −X0 in its past (the horizontal line). But if C1(X0) can have either X0 or −X0 in its past, then the occurrence of C1(X0) can hardly be said to constitute X0. Evidently, the occurrence of C1(X0) has no bearing on whether X0 occurs in the past. The argument is entirely general – it applies to any putative construction for a past event. In the branching model that we're contemplating, our constructive activities *don't* constitute the past.

Once again, there may be a way of dealing with these problems. But nothing quick and easy comes to mind. Certainly Hacking's description of the temporal problem of constructivism as a 'trivial paradox' seems inappropriately sanguine, as does Goodman's assertion that time 'raises no special difficulties'. There's no workable proposal on the table, and it obviously isn't a trivial matter to generate one. Under these circumstances, is there any excuse for continuing to treat Latourian or Goodmanian constructivism – a constructivism that allows for the reconstruction of the past – as a live option? When I put myself in as generous a frame of mind as I can muster, I get a glimmering of one: perhaps the conceptual innovation that constructivists have in mind is so radical that it's inexpressible by means of our current system of communication. I don't intend to enter into an exhaustive analysis of the ineffable, but a rough and ready distinction between *easy* and *difficult* conceptual innovations may serve to locate this final refuge for the non-coherent. Easy conceptual revisions are those where the new concepts can be introduced by defining them in terms of the old concepts. 'Grue' and 'bleen' are examples; and, despite its drastic effect on received modes of thinking, so is Freud's notion of an unconscious mental process. The difficult kind of conceptual revision is one that involves the introduction of new terms that have no definitional equivalents in the old scheme. The incommensurability problems discussed by Kuhn and Feyerabend were due to the putative impossibility of defining the concepts of new theories in terms of the preceding theoretical apparatus. The thesis of token identity between the physical and the mental provides us with another example: if mental events are only token-identical to physical events, then there would be no way to introduce the mentalistic concepts of intentional psychology into a purely physicalistic language by means of definitions.

If we want to effect a difficult conceptual innovation, we have to use indirection to convey our meaning. There's no telling *a priori* what might work. A well-timed shout, after the manner of the Zen masters, might do the job. So might the utterance of a judicious contradiction. It might also be the case that the very attempt to express the new idea in the old scheme issues in a contradiction. Here's an example of what I have in mind. The example draws its inspiration, appropriately enough, from a discussion of mystical ineffability (Henle 1949). Suppose that our system of communication is restricted to writing, and that each sentence is written by superimposing all of its component symbols, rather than by concatenation. Such a system can be adequate for expressing many varieties of facts. In particular, if the shapes of the symbols are chosen to avoid confounding readings, it should be possible to express propositions about symmetrical relations such as 'Bill and Sue are married' or 'Bill and Sue are not married'. The sentence for the latter might be the same as the sentence for the former, with a large X across it. But what if users of this language conceive of the idea of an asymmetric relation, such as 'is a parent of'? They can introduce a new symbol to stand for the new relation. But when they try to express the facts relating to 'is a parent of', they will find themselves inscribing contradictory sentences. The fact that Bill is a parent of Sue gets represented by the superimposition of the symbols for 'Bill', 'Sue' and 'is a parent of'; and the equally true fact that Sue is not a parent of Bill gets represented by the same superimposition with the large X of negation across it. There's no way that a space can be made for the new concept by operations that are permissible within the pre-existing system.

The suggestion is that constructivism might be saved by attributing its incoherencies to the same cause. It may be, as religious mystics have often suggested, that we labour under a fatally flawed conception of time, and that this conception is built into our very mode of communication, in the same way as the non-existence of asymmetrical relations is built into the superimposition language. When we try to express the truth about time in the current language, it comes out as gibberish. But the fault lies in the language, not in the idea that we're trying to express. I can conceive of being in a situation like this – of having an insight that can't be expressed in the current language. However, I confess to being blind to the ineffable insight of constructivism. The question is: what attitude should I have toward this ineffable doctrine? This is the question about mysticism that William James struggled with in *The Varieties of Religious Experience* (1902). In the end, he wasn't able to make any headway with it and settled for a bland agnosticism. It may be possible to do a little bit better than that. If constructivist talk about time is terminally incoherent, there are three ways to account for it. The first possibility is that constructivism is indeed related to our current temporal talk, as facts about asymmetrical relations are to the superimposition language. It's the attempt to force one's insight into an inadequate mould that results in a contradiction. The second possibility is that the would-be innovators are confused – that they think they have an insight, but they don't. The third possibility is that they're *faking it* – that they have no definite idea in mind at all – that they're engaged in the ancient philosophical practice of waving one's hands.

How can I tell which of the three hypotheses is the case? Well, I can't tell with any great degree of certainty. But it seems to me that I have a relevant clue. If the conceptual innovators really had an ineffable insight, and if they wanted me to share it, I would expect them to engage in a concerted attempt to iron out the incoherencies that arise when they first try to express themselves. In the case of the superimposition language, it may be immediately evident that asymmetrical relations can't be expressed. But this is an artificial example contrived to make a point. In real-life cases of apparent ineffability, it's not going to be obvious right from the start that a particular idea is inexpressible. Natural languages are so rich in expressive power that it would be precipitous to suggest that one's insight is ineffable unless and until one had made a serious and sustained attempt to eff it. This is the behaviour that I would expect from people who have an insight that they can't express. It's also what people would do if they erroneously believed they had such an insight. The bluffer and the hand-waver, however, have no project to work on. I would expect them to deliver their incoherent gloss and to change the topic as quickly as possible. This is what construc-tivists and their apologists have done. They've made no discernible effort to deal with the temporal paradoxes that their views generate. Hacking says that our temporal logic is at fault. But nobody seems to be trying to iron out the faults. This is cause for suspicion.

The repudiation of the mystical theory of constructivist time is the emotional climax of my discussion in this chapter. From a literary point of view, it would have been desirable to end on this high note. Unfortunately, there's some unfinished conceptual business that will have to be attended to post-climactically. I began this chapter with the observation that in the paradigmatic cases of socially constructed social facts, constructandum and constructans are always temporally conterminous. I stand by that claim. But there are some less-than-paradigmatic cases of constructed social facts in which the temporal congruence of constructandum and constructans isn't evident. For example, suppose that a legislative body passes a law that makes the smoking of tobacco *retroactively* illegal. It may be that retroactive laws are unjust. Indeed, our legal system prides itself in eschewing such laws. But the very fact that it prides itself in not indulging in retroactive legislation is evidence that it *could* indulge in it, if it so chose. Whether it's just or unjust, there's nothing to stop governments from branding and treating people as criminals for having smoked tobacco prior to the criminalization of smoking. But isn't this a case of constructing a new fact about the past? Suppose that the retroactive anti-smoking legislation is passed in 1996. Then didn't it become true in 1996 that smokers had been criminals in 1995? And isn't this a precise analogue to the putative fact that it became true in 1969 that TRH (i.e., a substance having the structure that was 'discovered' in 1969) had existed for aeons? If people can become criminals retroactively, then it would seem that we must believe that there is a coherent temporal logic that allows for the construction of past facts. At the very least, our encountering problems in formulating such a temporal logic can't be used as an argument against Latour or Goodman. These are problems that we *have* to live with.

My reply to this argument is that there are ways of dealing with the case of retroactive legislation that don't require any innovations in temporal logic. These alternative treatments, however, are not usable by strong constructivists like Latour and Goodman. Therefore (I will argue), the unsolved problems of temporal logic generated by Latour's and Goodman's claims count against these claims after all. The dilemma produced by retroactive legislation may be described as follows. When 1995 first rolled around, there were no laws against smoking, and smokers were therefore not criminals. After the retroactive legislation of 1996, however, it became true that smokers had been criminals in 1995. Thus smokers both were and were not criminals in 1995, which forces us to take refuge in alternative time lines and/or other obscure temporal novelties. The conclusion is that Latour's and Goodman's need to rely on the same obscure novelties doesn't count against their views. But do we really have to say that smokers both were and were not criminals in 1995? It seems to me far more natural, and certainly less problematic, to say that smokers were criminals in 1995 in one sense of the word 'criminal' and that they weren't criminals in 1995 in another sense of the word.

Were smokers criminals in 1995? The temptation to say that they weren't is due to the fact that in 1995, no law had yet been passed against smoking. Let's say that a *contempocriminal* is a person who breaks a law after it's been passed. The law in question may or may not retroactively criminalize that person's activity. But if the activity is criminalized retroactively, then that person is not a contempocriminal. Obviously, smokers were *not* contempocriminals in 1995. Nevertheless, they were subject to prosecution and punishment in 1996 for their 1995 non-contempocriminal activities. If their punishable activities were not contempocriminal, then what were they? They were *retrocriminal*. A retrocriminal is a person who commits an act that will retroactively be deemed illegal some time in the future. Obviously, smokers *were already* retrocriminals in 1995, although there was no way that anyone could know it until 1996. The important point is that they didn't retroactively *become* retrocriminals in 1996 – they were retrocriminals right from the start. Similarly, smokers became contempocriminals in 1996, but they didn't retroactively become contempocriminals in 1995. Smokers were and forever shall remain contempo-innocent in 1995. On this account, smokers never retroactively became anything: they never were and never will be contempocriminals in 1995, and they always were and always will be retrocriminals in 1995. The facts are all timeless; therefore there's no need to tinker with temporal logic. Moreover, there's nothing missing in this description of the relation between smoking and the law.

The foregoing account oversimplifies the situation in one respect: there may be successive reconstructions and deconstructions that make the story much more complicated. For example, smoking can be retroactively criminalized in 1996 and then *de*criminalized in 1997. Then are smokers retrocriminals or not in 1995? Clearly, the notion of a retrocriminal is too coarse-grained to deal with situations like these. We have to introduce temporally indexed varieties of retrocriminality, so that we can say that smokers in 1995 are 1996-retrocriminals but not 1997-retrocriminals. If our society goes through a lot of reconstructions and deconstructions, the account of the state of society at any single point in the past is going to get exceedingly complicated. This might lead someone to object that my account of the matter merely trades off complexity of temporal logic for complexity in the system of properties. But there's an enormous difference between the two realms of complexity. The complex temporal logic underlying Latour's and Goodman's claims, if it can coherently be formulated at all, would require us to alter some of our most basic ideas about the nature of the universe. The complex system of temporally indexed retroproperties that I've invoked may be just as ugly as the complex temporal logic, but it has no novel metaphysical implications – retroproperties are all straightforwardly definable in terms of everyday properties. In the scenario that I've developed, it's undoubtedly true and unproblematic that smokers in 1995 were 1996-retrocriminals. It's a fact of the same order as the undoubted fact that in 1995, a thirty-year-old is also a thirty-one-year-old-to-be-in-1996. I will henceforth ignore the complications introduced by the possibility of successive reconstructions and deconstructions.

Latour says (and Goodman would concur) that it became true in 1969 that TRH had existed for aeons. The analogous claim about retroactive legislation would be that it became true in 1996 that smokers had been criminals in 1995. What shall we say about this claim? Note, to begin with, that this kind of 'criminality' is not the same as either contempocriminality or retrocriminality – for, while it supposedly becomes true in 1996 that smokers had been criminals in 1995, it *remains false* in 1996 that smokers had been contempocriminals in 1995 – and while it isn't true before 1996 that smokers were criminals in 1995, it was *always true* that smokers were retrocriminals in 1995. What I want to say about the Latour–Goodman type of criminality is that:

1   it brings in its wake the need to make radical and highly dubious alterations in our temporal logic;
2   my account of retroactive legislation in terms of contempocriminality and retrocriminality seems to leave nothing out; and that
3   we should therefore altogether eliminate the Latour-Goodman concept of criminality from our repertoire.

To be sure, one can imagine a legislative body trying to invoke the Latour–Goodman conception by stipulating that, henceforth, past smokers shall be deemed to have been criminals all along. But one can also imagine legislative bodies trying to stipulate that P and that not-P (I seem to recall that a member of the Utah State Legislature once introduced a bill that would make pi equal to 3). In cases like these, we say that the legislature *can't* do what it purports to do, because what it purports to do is incoherent. There's no doubt that legislatures can impose penalties retroactively; but, if my analysis is right, they can't make it be the case that smokers shall have always been criminals.

But, if I'm right in claiming that retroactive construction requires no change in our temporal logic, then doesn't this provide Latour and Goodman with an escape route from the problems relating to the retroactive construction of natural facts? For example, consider the fact that electrons have spin. Latour and Goodman will want to say that this fact was constructed. Let's suppose that it was constructed by Goudsmit and Uhlenbeck in 1925. Now if we say that what was constructed in 1925 was the fact that electrons have always had spin, we inherit all the unsolved problems of temporal logic that were discussed above. So why don't we simply follow the pattern of my analysis of retroactive criminal laws? This strategy would have us say that prior to the construction of spin, electrons already had *retrospin*, but that they didn't have *contempospin*. Moreover, these facts about electrons never did and never will change. It was always true and will forever remain true that electrons had retrospin from the beginning of time, but that they didn't have contempospin until 1925. Thus we can have the construction of physical facts without altering our temporal logic in any way.

This escape route is not available to strong constructivists like Latour and Goodman. For the escape from the problems of temporal logic is predicated on our *never* simultaneously claiming, of any fact F, that F has always been a fact and that F is constructed. If we do make such a claim, then we must admit that there was a time when F was not a fact (because it hadn't yet been constructed) and F was a fact (because F has always been a fact) – which is the temporal paradox we've been trying to avoid. Consider once again the retroactive legislation against smoking. I claimed that it was always a fact that smokers were retrocriminals in 1995. This formula helps us to avoid temporal paradox so long as the fact in question is treated as an unconstructed, independent fact. To say that smokers were retrocriminals in 1995 is to say that certain constructive events take place some time later than 1995; but the fact that certain constructive events take place some time later than 1995 is not itself constructed – it's an independent fact. If the latter fact were constructed, then we would be able to reinstitute the temporal paradox at a higher level: there would be a time before the construction of 'Smokers are retrocriminals in 1995' when this was not a fact (because it hadn't yet been constructed) and it was a fact (because it's always been a fact). The same can be said about the retrospin of electrons. To say that it was always a fact that electrons had retrospin in 1924 enables us to circumvent the temporal paradox – so long as we don't add that the fact that electrons had retrospin in 1924 was itself constructed. But strong constructivists do make this additional claim. Therefore they don't escape from the charge of temporal incoherence.

14 Constructivism and logic

In representing the debate between constructivists and realists, I've assumed that both sides share certain broad inferential principles, such as the law of non-contradiction, the identity of indiscernibles, and inference to the best explanation. These principles differ from one another in enormously important ways. But the differences won't figure in this chapter. In fact, I will provocatively call them all rules of 'logic', by which I mean no more than that they're normative principles for making (not necessarily deductive) inferences. The question here is whether constructivists concede that there are any rules of inference that have independent validity – i.e., that are valid without being *rendered* valid by human activity.

Let's call the view that there are no independently valid rules of logic by the name of *logical constructivism*. Recall that a *strong constructivist* is one who claims that there are no independent (and ascertainable) contingent facts. It's clear that a strong constructivist can also be a logical constructivist. I leave it as an exercise for the reader to determine whether a logical constructivist may *repudiate* strong constructivism (the solution is at the end of the chapter). Those who hold that there are some independently valid rules of logic will collectively be referred to as *rationalists*. Presumably, logical constructivists want to distinguish their position not only from rationalism, but also from a blanket *irrationalism* that won't recognize any epistemic constraints on opinion or discourse. (There's a distinction here between rational belief and rational discourse that's of considerable import. I'll develop it in Chapter 17. At present, however, I'm going to try to paper over it as well as I can. I just want the reader to know that the equivocation is intentional, and that it will be remedied.) Unlike the irrationalists, logical constructivists are willing to say that some inference rules are valid. They just disagree with the rationalist thesis that the validity of logic is independent of human activity. The main question of this chapter is whether it's possible to maintain a distinctive logical constructivist stance that doesn't collapse into either rationalism or irrationalism.

Who are the logical constructivists? I'll show below that Latour and Woolgar should probably be counted among them, although I can't find an explicit endorsement in their book. One also thinks of Barnes and Bloor's

(1982) extensive discussion of the status of logic from the perspective of SSK. But, once again, Barnes and Bloor espouse a form of relativism that won't be dealt with until the next chapter. They want to replace the notion of logical validity with the notion of validity relative to a society. In Chapter 15 we'll see that this kind of relativism does indeed have conceptual connections to logical constructivism – connections that are reminiscent of the link between strong constructivism and ontological relativism that was discussed in Chapter 12. In this chapter, however, I have some things to say about logical constructivism that have nothing to do with the problems that entangle it with the relativistic thesis.

Now let's get to work.

For better or for worse, prevalent norms of proper discourse are steeped in realist and rationalist assumptions. Take the norm that we should endorse and promulgate the truth as we see it. This principle loses much of its allure in cases where the truth is socially constructed. For if the truth *depends* on our endorsements and promulgations, then to obey the principle is to make a political decision to support the status quo. Such a decision is surely optional. Presumably, everyone will agree that it's sometimes appropriate to challenge orthodox views. But, on the constructivists' own accounts, orthodoxies relating to socially constructed facts are always correct: socially constructed facts are still *facts*, and to endorse and promulgate their negation is to embrace the *false*. If scientific facts are constructed by broadly consensual processes, then every new scientific proposal that contradicts current views is false. If all facts are constructed by consensual processes, then the norm of adherence to the truth would brand any and all attempts to change current opinion as illegitimate. These are not propositions that constructivists want to endorse. Constructivists don't want to *stop* epistemic change – they just want to account for it without realist or rationalist assumptions. In brief, everyone agrees that constructed truths are not *ipso facto* binding on our epistemic activities.

When this general point about constructed truths is brought to bear on the thesis of *logical* constructivism, it precipitates the latter's collapse into irrationalism. Supposedly, logical constructivists differ from irrationalists in that they concede that the currently negotiated logic is valid, and they differ from rationalists in regarding this validity as socially constructed. But we've just seen that constructed truths don't provide any normative constraints on our epistemic activities. This means that logical constructivists don't have to capitulate to an ironclad logical argument against their position. After all, there are bound to be some logics where constructivism wins and some where it loses. (Consider the logic that contains the inference rule 'P, therefore constructivism is true', or the one with the rule 'P, therefore constructivism is false'.) Why should constructivists capitulate just because they have the bad luck of living under a regime which legislates a logic that renders their favourite thesis false? Why not try to overthrow the regime instead? The foregoing remarks don't constitute a valid argument for the permissibility of not capitulating to valid arguments. To claim otherwise would obviously be self-defeating. These remarks are addressed exclusively to rationalists, in order to make them realize the futility of constructing arguments against logical constructivism.

Let's try to contrive a difference between logical constructivists and irrationalists. The discussion so far has established that the former, like the latter, may violate any given rule of logic. But if rules of logic are constructed by a process of negotiation, this rule-breaking can't be entirely wanton. Negotiation would be impossible if neither party recognized any constraints on their behaviour, and one can't follow any set of constraints without respecting the rules of some logic. For instance, it's no use saying that you must honour the deals you make unless it's a consequence of this obligation that you must not *dis*honor the deals you make. Without logic, you can't distinguish adherence to the constraints from non-adherence. So while logical constructivists must be granted the latitude to disobey valid rules of inference, the scope of permitted invalidity has to be measured in some way. There have to be higher-order rules about how the first-order rules can and can't be broken. The suggestion is that logical constructivists are like irrationalists in that they don't regard any rule of logic as inviolable, but that they're unlike the irrationalists in that they deny that absolutely anything goes.

Once again, we stand at the brink of an infinite regress: if all rules of logic are constructed, and if constructed truths needn't be respected, then there's no compulsion to follow the higher-order rules that tell us how to break the first-order rules. This particular regress is of a more virulent strain than the relatively benign Niiniluoto–Collin regress of Chapter 10. This might be obscured by the fact that there is an argument that arises naturally at this juncture which *is* of the Niiniluoto–Collin type, and which sounds very much like the argument that I'm proposing. The relatively innocuous argument runs as follows. To negotiate, you need to have a logic of negotiation. But according to logical constructivism, all logics are negotiated. Therefore this logic of negotiation must itself have been negotiated. This can only have taken place in the context of a prior logic of negotiation, and so on. Every negotiation presupposes a logic, which presupposes another negotiation. This is the Niiniluoto–Collin argument in a slightly different guise. Like its predecessor, it's troublesome for constructivists, but not decisive. The fact that you can't negotiate without logic and that you can't have logic without negotiation doesn't preclude the possibility that both logic and negotiation develop together from some sort of proto-logic and proto-negotiation. This is admittedly hand-waving, but at least the argument leaves logical constructivists with the space to wave their hands in.

My argument is different. It's that the logic you need to negotiate is itself negotiable, *so you can break its rules*. For negotiation to be possible, there have to be higher-order rules about how the first-order rules can be broken.

But these too are negotiable – so you can break those too, and so on. The result is that there are no constraints on the moves that logical constructivists allow themselves to make. Therefore logical constructivism reduces to irrationalism.

Of course, the foregoing is itself a rational argument. The role of rational arguments in the dialectic between rationalists and irrationalists will be examined in Chapter 17. The present point is that there is no intermediate niche between rationalism and irrationalism that logical constructivists may occupy. To be sure, there's no logical reason why irrationalists can't claim to be logical constructivists who inhabit a position intermediate between rationalism and irrationalism. Since irrationalists don't recognize logical constraints, there's no logical reason why they can't say anything they want! Once again, this analysis is conducted exclusively for the benefit of rationalists. I want to tell them not to bother trying to argue against logical constructivists. If such an argument were to succeed, they'd just switch logics on you.

Look at what happened to somebody who didn't heed this advice. In the Postscript to the second edition of *Laboratory Life* (1986), Latour and Woolgar discuss an argument by Tilley (1981) to the effect that the anthropological data presented in the first edition support a Popperian philosophy of science, rather than the constructivism espoused by the authors. Now Latour and Woolgar don't clearly and unambiguously endorse logical constructivism. But then they don't clearly and unambiguously endorse anything. In Chapter 4 we saw that they sometimes comport themselves like instrumentalist constructivists and sometimes like strong constructivists. In their reply to Tilley they also reveal a logical constructivist streak. Whether Tilley's argument succeeds is not at issue. The important point is that he uses the *same logic* as Latour and Woolgar did themselves. Latour and Woolgar claimed that the best way to explain the anthropological data on laboratory life is a constructivist thesis; Tilley says that the best explanation for the same data is Popperian. Both sides appeal to the rule of inference to the best explanation. So how do Latour and Woolgar react to Tilley's challenge? One might have expected them to deny, whether cogently or wantonly, that Popperian philosophy of science *is* the better explanation. But they say nothing that suggests any inadequacy in Tilley's explanation. In fact they call it 'plausible' (281). What they say is that

> Tilley demonstrates that the resources at our disposal are insufficient to force our particular interpretation in preference to any other. At almost no cost, Tilley has been able to produce a diametrically opposed interpretation of the one we intended.

(281)

In brief, they don't even *try* to refute Tilley's argument. They let it stand. But they don't capitulate either. In fact, they interpret Tilley's success in terms of their views. They say: 'We lose, and moreover our hypothesis can explain why we lose.' They don't feel any pressure to give up their opinion as a result of Tilley's demonstration. They don't even feel any pressure to *defend* their opinion. This is what one might very well expect from logical constructivists who regard the dialectical victory of their opponents as a win within the rules of a negotiated, hence non-binding, logic.

What are we to say of such a move? From the logical constructivist's own point of view, it's rather like playing a game of chess, and then, when things start to go badly, reminding your opponent that the rules of the game are negotiable, and that if you and she were playing by different rules, *you'd* be the one that's ahead. This is undoubtedly in bad taste. But it's epistemically irreproachable. Tilley was wasting his time. A good argument against logical constructivism/irrationalism is a disengaged wheel. It leaves the status quo untouched. What are you going to accuse irrationalists of? Irrationality? The only way to defeat logical constructivists is to shoot them.

But this isn't to say that logical constructivism wins. After all, there are indefinitely many epistemic stances that possess the property of being impervious to criticism. For example, there's the Montypythonesque logic of utterances which stipulates that you should negate whatever your interlocutors say. If they claim that you've contradicted yourself, the indicated reply is 'No I haven't'. If they note that you said P and then said not-P, your reply is 'No I didn't'. There's no way that an adherent to this logic can ever be brought to admit defeat. There are indefinitely many silly games of this sort. The unbeatability of logical constructivism is not by itself anything very special. Moreover, if logical constructivists are at all concerned with bringing the rationalists over to their side, they're going to have to come up with an argument against rationalism that succeeds. From their own point of view, they're going to have to play a game of chess to the end and win it. I've argued that there can be no telling arguments against logical constructivism. It's by no means obvious that there can be such a thing as a telling argument *for* logical constructivism either. But neither is it obvious that there can't be. Maybe the derivation of a dilemma from rationalist assumptions would count as a sort of *reductio ad absurdum* of rationalism. Once again, we'll look into issues of this type in Chapter 17.

Even if there were an effective argument for logical constructivism, it still wouldn't constitute the sort of victory that logical constructivists can rejoice in unless their thesis can be differentiated from a blanket irrationalism. Failing that, it would be a victory for irrationalism. Once again, there's no reason why irrationalists can't call themselves logical constructivists. But by the same token, there's no reason why irrationalists can't call themselves anything they want. There's nothing particularly *constructive* about irrationalism.

Which brings us to the solution to the problem for the reader. Can logical constructivists repudiate strong constructivism? Sure they can. If logical constructivism reduces to irrationalism, and if irrationalists can repudiate or affirm anything they want, then logical constructivists can repudiate – or affirm – strong constructivism.

15 Relativism

In Chapter 1 I emphasized the fact that constructivism is not the same thing as relativism. Nevertheless, there are logical connections between the two doctrines. We've seen some of these connections already. The message of Chapter 12 was that strong constructivism (as well as other unreasonable forms of constructivism) becomes utterly untenable unless it's bolstered by ontological relativism. It's worth noting that relativism is implicated in the fate of logical as well as strong constructivism. The two-societies dilemma that precipitates the strong constructivists' appeal to relativism has an analogue that affects logical constructivism in the same way: if logic is socially constructed, what happens when two societies create two different logics? We can't simply say that they're both valid, for one of them may generate the conclusion that the other is *in*valid. Here again, it's tempting to try to escape from the dilemma by relativizing: if S1 constructs logic L1 and S2 constructs logic L2, then L1 is valid for S1, and L2 is valid for S2. But if each society constructs its own logic, then warranted belief can only be specified relative to a society. This is the thesis that goes by the name of *epistemic relativism*.

Supposing that epistemic relativism can itself be defended, the foregoing seems to be an adequate response to the two-societies problem of logical constructivists. It doesn't, for instance, generate the additional difficulties about inter-world relations that bedevil the ontological-relativist defence of strong constructivism. There's no reason why espousers of different logics can't have lunch together in the same world (though their conversation is apt to be strained). But of course the two-societies dilemma isn't the only problem that logical constructivists have to contend with. What about the collapse of logical constructivism into irrationalism? In the previous chapter, I argued that logical constructivism is unable to command adherence to the constructed logic, because what is once negotiated is always open to *re*negotiation. The result is that there can be no normative constraints on the logical constructivist's inferential practices, which means that logical constructivism is indistinguishable from irrationalism. It's just barely possible that relativizing logical validity will help with this problem as well. For epistemic relativists, 'breaking the rules of logic' can be assimilated to shifting one's allegiance from one system of logic to another. Such paradigm shifts don't preclude relativists from acknowledging the constraints imposed by whatever paradigm they currently adhere to. One might argue that this kind of relative obligation serves to distinguish relativistic logical constructivists from irrationalists, who recognize no inferential imperatives of any sort. I don't think that such an argument can be made to work. The counter-argument is that relativistic logical constructivism still allows for jumping the boat to another system at any time – and if everyone can do this *ad libitum*, then there still are no constraints on anybody's inferential practices. We've just redescribed 'breaking the rules of logic L1' as 'switching to an alternative logic, L2'.

In sum, it isn't clear sailing for logical constructivists, even if they're handed epistemic relativism on a silver platter. The same can be said about strong constructivism *vis-à-vis* ontological relativism: the arguments against strong constructivism presented in Chapters 11 and 13 don't depend on a repudiation of ontological relativism. But it's as certain as anything can get in philosophy that both constructivisms are lost causes if they're *deprived* of their relativisms. Yet the coherence of relativistic theses has been called to question by a succession of philosophers from Plato (1961) to Putnam (1981, 1983). Indeed, Putnam regards it as a 'truism among philosophers' that '(total) relativism is inconsistent' (1981: 119). It's incumbent on both types of constructivists to provide a defence against this charge.

The remainder of this chapter is devoted to an examination of the consistency, or lack thereof, of both types of relativism. It should not be forgotten, however, that relativism isn't merely an adjunct to constructivism. It may be true that you can't be a constructivist without also espousing some variety of relativism. But you surely can be either type of relativist without espousing constructivism (assuming, of course, that you can be a relativist at all). Ascertaining the status of relativism is an important philosophical task quite apart from its bearing on constructivism. But it's because the fate of relativism is so intertwined with that of constructivism that there's a chapter on it in this book.

I'll be dealing exclusively with arguments against relativism and the relativistic defences that they generate. What about arguments *for* relativism? The endemic justification for relativism among sociologists and anthropologists is that their empirical studies reveal an enormous diversity of substantive and methodological opinions. This is, of course, a *non sequitur*. Absolutism by itself doesn't entail that there will be universal agreement about anything. To get that result, you'd have to conjoin absolutism with the thesis that everybody gets it right. The only other pro-relativist arguments that I know of are found in Barnes and Bloor's (1982) manifesto for the strong programme. These are

1   that the social causation of our beliefs entails relativism, and
2   that absolutism makes a stronger claim than relativism without securing any philosophical advantage.

These arguments were discussed and repudiated in Chapter 2. Now let's see what, if anything, is wrong with relativism.

The most basic philosophers' objections to relativism have been pressed more or less continuously for thousands of years. Joseph Margolis (1991) regards this extraordinary perseveration as cause for suspicion. It's a major theme of his book that the need to rehearse the same simple arguments again and again is an indication that the arguments fail, again and again, to secure their conclusion, and that the absolutists' non-progressive repetition betokens a neurotic aversion to relativism. I think it must be agreed all round that the situation is abnormal: the continuous repetition of the same simple arguments for thousands of years, each time as though they were bearers of important philosophical news, clearly indicates that *somebody* is being neurotic. But the historical evidence alone doesn't tell us whether it's the absolutists or the relativists who are sick. To someone who doesn't already have an opinion about the merits of relativism, the data are amenable to either interpretation. Margolis' view is that absolutists are so irrationally wedded to their thesis that they repeat the same ineffectual arguments again and again, blind to the fact that these arguments never accomplish their aim. The other view is that *relativists* are so irrationally wedded to *their* thesis that they refuse to see that these simple arguments *do* the job, necessitating an endless repetition of the obvious. Let me speak for myself. I'm about to rehearse and endorse the classical arguments once again; but I'm confident that this endorsement is not precipitated by anti-relativistic prejudices. Before investigating the topic more closely, I used to *be* a relativist. I was familiar with the classical arguments, but always assumed that there must be an adequate relativistic rejoinder to them. Relativism might turn out to be untenable in the end, but it would surely take more than a three-step argument to overturn a world view that's shown itself to be so persistently attractive. After some reflection, however, I've come to the view that the three-step arguments leave relativists with very few avenues of escape, and that these avenues are easily blocked. This comes as a surprise to me.

    For ease of exposition, I'll conduct most of the analysis on the topic of epistemic relativism first, and then indicate briefly how it is that the same story can be told, *mutatis mutandis*, about ontological relativism. When I try to distil the classical anti-relativistic arguments to their simplest form, I come up with two equally simple formulations. The first one runs like this: if (epistemic) relativism is accepted, then we must say that all hypotheses can only be warranted relative to (say) a paradigm. But then relativism itself can only be warranted relative to a paradigm. So it's not warranted *tout court*. If we assume that relativism is warranted, we conclude that it isn't warranted. Therefore it isn't warranted. The second argument starts at the same place (the assumption that relativism is warranted) and ends at the same destination (the conclusion that relativism isn't warranted), but travels via a different route. Suppose, once again, that relativism is warranted. Then belief in *some* thesis is warranted, namely the thesis of relativism. But then relativism, the thesis that *nothing* is warranted *tout court*, is itself unwarranted. Therefore relativism isn't warranted.

It's easy to get these arguments mixed up, or mistakenly to count them as a single argument. These are harmless confusions, since they do pretty much the same work while utilizing the same resources. Friends and foes of relativism alike would agree that they're persuasive to an identical degree. Just for the record, however, they are different arguments. I keep them apart by noting that the crucial step in the first argument is a *universal instantiation* from 'all hypotheses can only be warranted relative to a paradigm' to 'relativism can only be warranted relative to a paradigm', while the crucial step in the second argument is an *existential generalization* from 'relativism is warranted *tout court*' to 'some hypotheses are warranted *tout court*'.

The foregoing description of the argument(s) against relativism is incomplete in one respect. What the argument says about relativism has its parallel in the liar paradox: the assumption that 'This sentence is false' is true leads to the conclusion that 'This sentence is false' is false. In the case of the liar paradox, the conclusion that the target sentence is false loses its force because that hypothesis in turn leads to the contradictory conclusion that the sentence is true. Thus we have no conclusion at all – it's a paradox. In the case of the warrantability of relativism, however, the assumption that relativism is unwarranted doesn't generate any paradoxical conclusions. So the complete argument runs as follows: if relativism is warranted, then it's not warranted; but if it's not warranted, no further problems ensue. Therefore relativism is unwarranted.

There are two traditional relativist responses to these and kindred arguments – and one non-traditional response. Meiland indicates the traditional options:

> That relativism is self-refuting ... is a myth which must be laid to rest. It *would* be inconsistent for the relativist to say both that all doctrines are relatively true and that relativism is not relatively true but instead is absolutely true. However, the careful relativist would not and need not say this. He would say either that all doctrines except relativism (and perhaps its competitors on the meta-level) are relatively true or false, or else he would say that his own doctrine of relativism is relatively true too. And saying that relativism is only relatively true does not produce inconsistency.

> (Meiland 1980: 121)

In this passage, Meiland talks about relativism about truth, rather than relativism about rational warrant. It's clear, however, that the issues remain the same with either formulation. I'll discuss Meiland's two relativistic rejoinders in reverse order. The second one can be characterized as an attitude of genial agreement toward the classical refutations: if you start with the assumption that (epistemic) relativism is absolutely warranted, then it indubitably follows that relativism is absolutely unwarranted. But relativists don't *want* to claim that their view is warranted absolutely. They're content to say that relativism is warranted relative to some paradigm and to admit that absolutism may be warranted relative to some other paradigm – or so it may be claimed. Let's call this position *relativistic relativism*.

There are two standard objections to relativistic relativism. The first is that the concept of relative warrant (or relative truth) is parasitic on the concept of absolute warrant (or absolute truth). What's supposed to follow from this parasitism is that you can't claim that anything has relative warrant unless you're also willing to say that something has absolute warrant. Meiland (1977) tries to defend relativistic relativism by showing that the relativized notions can be explicated without reference to the corresponding absolute notions. Commenting on this work, Siegel observes that

[t]his point is important for Meiland because, if it can be sustained, it rescues the relativist from the charge that she relies on the notion of absolute truth in holding a concept of relative truth, thereby refuting her own position by relying on a concept she expressly rejects.

(1987: 13)

Siegel proceeds to give a refutation of Meiland's defence of the independence of the relativized notions. But the ultimate disposition of relativistic relativism isn't placed in peril by Siegel's conclusion: Meiland was wrong to suppose that relativistic relativists need to worry about the parasitism issue. Grant that the concept of relative truth can't be defined without making reference to the concept of absolute truth. It follows that you can't *have* the relative concept without having the absolute one. But it doesn't follow that one's claims involving the relativized notion entail that there are absolute truths. More generally, conceptual parasitism doesn't entail anything about the logical relationships between sentences which assert that instances of the concepts occur or obtain. If it's a defining characteristic of an X that it be a non-Y, then the concept of an X is parasitic on the concept of a Y. But this doesn't mean that belief in the existence of Xs commits you to belief in the existence of Ys.

Despite his attempts to show that the concept of relative truth 'does not include the concept of absolute truth as a distinct part' (1977: 574), Meiland has also written passages that indicate his understanding of the fact that it doesn't *matter* whether the concept of relative truth includes the concept of absolute truth as a part. For instance, he considers the following charge of parasitism:

> When we talk about what Jones believes, we are presumably talking about what Jones believes *to be true* – and, apparently, about what Jones believes to be *absolutely* true. So it appears that [Protagoras'] variety of relativism cannot even be stated without recourse to a concept of absolute truth ... Relativism is supposed to eschew absolute truth entirely and it allegedly cannot succeed in doing so.
>
> (1977: 578)

He notes that this accusation misfires, for

> [t]he relativist can certainly admit that someone *believes* a statement to be absolutely true. The relativist will merely deny that this belief is itself absolutely true (although it may be relatively true – true for the person who believes it) and hence will also deny that the statement which is the object of that belief is itself absolutely true. The important point here is that in stating his position, the Protagorean relativist is not saying that anything is absolutely true; he is only allowing that some people believe that various statements are absolutely true.
>
> (1977: 579)

In this passage, Meiland correctly observes that *using* a concept of absolute truth – even using it in explicating the notion of relative truth – doesn't commit the relativist to *believing* that anything is absolutely true. One wonders then why he elsewhere tries so hard to show that relative truth can be defined without reference to the absolute notion. In any event, the parasitism argument against relativistic relativism misses the mark.

The second objection to relativistic relativism is that, in its attempt to evade the self-refutation arguments, it becomes so eviscerated that it fails to challenge the absolutist's beliefs:

> to argue that relativism is only correct for the relativist is to fail to join the issue with the opponent of relativism.
>
> (Siegel 1987: 24)

The idea here is that absolutists have no stake in denying, and are not challenged by, the thesis that relativism is true or warranted for relativists. Relativistic relativists try to avoid defeat by the simple expedient of claiming a lot less than their putative adversaries. To be sure, the thesis *that one cannot claim any more than what relativistic relativism allows* is a genuine rival to absolutism. But if relativists try to make this claim, they render themselves liable once again to the self-refutation arguments. In order to evade the reach of these arguments, relativists can't claim that their epistemic policy is better than the absolutists', except by their own lights – and this, once again, is not something that absolutists need to deny.

The foregoing argument shows that relativists are impotent to mount a philosophical attack on absolutism. This is already an important result: *the relativist has no case against absolutism.* But it doesn't yet show that absolutism wins. In order to claim more than a tie, absolutists have to come up with a telling critique of the relativistic relativists' self-imposed constraints. I think that one of Putnam's many anti-relativistic arguments fits the bill. However, Putnam's (1983) presentation contains several novelties which seem to me to be inessential to the argument. So, while I acknowledge that the idea that I'm about to present was inspired by his article, I refrain from claiming that it's identical to his idea. Anyway, here's the problem. Relativistic relativists generously want to assert the parity of their own views with those of their philosophical adversaries, the absolutists. Even so militant an anti-relativist as Siegel seems willing to grant that this assertion is coherent. The problem, according to Siegel, is that it's too weak to secure a victory:

> if the relativist defends relativism relativistically, she recognizes the equal cognitive legitimacy of absolutism … and thus the non-superiority of relativism and the arbitrariness of her commitment to it …
>
> (1987: 25)

But, having renounced any appeal to absolute warrant, it's not at all clear that relativists can lay claim to this parity. They proclaim themselves content to affirm only that relativism is warranted relative to the relativist paradigm. But, diminished as this claim is in comparison to the thesis that relativism is warranted *tout court*, it still claims too much. Relativists can't proclaim *absolutely* that relativism is warranted relative to the relativist paradigm. According to the epistemic relativist thesis, that relativized claim can itself be warranted only relative to some paradigm.

This double relativization is already problematic. As anti-relativists from Plato to Putnam have noted, our grasp of what this iteration of relativisms even means is hardly secure. But, of course, the problems don't stop here. Once again we find ourselves teetering on the edge of an infinite regress. However many relativizations are represented in our formulation of relativism, the resultant expression still seems to make a transcendental claim that relativists aren't entitled to entertain. It seems, in other words, that relativists are unable to come up with *any* formula that expresses the thesis that they want to endorse. Nor can this difficulty be remedied by allowing relativists to use infinitely long sentences. For suppose we say that the relativists' state of opinion is captured by the infinitely iterated expression:

' ' 'Relativism is warranted relative to paradigm S' is warranted relative to S' is warranted relative to S' ...

Let's abbreviate this unwieldy formula by $\{S_\infty, R\}$. Now the same dilemma can be run on $\{S_\infty, R\}$. Relativists can't affirm their belief in $\{S_\infty, R\}$ absolutely without violating their intention of never affirming anything absolutely. If they're going to preserve an across-the-board relativism, the most they can claim is that their belief in $\{S_\infty, R\}$ is warranted relative to their own paradigm. That is to say, the proposition $\{S_\infty, R\}$ still doesn't cleanly capture their state of opinion. It still claims too much. So it seems that epistemic relativists have no way of expressing what they want to say.

It's time to examine the second avenue of escape from self-refutation: exempting the thesis of relativism from its own scope. In the case of epistemic relativism, this would amount to saying that everything is only relatively warranted except this principle itself. Let's call this position *absolute (epistemic) relativism*. The opposite of absolute relativism – the view that eschews any and all absolutist claims – goes by the name of *total relativism*. Now, unless absolute relativism is going to be a bare and unconvincing posit, relativists are going to need to be able to adduce considerations in its favour. This capacity can only be purchased by exempting more than the thesis of relativism itself. Absolute relativists will need to concede the absolute warrantability of enough philosophical machinery to put together a decent case for their point of view. Moreover, the problem of inexpressibility doesn't just afflict the general thesis of relativism. For any first-order hypothesis X about the world, total relativists can't maintain that belief in X is absolutely warranted, or that belief in X is warranted relative to S, or that belief in 'belief in X is warranted relative to S' is warranted relative to S, etc. Relativists don't just find the general statement of their philosophy to be problematic – they find it equally problematic to express their specific states of opinion about tables and chairs. So the absolute relativists' concessions to absolutism have to be extended. They have to say that first-order hypotheses about the world are warranted only relative to paradigms, but that second-order hypotheses like 'belief in X is warranted relative to S' can be warranted absolutely. Actually, they don't have to say exactly this. They have the option of maintaining a relativistic stance for any number of levels – perhaps even for infinitely many levels. But if they want to talk about the world at all, it seems that they have to concede that every proposition P about the world has some transform like $\{S1, \{S2, \ldots \{Sn, P\} \ldots\}\}$ which is sufficiently relativized to be warrantable absolutely.

The standard absolutist reaction to this move from total to absolute relativism is to say that the new doctrine purchases coherence and expressibility at an enormous cost in newsworthiness. In fact, absolute relativism isn't relativism at all. It's a form of absolutism. Absolute relativists and traditional absolutists merely disagree over the details of what is and what isn't absolutely warranted. There's no doubt that the reduction in newsworthiness is considerable. Still, if absolute relativism were shown to be (absolutely) warranted, it would provide us with a significant insight about the world we live in. We would learn the non-trivial lesson that the world reveals different faces to different but equally rational investigators. This hypothesis is still sufficiently potent to arouse more traditional absolutists' ire. For instance, the relativism that Larry Laudan strives to get beyond in *Beyond Positivism and Relativism* (1996) seems to include absolute relativism.

In the present context, however, the most important point is that this modification of relativism renders it useless for the purpose of bolstering the case for logical constructivism. Absolute relativism can't help the logical constructivists with their two-societies problem. The problem here is what to say when S1 and S2 construct incompatible logics L1 and L2. The resolution via a full-fledged epistemic relativism is to say that L1 is valid for S1, and L2 is valid for S2. According to absolute relativists, however, there are some hypotheses that we're absolutely warranted in believing. But then there must be rules of inference that we're absolutely warranted in adopting, or else we could never arrive at an absolutely warranted opinion. The principle may be as stark and rudimentary as the rule that you can validly infer some fact X from null premises. But the existence of any absolute rule entails that logical constructivism is false. So, while absolute relativism is by no means devoid of interest, it's inadequate for the purpose at hand. Anyway, it's not relativism.

Let's turn now to Goodman's ontological relativism. Does Putnam's (1983) inexpressibility argument work against Goodman's thesis? Putnam doesn't refer to ontological relativism per se in his exposition. But there's an interesting bit of textual evidence to the effect that Putnam must regard Goodman's thesis as falling within the scope of his argument. In his discussion, Putnam states that his argument accuses relativism of the same fallacy as methodological solipsism, the view that each of us constructs the world from his or her own experience (Putnam 1983: 236). One year later, Goodman explicitly *likens* his own position to the methodological solipsist's (1996b: 153 – originally published in 1984). The fact that neither philosopher makes reference to the other in this context is surprising. These Harvard colleagues have a long history of commenting on each other's work. It's hard to imagine that Putnam should not have explicitly entertained the thought that his methodological solipsism argument applies to Goodman's relativism; and it's inconceivable that Goodman, writing one year later, didn't know about Putnam's analogy between relativism and solipsism. If Goodman recognized that his position *was* akin to the solipsist's, one would have thought that he'd try to deflect Putnam's critique. But, not a word.

In any case, the missing Putnamian argument against ontological relativism is easy to reconstruct. When society S1 constructs the fact X, and society S2 constructs the contrary fact −X, Goodman wants to say that X is true in world W1 and that −X is true in W2. But what about the fact that X is true in W1? Is that fact true only in one world, or is it true in all worlds? Can there be worlds whose inhabitants correctly judge that X is *not* true in W1? If we answer the last question in the affirmative, then we can't simply say that X is true in W1 *tout court*. We can at most say that 'X is true in W1' is true in W1 (and maybe in some other worlds as well). But this is the first step of the same regress that was encountered in the Putnamian critique of epistemic relativism. Once again, no number of relativizations – not even an infinite number – seems to weaken the claim enough to keep it within the bounds of a thoroughgoing ontological relativism. On the other hand, if we repudiate the regress – if we allow that X is true in W1 *tout court* – then there are trans-world facts about the universe that must be recognized by denizens of all the worlds – namely that X is true in W1. But this is to say that ontological relativism is false. Therefore ontological relativism is either inexpressible or false.

This argument forces Goodman to concede that there are some trans-world facts – a concession that parallels the forced march from relativistic epistemic relativism to absolute epistemic relativism described above. But, shorn of the protective shield of an uncompromisingly total ontological relativism, the thesis of *strong constructivism* can no longer be sustained – just as logical constructivism couldn't be sustained by absolute epistemic relativism. For if 'X is true in W1' is a trans-world fact, then no society can construct the fact 'X is not true in W1' – and it was shown in Chapter 12 that if any candidate fact can't be constructed, then strong constructivism is false. Therefore strong constructivism is false.

Let's summarize the dialectical situation for both epistemic and ontological relativism. The root problem is that you can't simply say that relativism is true (or warranted), because relativism entails the principle that nothing is true (or warranted) *tout court*. Absolute relativism tries to cope with the problem by weakening the relativistic thesis – specifically by conceding that relativism allows that some things are true. Relativistic relativism tries to cope with the problem by weakening the *epistemic status* of the thesis – specifically, by moving from 'relativism is true' to 'relativism is true relative to P'. Both these strategies fail. Relativistic relativism fails because it's inexpressible; and absolute relativism fails because it isn't relativism any more – it's not even relativistic enough to be of any use to constructivists.

Virtually all authors on both sides of the relativism issue have shared the presumption that these two strategies – absolute relativism and relativistic relativism – exhaust the relativist's options. But it seems that Joseph Margolis (1991) has come up with a third option for relativists: moving from the untenable 'relativism is true' to 'relativism is *truish*' (the term is my invention), where 'truish' is a third truth-value which shares some of the epistemically laudable qualities of 'true' while avoiding some of its more odious responsibilities. On the one hand, to say that relativism is truish is to commend it for its epistemic merits; on the other hand, it's not to say so much that the incoherence arguments can go through. For instance, while the truth of relativism conflicts with relativism's own claim that nothing is true, the weaker commendation that relativism is truish is compatible with the claim that nothing is true.

And what does it mean for something to be truish? Unfortunately, Margolis doesn't tell us. He satisfies himself with arguing that we *might* be able to develop a non-standard many-valued logic in which a non-self-defeating relativism *might* be formulated. We've seen this type of move before – in Hacking's apology for the apparent incoherence of the strong constructivists' talk about time. Hacking claimed that it's 'the grammar of our language' that's at fault: 'our very grammar has conditioned us towards the timeless view of facts' (Hacking 1988: 282). In effect, Margolis makes the parallel claim that our habitual bivalent logic has conditioned us toward the absolutist view of truth.

Now I don't want to say that this is an absurd or unthinkable type of move to make in any circumstance. But neither can I forget that repudiating the logic is a facile means of extricating oneself from any and all conceptual difficulties. When confronted with such a response, what I want to say is: okay, let's see what the better logic looks like. Neither Hacking nor Margolis comes across with the goods. They both content themselves with the broadest of programmatic statements. Hacking assures us that it's all right to say that a fact about the distant past was recently constructed; and Margolis assures us that it's permissible to say that relativism isn't true, but that it isn't false either. In both cases, these isolated fragments of an alternative logic give us no clue as to how to answer various further questions about time or truth. Hacking's gloss doesn't tell us what we're to say when an event at time t0 is constructed at t1 and deconstructed at t2. Margolis' gloss doesn't tell us why we couldn't say that, while relativism may be truish, the metaclaim that relativism is truish is *true*, thereby precipitating the same incoherence arguments all over again. Perhaps there are viable logics that disallow this move. But responding to a difficulty merely by noting that there may yet be a way out of it doesn't count as *disposing* of the difficulty. Margolis says that the non-standard logic gambit gives the relativist team 'another inning' when everyone had thought that the game was over. Maybe so. But this is an inning that's forever available to any team. If you get to question the logic, then the game is never over. The mere availability of these extra outs isn't worth mentioning. The play only gets interesting when someone steps into the batter's box to take a swing.

16 Semantic constructivism

Many of the people who call themselves constructivists subscribe to the slogan that nature plays no role in our epistemic decisions. This slogan is amenable to various interpretations, however. The previous chapters have been largely devoted to one gloss on the constructivist slogan – the metaphysical claim that there are no unconstructed natural facts. Another way to cash in on the same formula is to say that nature plays no role in our epistemic decisions, not because it doesn't exist, but because our epistemic decision-making procedures make no use of it. Such a state of affairs would obtain if, for example, we decided what to believe by randomly assigning all hypotheses a number and accepting only the even-numbered ones. A number of constructivists have argued that our epistemic practices do, in fact, have this character of being divorced from what may or may not happen in the world (Barnes 1982; Bloor 1983; Collins 1985).

Now to say that our epistemic practices make no use of nature is to make a historical claim which may be of little epistemological significance. The claim would be true, for instance, if we inveterately played the game of accepting the even-numbered hypotheses. But the appropriate reaction to such a state of affairs wouldn't be to become constructivists – it would be to reform the epistemic practices. However, Barnes, Bloor and Collins all argue that *there cannot be* an epistemic enterprise that takes nature into account. They endorse an argument of Kripke's (1982) to the effect that sentences have no determinate truth conditions. Kripke in turn represents his argument as a reconstruction of the main message of Wittgenstein's (1953) *Philosophical Investigations*. The argument runs as follows.

I think that I've learned what tables are, and that I can correctly apply 'table' to indefinitely many items in the future. Suppose, then, that I visit the Eiffel Tower for the first time, see a table at its base and identify it as such. My companion, however, makes the following startling claim: according to *my own past linguistic usage*, the object in question isn't a table at all – for when I look at all the past instances of objects that I've called a 'table', as well as all the instances of objects whose tablehood I've denied, I find (my companion claims) that by 'table', I've meant *tabair*, where a 'tabair' is anything which is a table not found at the base of the Eiffel

Tower, or a chair found there. As for my present inclination to call the object before us a table, she attributes it to a temporary aberration, induced perhaps by too much French wine. How can I answer my companion? To be sure, the history of my usage of 'table' doesn't support her hypothesis any better than it supports my own hypothesis that by 'table' I've always meant *table*. But I need more than a tie here. How do I establish to my own satisfaction that 'table' refers to tables?

Evidently, the history of a term's past usage doesn't by itself determine the course of its future applications. Kripke considers various hypotheses about what other facts there may be which establish the meaning of the word 'table' and finds them all to be deficient. It isn't feasible for me to go over these arguments in enough detail to be persuasive. I refer the reader to Kripke's exceptionally lucid text. Here, however, is a brief impression of some of the ground that's covered. It obviously won't help to say that the meaning I assigned to 'table' is determined by a verbal definition, for that would merely push the problem to another place: my companion could then come up with non-standard interpretations of the words used in the definition. What about saying that to mean *table* by 'table' is to be disposed to call tables, and nothing else, by the name of 'table'? One of several problems with this suggestion is that I'm *not* disposed to call tables and nothing else by the name of 'table'. Sometimes, when it's dark and I'm groggy from having just awakened, I've incorrectly identified chairs as tables. On the dispositional account of meaning, there could be no such thing as a labelling error. What about saying that there's an introspectible experience, a special feeling, which corresponds to my meaning *table* when I say 'table', and which would be different if I meant *tabair*? Suppose there are such experiences. How on earth, asks Kripke, would I be able to know which feeling is which? Perhaps the feeling that I take to be the feeling of meaning *table* is really the feeling of meaning *tabair*. In desperation, I might posit that meanings are non-mental, non-behavioural, independently existing Platonic entities, and that 'table' means *table* by virtue of naming the appropriate Platonic form. Of course, in order to explain how it is that *I* mean 'table' by *table*, I need to add when I say 'table', I'm in a special relation to the form of *table* and not to other forms. But then how do I know that I've got the form right? Maybe what I think is the form of *table* is really the form of *tabair*. And so on.

What seems to follow from this analysis is that there's no fact of the matter whether I mean *table* or *tabair* by 'table'. Since the dilemma is entirely general, it further follows that *sentences have no determinate empirical content*. If this conclusion is right, then it's indeed the case that nature can play no role in determining which sentences we are to accept. I call this doctrine *semantic constructivism* in order to emphasize that, like metaphysical constructivism, it's a way to construe the generic constructivist slogan ('Nature plays no role ...'). More precisely, semantic constructivism is the view that nature does not place any normative constraints on which sentences we should accept as true. Barnes, Bloor and Collins are all semantic constructivists on the basis of the Kripkean conclusion that sentences have no determinate empirical content. But the thesis that sentences have no empirical content isn't a part of my definition of semantic constructivism. In fact, I'm going to discuss an argument for semantic constructivism a little later which allows that sentences *may have* determinate empirical content. But that's not Barnes *et al.*'s argument. Until such time as I do present the alternative argument, I'll use 'semantic constructivism' to refer indiscriminately either to the more general thesis that nature does not place any normative constraints on what we accept as true, or to the more specific thesis that this is so because sentences have no determinate empirical content.

If nature places no constraints on what to accept, then what *does* determine which hypotheses get accepted? According to the semantic constructivists, there's only one other possibility: social negotiation. Barnes *et al.* write as though the negotiated nature of all putative facts is an immediate corollary of semantic constructivism. But it's at least *prima facie* possible to be a semantic constructivist and to offer a different account of our epistemic practices. If nature plays no role in our epistemic decisions, then maybe these decisions are entirely random, or maybe they're divinely (or diabolically) directed. So, even if the Kripkean argument succeeds, semantic constructivists who want to be *social* constructivists owe us another argument. But let's start with semantic constructivism proper.

It's helpful to start by contrasting semantic constructivism with other related theses. The main contrast is, of course, with *metaphysical constructivism*, which includes the strong constructivism and scientific constructivism that have been my main focus so far. Unlike metaphysical constructivism, semantic constructivism isn't an ontological thesis. It doesn't claim that there is no independent world. It claims that the nature of language precludes our utilizing the independent world in our epistemic practices. This sounds rather like *scepticism*. Indeed, it can appropriately be regarded as a form of scepticism, so long as it's understood that it's significantly different from – and much more radical than – the more traditional forms of scepticism. Classical sceptics worry about how to justify our acceptance of hypotheses. Their worry would be laid to rest if only they could persuade themselves that it's legitimate to accept some assumptions without offering any justification. For semantic constructivists the problem is more fundamental. According to semantic constructivists, you can't make any assumptions, even if you want to. To be sure, you can select some sentences and treat them in a privileged manner. But these sentences don't represent substantive assumptions about the world, because sentences don't *say* anything about the world.

Semantic constructivism is also more radical than Quinean *holism* (Quine 1951). Both principles entail that any sentence can be held true 'come what may'. But semantic constructivism goes further. Holism is a thesis about the *apportionment* of empirical content to individual sentences, while semantic constructivism is the thesis that there is no empirical content to apportion. Like the semantic constructivists, Quine denies that individual sentences have a determinate empirical content. But he's evidently willing to ascribe a determinate empirical content to the system of accepted sentences as a whole. This is evidenced by the fact that, according to Quine, we're supposed to know when our total system of beliefs has been violated in a way that necessitates some adjustment to the system. It's just that we have a wide latitude in how the adjustment can be made. If semantic constructivism is right, then there's no fact of the matter concerning whether an adjustment in our web of belief is required. The decision to make an adjustment – or not to make it – is entirely conventional.

Before subjecting their thesis to critical scrutiny, it's worth mentioning that Barnes, Bloor and Collins have all expressed other views that don't sit well with their semantic constructivism. Barnes and Bloor, for instance, are just as famous (or infamous) for their *epistemic relativism* as for their semantic constructivism. But there's a tension between these two doctrines. It makes sense to deny them both – to claim that sentences have determinate truth values and that we're sometimes (absolutely) warranted in believing them. It's also feasible to deny semantic constructivism and affirm epistemic relativism (or rather, this would be feasible if epistemic relativism weren't untenable all by itself). Someone holding such a view would maintain that sentences have definite meanings, but that there is no absolute warrant for believing any of them. It may even be possible to affirm that sentences have no meaning and to hold an absolutist conception of knowledge. Perhaps an appeal to tacit knowledge will do the job: sentences have no meaning, but our tacit non-verbal expectations are sometimes absolutely correct. But how can one assert both that sentences have no meanings and that our beliefs are warranted or fail to be warranted relative to a paradigm? The appeal to tacit knowledge is much more problematic here, for the idea that a belief can at once be tacit and true-relative-to-a-system is an oxymoron. In any case, the relativism that Barnes and Bloor talk about is a thesis about the warrantability of *sentences*. But their semantic constructivism undercuts the relativism/absolutism issue for sentences completely. Semantic constructivists might say that sentences can be believed *ad lib*, or that they can't be believed at all. But if sentences have no determinate meaning, there's no issue about whether belief in them is warrantable absolutely or relative to a system.

Collins, for his part, correctly characterizes the semantic constructivist line of reasoning as leading to a thoroughgoing conventionalism: it's up to us to *decide* which sentences to take as true. He acknowledges this explicitly, chiding Barnes for holding back from this radical conclusion to the argument (Collins 1985: 172–3). But he also has things to say about the conditions that foster scientific progress (160). It's hard to see how any scientific change can be regarded as progressive from an uncompromisingly conventionalist point of view. After all, isn't every instance of scientific change merely a matter of replacing one convention with another? If we agree to regard progressive change as desirable, why don't we simply agree that it's happening? This incongruity in Collins's thinking comes to a head in the grand finale of his book:

> Professional scientists are the experts to whom we must turn when we want to know about the natural world. Science, however, is not a profession that can take from our shoulders the burden of political, legal, moral and technological decision making. It can only offer the best advice that there is to be had. To ask for more than this is to risk widespread disillusion with science with all its devastating consequences.
>
> (167)

A semantic constructivist might appropriately claim that the advice offered by science is *as good* as any that there is to be had. But 'the best'?

What about Collins's argument for conventionalism? The argument is that concepts have no determinate extensions (this is the Kripkean part), so we can't explain our co-ordinated linguistic practices by an appeal to common meanings – the co-ordination has to be negotiated. Finn Collin (1993) has objected to this argument as follows. To say that our linguistic practices are co-ordinated is to classify them as instances of the concept 'co-ordinated'. But if concepts have no determinate extensions, then there's no fact of the matter as to whether our linguistic practices *are* co-ordinated. Harry Collins's solution to the problem of co-ordination has this drawback – that, if he's right, then there is no problem requiring a solution. Therefore it can't be the right solution to the problem. Conversely, if there *is* a problem – if there's a need to explain how people manage to 'go on in the same way' – then it's a determinate fact that people *do* go on in the same way. And then Collins is wrong again.

Finn Collin says that this argument is a *reductio* of the assumption that concepts have no determinate extensions (1993: 40). But this goes too far. Let's review Harry Collins's line of thinking: he gives the Kripkean argument, draws the conclusion that nature can play no role in our epistemic practices, and then adds that only negotiation can explain these epistemic practices. Finn Collin's argument shows that the last addition is undermined by the semantic-constructivist hypothesis that it's designed to supplement: if semantic constructivism is accepted, then there are no determinate 'epistemic practices' to explain. Semantic constructivism doesn't lend credence to anything as constructive as a sociological analysis of our epistemic practices. Later in this chapter, I'll argue that an argument for semantic constructivism is an argument for irrationalism. The point here is that Finn Collin's argument refutes Harry Collins's sociological addendum, but it leaves the argument for semantic constructivism untouched.

What about the Kripkean argument itself? Well, it's a strong argument, but it isn't conclusive. For one thing, there are some philosophers who think that Kripke hasn't disposed of all extant solutions to the sceptical paradox. Boghossian (1989), for instance, thinks that Kripke's arguments don't rule out the possibility that my meaning *table* by 'table' is an unanalysable state which can't be reduced to any experiences or behavioural dispositions. More importantly, the argument wouldn't be conclusive even if there were no unrefuted explanations of meaning on the table (or on the tabair) – for the form of the argument *guarantees* that it will be inconclusive. Kripke argues for the claim that there's no solution to the problem of meaning by considering all the candidate solutions that he and others are able to think of, and showing that none of these works. Obviously, this doesn't rule out the possibility that there is a candidate solution that hasn't yet been thought of which will turn out to do the job. Even the admission that nobody will ever come up with a solution wouldn't establish beyond doubt that words have no meanings. After all, there's no reason to believe that the human cognitive apparatus is capable of discovering and comprehending the solution to every problem that *has* a solution. Indeed, McGinn (1989) has urged us to take this line with the mind–body problem. It's notoriously the case that all the extant theories about the relation between mind and body suffer from severe conceptual difficulties. McGinn suggests that the solution to the problem is beyond human capacity. In fact, he suggests that the correct explanation of the mind–body connection could be entirely naturalistic and *still* be undiscoverable by the human mind. By the same token, the failure of all the solutions to Kripke's problem could be due either to the fact that there is no solution to be found, or to the fact that the solution is beyond human ken.

It might be objected that one can always make this move to save a favoured thesis. But this isn't the case. McGinn's rejoinder is available when the argument tries to establish a thesis by eliminating all its possible rivals. Such an argument by elimination always allows for the logical possibility that there's another rival, not yet thought of or perhaps unthinkable by human minds, that has no refutation. But not all arguments have this structure. For example, we sometimes support a thesis by claiming that it's implied by principles which are firmly accepted by the person we're trying to convince. McGinn's rejoinder has no purchase on such a direct demonstration. I will present a direct proof of this type for the thesis of semantic constructivism immediately below. I don't present this argument because I think that the Kripkean argument fails. On the contrary, I think the Kripkean argument is enormously persuasive. But, by virtue of eliminating the feasibility of McGinn's rejoinder, a direct proof of the same thesis makes the case for semantic constructivism stronger still. Here's the argument.

Suppose that sentences *do* have absolutely determinate empirical contents. Moreover, suppose that we all know what these empirical contents are. These aren't necessary premises of the argument – they're concessions to the opposition that the argument can afford to make. (A minor variant of the argument will work just as well if we start with the assumption of Quinean holism.) Suppose now that the sentence P is in my stock of beliefs, and that P is disconfirmed. Then either of two things may happen: I can give up my belief in P, or I can change the empirical import of P. For example, if I believe that all swans are white and I encounter a black swan, I can either cease to believe that all swans are white, or I can change the extension that I attach to 'swan' in such a way that the truth of 'All swans are white' is preserved. That both options *have* to be available is evidenced by the fact that I had to *learn* the extension of the term 'swan' in the first place. When we're learning a language, it routinely happens that we have to make a choice between regarding a sentence as disconfirmed and altering the extensions of our concepts. In what may have been my first conceptual controversy, I once argued vehemently that mushroom is a type of meat.

How do we decide which course to take? The issue comes up for Fred Dretske in the course of his defence of a causal theory of mental content. According to Dretske, we have to distinguish between two phases in our relationship to the language: the *learning situation*, during which time we acquire its concepts, and the *post-learning situation*, during which we utilize the concepts with a fixed extension (Dretske 1981: 194–5). Suppose now that we believe that all swans are white and we encounter what seems to be a black swan. If we're in the post-learning situation, we take this to mean that we must give up our belief in the universal whiteness of swans; if we're in the learning situation, however, we modify our concept of 'swan' (or conceivably of 'white'). No doubt these observations have a rough-and-ready validity: this is more or less what happens. But they can hardly be taken as a principled solution to the problem. As Fodor points out,

> the distinction between what happens in the learning period and what happens thereafter surely isn't principled; there is no time after which one's use of a symbol stops being merely shaped and starts to be, as it were, in earnest.

(Fodor 1987: 103)

So what determines which course we will take? Why did I lose the argument about mushrooms? We're tempted to say that it's things like the status difference between the disputants, which results in one of them being assigned the role of teacher and the other being relegated to the role of learner – in brief, that it's a process of social negotiation. We don't have to say this – appeals to divine or diabolical intervention are still logically available. But one thing is certain: it's not the independent properties of nature that settle the issue. The fact that 'All swans are white' *has* a determinate empirical content is neither here nor there. In effect, the role of empirical content drops out of the picture in our account of the process whereby we take certain sentences to be true. *Given* a set of extensions for our concepts, then there's a fact of the matter concerning which sentences are true. But extensions are never – can never be – 'given' in the requisite sense. There can be no epistemic compulsion to continue to adhere to any set of extensions. If there were, then we could never learn what these extensions are supposed to be in the first place, for conceptual learning is a process of successive modification of these extensions. The corollary is that it's not an epistemic error to champion an alternative extension for some concept. It's epistemically permissible, for instance, to promulgate the hypothesis that a whale is a fish. At the very worst, it's merely a losing proposition. Nor can it be claimed that it's an epistemic error to say 'A whale is a fish under the current extensions', for the extension of 'current extension' is also up for grabs. Freud's claim that there are unconscious mental processes provides us with a historical example of this possibility: Freud knew that the claim was self-contradictory according to then-current meanings, but he said it anyway, and he wasn't guilty of any epistemic error for saying it (see Chapter 13). There's no principled limit to the conceptual revisions that we might champion. We can claim that trees are fish too, or that unconscious mental processes are fish, or that there are no fish. Evidently, the independent properties of nature, even if they exist, are powerless to dictate which sentences we accept as true.

Let's examine the difference between the foregoing argument for semantic constructivism and the Barnes–Bloor–Collins argument. Barnes *et al.* claim that concepts have no extensions, so that we have to decide anew each time whether a putative instance of the concept C shall be deemed an actual instance of C. I grant that C has a definite extension, but claim that we *still* have to decide anew each time whether a putative C is an actual C. The reason for this is that we're forever confronted with the choice between leaving the extension unchanged, or changing it so as to accommodate the putative instance. You can't avoid having to make the decision anew each time, and either course is epistemically irreproachable each time. Even if I know how my language teachers want me to go on in the identification of candidate swans or candidate fish, there are no epistemic considerations that would oblige me to accede to their expectations. It wouldn't be an epistemic error for me to try to make my alternative way of going on prevail.

Here's another description of the difference between the two arguments for semantic constructivism. In the course of combating Goodmanian relativism, Putnam writes:

> One perfectly good answer to Goodman's rhetorical question 'Can you tell me something that we didn't make?' is that we didn't make Sirius a star. Not only didn't we make Sirius a star in the sense in which a carpenter makes a table, *we didn't make it a star*. Our ancestors and our contemporaries (including astrophysicists), in shaping and creating our

language, created the concept *star*, with its partly conventional boundaries, and so on. And that concept *applies* to Sirius.

(1996: 183)

In this passage, Putnam *presupposes* that semantic constructivism is false.
This is a fair presupposition for him to make, because semantic constructivism isn't at issue in his disagreement with Goodman. The issue between
them is metaphysical constructivism. But, in the course of making his point,
he has occasion to negate the central claim of the Kripkean argument for
semantic constructivism: Barnes *et al.* would never agree that 'our ancestors
and our contemporaries ... created the concept *star*, with its partly
conventional boundaries'. Barnes *et al.* don't think that concepts *have*
boundaries. Naturally, this would lead them to reject Putnam's conclusion
that the concept of a star *'applies* to Sirius'. My argument for semantic
constructivism is that, even if our ancestors *did* create the concept *star* with
certain boundaries, there's still no fact of the matter as to whether that
concept applies to Sirius, because its continued application depends on our
continued adherence to our ancestors' decisions.

Am I arguing for anything more than the truism that the meanings of
words aren't fixed by nature? Well, I'm pointing to an unappreciated
corollary to this truism. The picture underlying a lot of philosophical and
psychological discourse about concepts is that their meanings are socially
negotiated, but that, once the negotiations are over, the meanings are fixed
– we can thereafter treat them as though they were independent facts of
nature. This view is made explicit in Dretske's distinction between the
learning situation and the post-learning situation. It's also evidenced in
Putnam's pronounless, impersonal locution: the concept *star* applies to
Sirius (as opposed to 'We take the concept *star* to apply to Sirius, and may
stop taking it so at any moment'). Negotiated outcomes are never fixed in
the same way as facts of nature are fixed. We can't decide to change the
independent facts of nature; but negotiated results are *always* liable to
renegotiation. When someone insists that whales are fish, we may regard
him either as mistaken or as a conceptual innovator. The course we take
depends on whether we want to go along with him.

It might be objected that there's an important asymmetry between going
along with our ancestors' conceptual boundaries and altering them. To be
sure, the received boundaries are open to renegotiation at any time. But
keeping the extensions unchanged is the *default* option. This would account
for – and excuse – our treatment of linguistic facts as though they were fixed
facts of nature. Putnam's unqualified statement that the concept *star* applies
to Sirius would then be the right thing to say even though we may choose at
any moment to exclude Sirius from the realm of stars. I have two replies to
this objection. The more important one is that it doesn't make any difference
to the argument for semantic constructivism that I've presented. The fact
that one choice is an automatic default, whereas the other requires explicit

intervention, doesn't affect their equal availability. It's still always equally 'correct' either to go along with the received extensions or to change them.

The second reply is less important, but it leads to some interesting observations. If it's a default option to keep the extensions fixed, then it's so because of a policy that we've adopted. There's nothing inherent about language that requires us to adhere to this policy. We could just as well adopt a contrary policy. For instance, consider this one, which I call the *astrological* policy: when one of the sentences we accept appears to be disconfirmed, the default is automatically to adjust the conceptual extensions in such a way as to preserve the truth of the sentence. If we follow the astrological policy in astrology, we don't give up the notion that Capricorns all have a distinctively Capricornian personality just because we encounter an anomalous case. The default is to take every encounter with a Capricorn as informative of the boundaries of the concept *Capricornian personality*. It's a frequent charge against astrology that it actually operates in this manner. But it's not immediately obvious that such a policy is, in itself, epistemically reprehensible. In fact, it's probably the policy that's followed in what Dretske calls the learning situation. When we're acquiring a conceptual repertoire from scratch, there's probably no other way to proceed than by adopting a *prima facie* presumption that the authoritative utterances of the experts are correct, and adjusting our conceptual boundaries accordingly.

But if we can follow the astrological policy as conceptual learners, there's no principled reason why we can't continue to do so forever. That may not be what we do in fact – but we could. We could play a language game wherein there's an independent source of sentences which are assigned the truth value 'true' by default. These could be the sentences found in the Bible, the deliverances of the Azande chicken oracle, or whatever. Any apparent disconfirmation of the canon would automatically be taken to require an alteration of conceptual boundaries. If the Bible says that all swans are white, and we encounter what seems to be a black one, we just have to change the extension of 'swan' (or of 'white'). If generally adopted, such a policy would result in everybody's endorsing the same set of sentences regardless of what happens in the world. It might be objected that such a game wouldn't count as a *language*: if everybody says the same things regardless of what happens, then their acoustic behaviour is no more linguistic than are bird calls. But this isn't so. Even if we all adhere to the astrological policy, our verbal behaviour (unlike bird calls) continues to be thoroughly conventional. What we say may be fixed in a manner which disregards what happens in the world, but it's not fixed in its fixity, nor is there anything that anyone can do to *make* it fixed in its fixity. The option of abandoning the astrological policy at any time can't be lost or taken away from us.

In effect, to follow the astrological policy is to abide in Dretske's learning situation. The fact that there's no principled distinction between the learning situation and the post-learning situation is already enough to insure that following the astrological policy is a viable and epistemically irreproachable practice. When we follow the astrological policy, we regard ourselves as perpetual language learners, never as language experts. There's nothing to stop us from designating ourselves as experts at any time. But neither is there anything to force us to so designate ourselves. Imagine a Lord-of-the-Flies scenario in which all the adult linguistic authorities disappear, leaving behind a society of children who designate themselves as language learners. It seems plausible that, for a while at least, this society would not abandon any of the received views that came from the now-defunct elders. If the children had been told that all leaves are green, then, upon encountering what seems to be a brown leaf, the default conclusion might be that they had the boundaries of 'leaf' (or of 'green') wrong. Eventually, some of these children would no doubt designate themselves as experts. That is to say, they would give up the astrological policy. But we certainly wouldn't want to say that, prior to the evolution of experts, these children's practices didn't constitute a language. Moreover, there's clearly no time limit that the development of linguistic experts has to meet. In fact it may never happen. Therefore a community adhering to the defaults of the astrological policy is still talking a language.

It was noted at the very beginning of this chapter that what unites semantic and metaphysical constructivism is that they're both glosses on the slogan that nature plays no role in our epistemic practices. If adherence to this slogan is the core belief that impels a person to fly under the banner of constructivism, then there's a lot to be said for giving one's constructivism a semantic as opposed to metaphysical turn. Semantic constructivism purchases the slogan, while avoiding the paradoxes that are generated by the metaphysical thesis. For instance, there's no need to multiply worlds, *à la* Goodman, in order to account for the construction of X and not-X by two different societies. We can just say that each society ascribes a different empirical content to the sentence 'X'. A similar move also obviates the need for elaborate models involving multiple time lines to account for the problem of the two eras. To say that X is constructed at t1 and decon-structed at t2 is simply to say that the empirical content of 'X' is changed. Semantic constructivism also has the resources for explaining the Duhemian asymmetry. Changing the empirical content of a sentence often *is* a species of Duhemian manoeuvre: one side or the other in a controversy may be impelled to do it in order to preserve a valued thesis in the face of an apparent disconfirmation. Now the new argument for semantic construc-tivism allows that sentences *have* empirical content – it's just that we're allowed to change them. Thus there's a simple answer to the question: who initiates the Duhemian manoeuvre? It's the side whose hypothesis is disconfirmed, given the empirical content that's currently assigned to the hypothesis.

So if you're going to be a constructivist, I recommend the semantic variety – or rather I *would* recommend it if it didn't, like *logical* constructivism, collapse into irrationalism. I noted that Collins correctly affirms that semantic constructivism leads to a total conventionalism: it's up to us to *decide* what's true and what's false. But total conventionalism is, in the end, the same thing as logical constructivism, which in turn collapses into irrationalism. In logical constructivism, the irrationalist absence of epistemic constraints on what to say comes from the fact that all logical principles are up for grabs. Now the rules assigning empirical contents to sentences are themselves little logical principles. One of them, for instance, is the rule that 'Snow is white' means that snow is white. On my account, semantic constructivism is the thesis that *these* principles are up for grabs in exactly the same way: they're negotiable, hence we can break any one of them at any time. So semantic constructivism is a *sub*thesis of logical constructivism.

Now the average subthesis is logically weaker than the full thesis of which it's a part. For example, it's also a subthesis of logical constructivism that the rule of inference to the best explanation is up for grabs. If you adopt only that portion of logical constructivism, you don't become a raving irrationalist. You become the courteous and surpassingly reasonable philosopher of science who goes by the name of Bas van Fraassen. But if you adopt that portion of logical constructivism which states that the rules assigning truth conditions to sentences can be broken, then you get the whole of logical constructivism. Here's one way among many to see this. If the meanings of words can be changed *ad lib*, then the meaning of 'and' can be changed *ad lib*, and then you can't fault someone who wants to infer 'X and Y' from X, for all X and all Y. The point is obvious, really: *if you can change the meanings of words ad lib, then you can say anything at any time.*

There's a hugely important difference between the general argument that logical constructivism leads to irrationalism that I gave in Chapter 14 and the new argument that semantic constructivism leads to irrationalism: the antecedent of the new argument is much more difficult to resist. Rationalists will not feel threatened by the earlier, more general argument, because they simply won't concede that the validity of deductive principles is a matter of convention. But who can deny that the meanings of words are a matter of convention? The case for semantic constructivism seems to require no more than the admission of this truism; and the move from semantic constructivism to irrationalism seems to require no more than the equally compelling principle that conventions can be broken.

Let's recapitulate. I've presented an argument to the effect that semantic constructivism is true, and another argument to the effect that semantic constructivism entails irrationalism. It would seem to follow by *modus ponens* that irrationalism is true. But of course the situation isn't as simple as that. The argument that semantic constructivism leads to irrationalism doesn't merely uncover an unsuspected entailment of the former thesis. It's a *collapse* of the former thesis. Irrationalism is the practice of eschewing all epistemic constraints on what we say. Thus, if a hypothesis X leads to irrationalism, one has just as much warrant for espousing *not*-X as for espousing X. It's a *criticism* of semantic constructivism that it entails irrationalism, and not just a revelation of one of its consequences.

But what if nobody can find a mistake in the argument for semantic constructivism, or in the argument that semantic constructivism entails irrationalism? Does that mean that a compelling case has been made for becoming an irrationalist? Can there be such a thing as a good argument for – or against – irrationalism?

17 Irrationalism

Can there be an argument for irrationalism? One might take the view that such arguments are illegitimate, because their proponents are helping themselves to resources to which they're not entitled. They reject the claims of logic; therefore they forfeit the right to use logical argumentation to advance their position. Now it's true that rationalists can claim to their satisfaction that any and all arguments against rationalism must count for nothing *among the irrationalists*. This is undoubtedly so, since irrationalists don't recognize any normative constraints on their inferential practices. Even if she thinks of a clever argument that seems to undo rationalism, one wouldn't expect an irrationalist to say: 'I *thought* that rationality was untrustworthy – and now I have proof!' More exactly, an irrationalist might say this, by virtue of the fact that irrationalists might say anything. But there's no more logical reason for an irrationalist to say this than to say anything else – because there are no logical reasons for irrationalists. So rationalists may indeed reassure themselves that the irrationalists are engaging in persuasive endeavours that have no normative force by their own lights.

But that doesn't yet get the rationalists off the hook. The fact that an argument has no force for the giver doesn't entail that it has no force for the recipient. We need to distinguish two varieties of dialectical victory: winning the argument by one's own lights, and winning by one's *opponent's* lights. Ideally, of course, one would like to do both. But it's obvious that a double victory is going to be out of reach whenever the two lights are sufficiently disparate. In these cases, winning by one's opponent's lights still provides a possible avenue for resolving a difference of opinions. Suppose, for example, that biblical fundamentalists cite a passage from the Bible which conflicts with the theory of evolution. This citation has no force for me and you, because the Bible carries no special authority for us. But suppose *we* find a passage in the Bible that unambiguously *endorses* an evolutionary view. By our lights, this discovery would be irrelevant to the question whether human beings evolved from non-human origins. Nevertheless, it's fair to say that our biblical discovery would strike a devastating blow to the anti-evolutionary fundamentalists' case. In this scenario, we win the dispute with an argument whose force we ourselves don't acknowledge. (The argument in question isn't that our opponent's anti-evolutionary fundamentalism is internally incoherent – that's an argument whose force we *do* recognize. I'm talking about the argument that evolutionary theory is true.)

There is, to be sure, this difference between the rationalism–irrationalism dispute and the dispute between fundamentalists and biologists: the latter is a conflict between two logics (i.e., inferential practices), while the former pits one logic against *no* logic. But surely this can't make a difference to the recipient of the argument. To suppose that it does is to say that the cognitive state of our opponent determines the force of his argument against us. But an argument has the same force whether it's presented in jest or in earnest. In fact, it has the same force even if it's 'presented' through no intentional agency at all. Rationalists – and fundamentalists – can, if they wish, regard the arguments of their opponents just as they would the output of the proverbial typing monkeys, or patterns in the sand made by the blowing wind. If the monkeys happen to type out a series of characters that brings to mind a telling argument against my views, I'm in the same epistemic situation as if I'd thought of the argument myself.

There's another, more fundamental difference between the rationalism–irrationalism dispute and the dispute over evolution: in the former, what's at stake isn't simply a hypothesis which receives different truth values when viewed by the disputants' two lights – it's the status of one of the lights itself. A closer analogy would be to a debate between scientists and fundamentalists over the validity of the scientific method, or of fundamentalism. An argument against rationalism would be akin to citing a passage in the Bible which tells us not to believe anything just because we find it written in a book. By their own lights, how should fundamentalists react to the discovery of such a passage? The answer depends on the details of their methodology. One crucial detail concerns the relation between deductive logic and biblical citation. Suppose first that they regard biblical citation as prepotent over every other consideration, including deductive logic. This is more easily said than done. Even these extremists among fundamentalists need to use *modus ponens* in order to transfer passages from the Bible into their system of beliefs. Fundamentalism is, after all, a species of rationalism (i.e., it's not irrationalism), and there can be no rationalism without logic. To say that biblical citation is prepotent over logic is really to say that a non-standard logic is being used – one in which any conclusion that P is true is incorrigible so long as 'The Bible says that P' is available as a premise. In this case, the problematic passage doesn't cause a crisis. This type of fundamentalist will be content to assert both that one shouldn't believe anything because we find it written in a book, and that we should believe anything that we find written in the Good Book. Suppose, on the other hand, that fundamentalists regard standard deductive logic and biblical citation as equally indispensable ingredients of their paradigm. In that case, the problematic passage strikes a mortal blow to their system of beliefs: it forces them to choose between the Good Book and Good Deduction.

In the end, there's nothing about their dialectical situation which renders it impossible or impermissible for irrationalists to contrive a telling argument against their rationalist adversaries. When I say that such an argument is possible, I mean it in the sense that a mathematical proposition that's been neither proved nor refuted is still possibly true or possibly false. The preliminary objection that irrationalists don't recognize the force of arguments doesn't preclude their using arguments to discomfit their foes; nor does the fact that the issue concerns the status of the methodology of one of the disputants – some methodologies leave themselves open to refutation, and some don't. The question is: which type of methodology is at stake in the debate about rationalism? It's worth noting that if there *is* a rational refutation of rationalism, it will have some peculiar properties. It will have no force whatever on those who accept its conclusion; but it will force those who *don't yet* accept the conclusion to do so forthwith. A rational refutation of rationalism would be a one-way ticket to a place where the validity of the ticket isn't recognized. But it wouldn't matter, because you'd already be there. The same is true, of course, of any paradigm-busting argument.

Here's an argument showing that irrationalists *can't* come up with a winning argument – equivalently, that there can be no rational refutations of rationalism. (This argument is a rational refutation of rational refutations of rationalism.) As was indicated in our discussion of fundamentalism, there are many logics. There are even academically respectable logics that tolerate a certain amount of inconsistency (Rescher and Brandom 1980). Thus the worst thing that can happen to rationalism is that it's refuted by an argument *which relies on some particular logic L*. But, given that this worst-case scenario takes place, rationalists always have the option of engaging in Duhemian manoeuvres. Rather than abandoning rationalism, they can always abandon L for another logic in which the argument can't be carried through to its conclusion.

In fact, the worst-case scenario has already happened. Russell's discovery of the inconsistency of set theory was as much of a blow to rationalism as there can ever be. Yet it didn't result in wholesale defections to the irrationalist camp. Mathematicians preferred to adopt even such patently ad hoc patches as the Zermelo–Fraenkel axioms. In brief, when the rules of rationality proved to be untrustworthy, rationalists just changed the rules. Every paradox is an invitation to irrationalism. But it's an invitation that can always be declined.

What about the possibility of a general argument to the effect that *all* logics are untrustworthy? An example might be the argument for semantic constructivism given in the previous chapter. The problem, of course, is that any such argument is always going to be formulated within some specific logic. A putative proof that all logics are untrustworthy is just another paradox within a single logic. Therefore it, too, can be dealt with by rejecting that particular logic. So, while irrationalists can make trouble for a particular logic, they can't make trouble for rationalism as a whole – or, rather, they can make trouble, but the rationalist always has an out.

It might be objected that the foregoing argument is too strong: Duhemian manoeuvres are always available in every kind of intellectual dispute. If this availability permitted us to conclude that the target thesis avoids defeat, then no thesis would ever be defeated. As it stands, this defence of rationalism leads to an across-the-board scepticism. To avoid the scepticism, one has to say something like the following. The availability of a Duhemian defence might entail that hypotheses are immune to *immediate and catastrophic* defeat. But if a hypothesis needs to be continually defended against new problems, it loses credibility by degrees. I'm sure this is more or less correct for the general run of hypotheses. In the special case where the hypothesis is rationalism, however, there's a further argument to the effect that engaging in a Duhemian defence is *always* rationally to be preferred over giving up on rationalism altogether. It goes like this.

Suppose there is a rational refutation of rationalism – i.e., an argument the conclusion of which is that all logical arguments are untrustworthy. Call this argument R. Now R itself is either trustworthy or untrustworthy. Suppose it's trustworthy. Then we should accept its conclusion, which is that all logical arguments are untrustworthy. But then, by universal instantiation, R itself is untrustworthy. Therefore it's untrustworthy. That is to say, we may ignore its dictates. This argument evidently has the same structure as the universal instantiation argument which shows that relativism is false (see Chapter 15). There's also a rational refutation of rational refutations of rationalism that parallels the existential generalization argument against relativism: if we suppose that the rational refutation of rationalism is trustworthy, it follows that there are trustworthy arguments, which means that rationalism is true – therefore the rational refutation of rationalism isn't trustworthy.

Having concluded that R is untrustworthy, we might want to ascertain where it goes wrong. There are three possible outcomes of such an investigation. We might discover that R utilizes a false premise; we might discover that it commits a misstep which our logic condemns as fallacious; or, most interestingly, we might be unable to find either false premises or missteps. If we are unable to find falsehoods or missteps in R, then the foregoing argument indicates that we must conclude that our current logic needs to be revised. This is an immediate consequence of the conclusion that R is untrustworthy, together with the assumption that no false premises have been used and no missteps have been committed. Our current logic *stipulates* that, when faced with a faultlessly executed paradox, we should always change the logic rather than abandon logic altogether. Therefore rationalism can never lose to irrationalism.

The conclusion encapsulated in the last sentence needs a minor modification. Strictly speaking, it's only a *certain type* of rationalism that's immune to irrationalist refutation – a rationalism that relies on logical machinery which permits the foregoing argument to be brought to its conclusion. One can envision rationalisms based on logics that don't have this feature – rationalisms that stipulate that we *should* give up on logic altogether if we're faced with a faultlessly executed paradox. The difference between these two types of rationalism is like the difference between the biblical fundamentalism that's prepared to jettison standard deduction if necessary and the fundamentalism that regards standard deduction as equipotent with biblical citation. The former is impervious to refutation, while the latter leaves itself vulnerable. A rationalism that leaves itself vulnerable to refutation is a possible form of rationalism, but it isn't our form. In fact, it's nobody's form. This isn't surprising from an evolutionary point of view. If there ever were rationalists of so feeble a stripe, they would have been extinct by the time of Epimenides.

In Chapter 14, I argued that the logical constructivists' prerogative to change their logic leads to the collapse of their thesis to irrationalism. Don't we have to say the same thing here about rationalism? If it's allowed that rationalists can change their logic, then aren't they in the same boat as the logical constructivists? They aren't. What precipitates the collapse of logical constructivism to irrationalism is the licence to change logics *ad libitum*. It's indeed the case that if you can change logics any time you like and in any way you like, then you're an irrationalist. But rationalists don't have to take this line. To begin with, they don't have to admit that one can change logics at any time. They may stipulate that the rules are to be changed only under certain conditions – e.g., when confronted with a perfectly executed paradox. Secondly, rationalists don't have to admit that one ever has a totally free choice of logics. Our current logic may itself stipulate how it's to be changed in the event of an irresolvable paradox. For example, it might stipulate that we should follow a principle of conservatism, striving to leave as much of our logical repertoire unchanged as we can. Both these features serve to distinguish irrationalists from rationalists who allow that they may change their logic. The rational refutation of rational refutations of rationalism stands.

Of course, the rational refutation of their critical arguments has no more force among the irrationalists than the critical arguments themselves do. The rational refutation of rational refutations of rationalism isn't a criticism of irrationalism. But it does render the rationalists permanently immune to irrationalist attack. Conversely, rationalists can't make any trouble for irrationalists either. There's no point presenting irrationalists with a logical argument to the effect that logical arguments have normative force. Even if one could find such an argument, it would have no force among the irrationalists. Rationalism and irrationalism are therefore *irreconcilable* positions: neither side possesses the resources for persuading the other side that it's wrong by its own lights. The rationalists can't logically persuade the irrationalists to change, because the irrationalists don't recognize the force of any logical argument; and the irrationalists can't logically persuade the rationalists to change, because the rationalists' logic stipulates that, if they lose, they should simply change the rules.

Let's look at the situation through rationalist eyes. My commitment to rationalism (really, to the prevalent brand of rationalism) makes abandoning logic into an epistemic error under any and all circumstances. I am not allowed to leave the confines of rationality. But outside my epistemic prison, I see gambolling irrationalists who allow themselves to say anything they want, and who reply to my tortuous arguments with derisive laughter – all this *without incurring epistemic blame*. By my own lights, it would be a mistake to cast off my shackles and join them. But one mistake and I'm home free. It's tempting to make a dash for it. To do so would be akin to knowingly taking a mind-numbing drug that causes me to lose the ability to tell moral right from moral wrong. Before taking the drug, I know that it's morally wrong to do so; but I also know that after I take the drug, I'll no longer know that it or anything else is wrong – and then a world of illicit pleasures will open itself to me. In brief, there's the possibility of a utilitarian argument for taking the drug, or for going over to the irrationalist side. In the case of going over to irrationalism, there's no getting around the fact that it's an epistemic error to do so. But that doesn't prevent the question from being posed: epistemic considerations aside, would I prefer life as an irrationalist? The benefits of irrationalism have already been noted: it's so deliciously free and easy – you can say anything you want! What are the costs?

Rationalists do sometimes present non-epistemic reasons for their continued adherence to the hard option. A common rationalist reaction to the prospect of irrationalism, just past the incredulity, is fear. To begin with, there's the professional fear that discourse will become or prove to be chaotic and absurd – and then how will we justify our continued employment as philosophers? There's also a deeper fear that if we all become irrationalists, life itself will become dangerous. Without the restraining hand of reason, what's to stop people from blithely stepping out of ten-storey windows, or sticking their thumbs in their eyes when they intend to get a cup of coffee? Then there's the often-encountered *Nazi* argument: without the constraints of rationality, there's nothing to prevent us from all becoming Nazis. My most recent encounter with the Nazi argument has been provided by Putnam:

> the thrust of Derrida's writing is that the notions of 'justification', 'good reason', 'warrant', and the like are primarily repressive gestures. And *that* view is dangerous because it provides aid and comfort for extremists (especially extremists of a romantic bent) of all kinds, both

left and right. The twentieth century has witnessed horrible events, and the extreme left and the extreme right are both responsible for its horrors. Today, as we face the twenty-first century, our task is not to repeat the mistakes of the twentieth century. Thinking of reason as just a repressive notion is certainly not going to help us to do that.

(Putnam 1996: 197)

In this passage, Putnam doesn't criticize irrationalism directly – he attacks 'thinking of reason as just a repressive notion'. But it's clearly not this specific hypothesis about the relation between reason and repression that upsets him. It's a consequence of this hypothesis – the consequence that we will cease to take the constraints of reason to heart. Putnam would undoubtedly be just as upset with writers who promulgate the view that reason is uncool.

These worries are unfounded. The safety of daily life and the benignancy of human action don't depend on our making decisions based on rational considerations. This is a corollary of the fact that safety and benignancy don't depend on our making decisions at all. The truth of the broader principle is brought home to us by the contemplation of cats and dogs. These beings are capable of living safely and harmoniously; yet it seems highly implausible to suppose that feline and canine behaviour is preceded by a process of deliberation which terminates in an explicit choice among alternatives (Fido says to himself: 'Yes! I'm going to greet my master enthusiastically!') If the reader is tempted to attribute deliberation to cats and dogs, I would switch the example to spiders and ants. Surely *these* beings act 'spontaneously', i.e., without working out what their course shall be in advance. Yet it's only in pathological cases that they do the brutish equivalent of sticking their thumbs in their eyes, or of becoming Nazis.

The fallacy of the Nazi argument is pinpointed by the archery master in Herrigel's account of Zen in the art of archery:

You think that what you do not do yourself does not happen.

(Herrigel 1953: 51)

Order isn't exclusively created by our heeding of normative constraints, or indeed by any deliberate activity on our part. Sometimes order happens by itself, as a result of natural causes. In the chapter on semantic constructivism I argued that we're allowed to alter the meanings of words *ad lib*, and that this latitude seems to open the door to irrationalism. The apparent fact that most conversations are smoothly co-ordinated and foster a sense of mutual understanding is not incompatible with this thesis. There may be no *normative* constraints against changing the meanings of words *ad lib*, yet we may not *utilize* this freedom because there are certain *causal* constraints to our doing so. For example, we may be subject to a *law of ossification* for meanings: after a critical learning period, we may become constitutionally disinclined to alter the extensions associated with the terms of our language. Normatively speaking, we *could* alter the extensions at any time. But we happen to be the sorts of creatures that *don't*, and this is why conversation is possible. Nevertheless, the availability of a naturalistic theory that explains how we manage to co-ordinate our talk doesn't negate irrationalism. Irrationalism is a *normative* thesis – it's the null thesis which says that there are no epistemic norms. If irrationalism is right, then we can't accuse someone who says that whales are fish, or that numbers are fish, of *making an epistemic error*. This is entirely compatible with the law of ossification. If the law of ossification were true, it might still not be a mistake to say that numbers are fish. It's just that we wouldn't be inclined to say it.

So, when contemplating the switch from rationalism to irrationalism, fear of chaos is not a weighty consideration. Fear of unemployment for philosophers is also uncalled for, but this is perhaps not as obvious. My therapy for fear of unemployment takes the form of a quasi-historical disquisition, like Putnam's Nazi argument. I call these 'quasi-historical' because they're not based on historical scholarship. They're merely plausible stories that respect a handful of historical platitudes (e.g., that extremists of both the left and the right have committed atrocities). Quasi-historical arguments have force to the extent that the point being made doesn't require more than that the story be plausible. I'm not so sure that Putnam's argument satisfies this condition – for his claim that irrationality leads to atrocious behaviour isn't based on any conceptual connection between irrationality and evil. If it turned out that irrational extremists *hadn't*, as a matter of hard historical fact, committed atrocities, there would be no reason to accept Putnam's thesis. My use of quasi-history isn't of this sort. I don't at any stage of the argument require the hypothesis that events really happened in the way that I depict. It's enough for my purpose that events might have happened in this way.

Something very much like the switch from rationalism to irrationalism has happened at least once before, in the history of Western painting. It used to be thought that there was an epistemically privileged way to paint – a 'realistic' way, which rendered the world as it 'really' looked. It was conceded all round that no painting had ever achieved perfect realism. But realism was a regulative ideal, and pictures were routinely ranked on this normative dimension. This approach to painting gradually unravelled in the closing decades of the nineteenth century and the early decades of the twentieth. In part, the turn-of-the-century liberation from former constraints might be described as the realization that one didn't have to paint realistically. But the critique of realism went further than that. The very coherence of realism as a regulative ideal came under attack. It wasn't merely that one didn't have to paint realistically – it was that the imperative to paint realistically didn't make any sense.

Nevertheless, the painters who laboured under this conceptual confusion produced works of art, some of them of enormous aesthetic merit.

Evidently, conceptual clarity isn't a necessary precondition for the production of significant art. Moreover, the output of those who strove in vain to achieve epistemic correctness has a certain recognizable look. There's a more or less unitary style which was fostered by the incoherent goal of epistemic correctness, as that goal was understood in recent centuries in Europe. This style also goes by the name of 'realism'.

Now it's an interesting historical fact that painting in the realist style virtually disappeared around the turn of the century. For the next half-century, it was impossible to paint realistically and be taken seriously as an artist. What precipitated this exclusion? The following account is at least arguable. Just as painting in the realist style was fostered by a conceptual confusion, so also was the *cessation* of painting in the realist style due to a confusion. The second confusion was this: the incoherence and false pretensions of realism having been exposed, the lesson was derived that one ought not to paint realistically. To derive this lesson is to be confused about the nature of the first confusion. The first confusion was to suppose that one could paint realistically, where 'realistically' means 'in the epistemically correct manner'.

The second confusion is to suppose that this insight warrants the recommendation that one ought not to paint realistically. There's *no* recommendation or prohibition for painters that can be derived from the clarification of the first confusion. There's certainly no point telling them that they shouldn't paint realistically in the *epistemic* sense of the word, since the clarification of the first confusion is precisely that the idea of painting realistically in this sense is incoherent. One couldn't paint realistically in this sense even if one tried. To the extent that a stricture against certain sorts of paintings was imposed, it had to be against realism as a *style*. But the clarification of the first confusion has no bearing on the merits or demerits of realism as a style. To suppose otherwise is the second confusion. In recent decades, there's been a resurgence of paintings in a realist style. But this resurgence has not, as far as I can tell, been accompanied by a relapse into the first confusion. So while the style of realism might never have been forged if the first confusion hadn't taken place, it seems that this style can survive the dissipation of the confusion.

Let's turn now from painting to the world of ideas. It's arguable that a movement from rationalism to irrationalism has been taking place that exactly parallels the story I've just told about painting. My point doesn't depend on the truth of this socio-historical thesis, however – nor even on the truth of the story that I told about painting. All I require is that the story about painting be plausible. If it is, then it provides a model for how philosophy isn't precluded by irrationalism. For realism in painting, substitute rationalism in the world of ideas – the former is the doctrine that there's an epistemically privileged mode of painting, the latter that there are epistemically privileged sequences of ideas. The early twentieth-century devaluation of realism corresponds to the contemporary devaluation of reasoned philosophical discourse. In both cases, the devaluations can be due to a superficial or a deep reason. The superficial reason is that one simply loses interest in epistemic matters. There would be no imperative to paint realistically even if 'painting realistically' made sense. One might prefer to make abstract wallpaper patterns. By the same token, there's no imperative that idea-mongers be rationalistic philosophers, even if rationalistic philosophy is the royal road to the truth. People who take pleasure in dealing with ideas might prefer to write novels, or do stand-up comedy. The deeper reason for the devaluation of realism in painting is that it's an attempt to chase after an incoherent goal. Some idea-mongers like Rorty (1979) have suggested that the same thing is true of rationalistic philosophy: the problem isn't merely that its goal is optional – it's that the pursuit of its goal is based on a confusion.

In this book, I'll refrain from expressing my opinion of Rorty's thesis. Let's grant that rationalists are guilty of the equivalent of the first confusion – trying to chase after an unchaseable goal. My point is that, even if this is so, there are some contemporary idea-mongers who are guilty of the second confusion – the passing of injunctions against impossible pursuits. The clearest example is Lyotard's (1984) notorious stricture against 'metadiscourses' of the type that rationalistic philosophers have tried to provide. The peculiarity of Lyotard's stance has often been remarked upon. Second-level discourses are deemed to be reprehensible, but apparently third-level discourses like his own are okay. What would be Lyotard's opinion of fourth-level discourses like the one I'm engaged in right at this moment? Is there a problem with all even-numbered levels? It's hard to avoid the impression that Lyotard's stricture is a gerrymandered criterion designed to exclude something preconceived. In any case, Lyotard's exclusion is the isomorphic element to the exclusion of realist paintings in the early twentieth century. It's based on the second confusion – confounding the repudiation of an epistemic goal (realism in painting, rationalism in philosophy) with the repudiation of a style. It may be true that the realist style of painting would never have developed if painters hadn't been victims of the first confusion. But this historical fact is not a criticism of the realist style. Similarly, even if it's true that rationalistic philosophy was born out of a sort of first confusion, it doesn't follow that you can't or shouldn't write in the *manner* of rationalistic philosophy after that confusion has been dispelled. If, as the point has sometimes been put, all writing is literature, then the moral isn't that philosophy is illegitimate writing – it's that philosophy is literature.

To be sure, postmodern, unconfused realist paintings have a distinctive look that sets them apart from the products of the confused and pretentious realism of an earlier era. By the same token, it's to be expected that a postmodern, unconfused rationalistic philosophy would have its own stylistic features that make it discriminable from the (putatively) confused and pretentious brand of old-style rationalistic philosophy. But there's going to be a preponderance of common stylistic elements in both cases. Postmodern rationalistic philosophy is still going to strive after a maximal economy of means in achieving its effects, and it will still eschew the intentional cultivation of obscurity – in brief, it will continue to be an expression of the classical as opposed to the romantic sensibility. It will also continue to prefer the linear to the painterly, the systematic to the impressionistic, and so on. In sum, rationalistic philosophers contemplating irrationalism needn't worry about unemployment. There'll still be plenty of scope for the pursuit of their interests and the exercise of their talents after the Big Switch.

18 Conclusions

Here are my conclusions in summary form. First, there's nothing wrong with the strong programme of seeking out the social causes of any and all beliefs (Chapter 2). But the strong programme isn't yet constructivism, if by that term we mean the thesis that certain classes of facts are constituted by human activity. Among constructivisms, the only variety that isn't beset by serious conceptual problems is the type that I called *reasonable* constructivism (Chapter 12). This is the unadventurous thesis that every society is able to construct facts about itself. At the other end of the scale of credibility is the strong constructivism which asserts that all ascertainable facts are constructed. This position is as indefensible as any philosophical stance can be. Strong constructivists have yet to show that the infinite regress of constructions generated by their thesis isn't vicious (Chapter 10), or that the temporal incongruities generated by their thesis admit of a coherent resolution (Chapter 13). They also haven't accounted for what happens when two societies construct incompatible facts (Chapter 12). To my mind, the most telling argument against strong constructivism is also the simplest (Chapter 11): if facts are all negotiable, then why does anybody ever feel the need to defend a favoured thesis against a factual objection? Why not simply deny the problematic fact? In light of all these unresolved difficulties, I think we're justified in drawing the firm conclusion that the world exists. I've called the Science Editor of the local television station with news of my discovery, but he won't answer my calls.

What about scientific constructivism, the thesis which claims that scientific facts are constructed, but which allows that there may also be independent facts? This retrenchment provides constructivists with an avenue of escape from all the above problems except one: the problem of accounting for what happens when two societies construct incompatible facts (Chapter 12). But one unresolved conceptual difficulty is enough. The ball is in the scientific constructivists' court.

There are other conceivable constructivisms. For instance, there's *chronological constructivism*, which is defined as follows. Let S1, S2, ..., Sn represent all the societies there ever were or will be in chronological order. Then chronological constructivism is the thesis that each society Si is able to construct social facts about the successor society S(i+1). Chronological constructivism obviously isn't reasonable (in the technical sense of the word). It also isn't the same thing as scientific or strong constructivism, since it allows that non-social scientific facts may be unconstructed. Nevertheless, it's liable to a variant of the galactic conspiracy argument that was wielded against scientific constructivism in Chapter 12 – for it allows that the society immediately preceding our own may have constructed some facts that are binding on us, even though we may have no inkling of that society's existence. I bring up this outlandish possibility only to make the point that the constructivist hypotheses that were evaluated in this book don't exhaust the realm of conceivable constructivisms. So it's possible that there's an as yet unformulated constructivism that has implications that go beyond those of reasonable constructivism, but that nevertheless avoids all the conceptual problems that were developed in the previous chapters. Try as I might, I can't think of a non-reasonable constructivism that simultaneously circumvents the galactic conspiracy argument and isn't so totally ad hoc that nobody would have an interest in maintaining it. Under the circumstances, I think that it's rational to adopt the view that nothing can be constructed, in the constitutive sense of the word, except facts about our own society. If this is right, then non-reasonable constructivist hypotheses are all *un*reasonable. This conclusion will, I hope, create a little more of a stir than the news that the world exists.

The analysis of metaphysical constructivism takes up the first thirteen chapters of the book. The last four chapters are different. Chapters 14 and 15 deal with auxiliary issues that arise in the course of the critique of metaphysical constructivism. That critique was conducted without calling into question the prevailing standards of scientific rationality. But of course many constructivists regard these standards themselves as socially negotiated results. This *logical* constructivism casts the prior critique in a new light: if the standards of rationality are negotiable, then the fact that metaphysical constructivism is a non-starter according to prevailing standards might just mean that constructivists need to negotiate new standards. In Chapter 14 I explore the implications of taking this line, and find that it leads to a blanket irrationalism according to which there are no standards of rationality, not even negotiated ones. So there's no hope of justifying one's metaphysical constructivism by that route.

The critiques of both metaphysical and logical constructivism are such that they could conceivably be mollified if the constructivist thesis is conjoined with some form of relativism. It therefore becomes necessary to examine the bona fides of relativism to settle the status of constructivism once and for all. I do this in Chapter 15 and conclude that Plato was right: relativism is incoherent. Thus is the last nail driven into the coffin of unreasonable constructivism. Or is it?

Having dealt with the issue of relativism as well as metaphysical constructivism, I found that I had touched on all the hypotheses that go by the name of 'constructivism' except for the semantic thesis that past linguistic usage doesn't determine future usage. For the sake of completeness, I decided to add a chapter that canvassed the issues relating to this type of *semantic* constructivism. I found that this thesis, like logical constructivism, entails irrationalism (Chapter 16). There's a big difference between the two entailments, however. From a rationalist's point of view, the demonstration that logical constructivism leads to irrationalism is unproblematic – it just means that we should reject logical constructivism by *modus tollens*. Rationalists can't take an equally cavalier attitude toward the demonstration that semantic constructivism leads to irrationalism, however. In this case, they can't simply conclude that the antecedent is false, because there are two independent and unrefuted arguments purporting to show that the antecedent is *true*: Kripke's and mine. Unless and until these arguments are defused, I seem to have inadvertently made a case for irrationalism. Now an argument for irrationalism – an argument to the effect that arguments have no normative force – is a peculiar conceptual entity. It's not immediately clear what moral, if any, may be derived from the existence of such an entity. So I felt impelled to write still another chapter in which I tried to sort out what to make of arguments of this type (Chapter 17).

It's my impression that some of the more extreme constructivists are openly rooting for irrationalism to win. Recall Ashmore's reaction to the logical problems of logical positivism:

> I have no intention of *arguing* with this wonderful piece of irony – for those who live by logic to die by logic is an eminently satisfying state of affairs ...
>
> (Ashmore 1989: 88)

Even more diagnostic is the following remark by Latour:

> Amateurs of self-reference will have noted with delight that these last two paragraphs are self-contradictory: I am glad to offer them this delight.
>
> (Latour 1988: 170)

Perhaps Latour and Ashmore hope to defuse rational criticism of their position by repudiating rationality itself. But I don't see how the repudiation of rationality can advance any of their interests. On the one hand, it doesn't render their thesis epistemically more acceptable, since irrationalism is the view that nothing is epistemically more acceptable than anything else. If they reject rationalism, then their favourite constructivist theses have exactly the same status as pieces of speculative fiction or bawdy limericks. On the other hand, if they're willing to accept that characterization of their work, then they needn't have engaged the rationality issue at all. There's no law against writing speculative fiction even if there are universally valid principles of reasoning. The repudiation of rationality doesn't make available any hitherto thwarted enterprises.

Ironically, if unreasonable constructivists were to remain faithful to rationalism in its time of trouble, they would find a new hope for vindication. I noted in Chapter 17 that rationalism does not allow for the possibility that irrationalism might win. Faced with a faultless argument for irrationalism, the rational conclusion is that we must change the logic in such a way that the argument no longer goes through. If a mistake can't be found in the argument that semantic constructivism is true and that it leads to irrationalism, then we're going to have to change some inference rules – just as the rules of set theory were changed to block Russell's paradox. But if the rules are going to change, there's no way of knowing ahead of time what other established results might be reversed. Maybe the new logic will countenance some unreasonable forms of constructivism after all. We won't know for sure until we know how to dispose of the argument from semantic constructivism to irrationalism. So it has to be admitted that the status of scientific constructivism, and even that of strong constructivism, remains open. Of course, this is a sense in which the status of every hypothesis remains open. It's conceivable that the new logic will vindicate the view that the earth is flat, that perpetual motion is physically possible, or that angles can be trisected with a ruler and compass. Unless and until the vindication comes, this is the company in which all but the most pallid of constructivist theses belong.

References

Ashmore, M. (1989). *The reflexive thesis: Wrighting sociology of scientific knowledge*, Chicago: University of Chicago Press.

Barnes, B. (1982). 'On the extensions of concepts and the growth of knowledge', *Sociological Review, 30*, 23–44.

Barnes, B. and Bloor, D. (1982). 'Relativism, rationalism and the sociology of knowledge', in M. Hollis and S. Lukes (eds), *Rationality and relativism*, Cambridge MA: MIT Press (pp. 21–47).

Bloor, D. (1976). *Knowledge and social imagery*, London: Routledge & Kegan Paul.

——(1981). 'The strengths of the strong programme', *Philosophy of the Social Sciences, 11*, 199–213.

—— (1983). *Wittgenstein: A social theory of knowledge*, London: Macmillan.

Boghossian, P.A. (1989). 'The rule-following considerations', *Mind, 98*, 507–49.

Boyd, R. (1984). 'The current status of scientific realism', in J. Leplin (ed.), *Scientific realism*, Berkeley: University of California Press (pp. 41–82).

Brown, J.R. (1989). *The rational and the social*, London: Routledge.

Callon, M. and Latour, B. (1992). 'Don't throw the baby out with the Bath school!', in A. Pickering (ed.), *Science as practice and culture*, Chicago: University of Chicago Press, 343–68.

Cantor, G.N. (1975). 'A critique of Shapin's social interpretation of the Edinburgh phrenological debate', *Annals of Science, 33*, 245–56.

Chomsky, N. (1986). *Knowledge of language: Its nature, origin, and use*, New York: Praeger.

Collin, F. (1993). 'Social constructivism without paradox', *Danish Yearbook of Philosophy, 28*, 24–46.

Collins, H.M. (1981). 'What is TRASP? The radical programme as a methodological imperative', *Philosophy of the Social Sciences, 11*, 215–24.

—— (1985). *Changing order: Replication and induction in scientific practice*, London: Sage.

Collins, H.M. and Pinch, T J. (1993). *The golem: What everyone should know about science*, Cambridge: Cambridge University Press.

Devitt, M. (1991). *Realism and truth* (2nd edn), Oxford: Blackwell.

Dretske, F. (1981). *Knowledge and the flow of information*, Cambridge MA: MIT Press.

Duhem, P. (1951). *The aim and structure of physical theory*, Princeton NJ: Princeton University Press.

Durkheim, E. (1915). *Elementary forms of religious life*, London: George Allen & Unwin.

Fine, A. (1984). 'The natural ontological attitude', in J. Leplin (ed.), *Scientific realism*, Berkeley: University of California Press (pp. 83–107).

—— (1996). 'Science made up: Constructivist sociology of scientific knowledge', in P. Galison and D.J. Stump (eds), *The disunity of science: Boundaries, contexts, and power*, Stanford: Stanford University Press (pp. 231–54).

Fodor, J.A. (1987). *Psychosemantics: The problem of meaning in the philosophy of mind*, Cambridge MA: MIT Press.

Franklin, A. (1990). *Experiment right or wrong*, Cambridge: Cambridge University Press.

Freud, S. (1973a). *Introductory lectures on psychoanalysis*, Harmondsworth: Penguin Books. (Original work published 1917.)

—— (1973b). *New Introductory lectures on psychoanalysis*, Harmondsworth: Penguin Books. (Original work published 1933.)

Friedman, M. (1998). 'On the sociology of scientific knowledge and its philosophical agenda', *Studies in History and Philosophy of Science, 29*, 239–71.

Goodman, N. (1978). *Ways of worldmaking*, Indianapolis IN: Hackett.

—— (1996a). 'Comments', in P.J. McCormick (ed.), *Starmaking: Realism, anti-realism, irrealism*, Cambridge MA: MIT Press (pp. 203–13).

—— (1996b). 'Notes on the well-made world', in P.J. McCormick (ed.), *Starmaking: Realism, anti-realism, irrealism*, Cambridge MA: MIT Press (pp. 151–9).

Hacking, I. (1983). *Representing and intervening*, Cambridge: Cambridge University Press.

—— (1988). 'The participant irrealist at large in the laboratory', *British Journal for the Philosophy of Science, 39*, 277–94.

—— (1999). *The social construction of what?*, Cambridge MA: Harvard University Press.

Hempel, C. (1996). 'Comments on Goodman's "Ways of worldmaking"', in P.J. McCormick (ed.), *Starmaking: Realism, anti-realism, irrealism*, Cambridge MA: MIT Press (pp. 125–32).

Henle, P. (1949). 'Mysticism and semantics', *Philosophy and Phenomenological Research, 9*, 416–22.

Herrigel, E. (1953). *Zen in the art of archery*, New York: Pantheon.

James, W. (1902). *The varieties of religious experience*, New York: Longmans, Green & Co.

Knorr-Cetina, K. (1983). 'The ethnographic study of scientific work: Towards a constructivist interpretation of science', in K. Knorr-Cetina and M. Mulkay (eds), *Science observed: Perspectives on the social study of science*, London: Sage (pp. 115–40).

—— (1993). 'Strong constructivism – from a sociologist's point of view: A personal addendum to Sismondo's paper', *Social Studies of Science, 23*, 555–63.

Kripke, S.A. (1982). *Wittgenstein on rules and private language: An elementary analysis*, Oxford: Blackwell.

Kuhn, T.S. (1962). *The structure of scientific revolutions*, Chicago: University of Chicago Press.

Kukla, A. (1994). 'Scientific realism, scientific practice and the natural ontological attitude', *British Journal for the Philosophy of Science, 45*, 955–75.

—— (1996). 'The theory-observation distinction', *The Philosophical Review, 105*, 173–230.

—— (1998). *Studies in scientific realism*, New York: Oxford University Press.

Lakatos, I. (1978). *The methodology of scientific research programmes*, Cambridge: Cambridge University Press.

Latour, B. (1987). *Science in action*, Milton Keynes: Open University Press.

—— (1988). 'The politics of explanation: An alternative', in S. Woolgar (ed.), *Knowledge and reflexivity: New frontiers in the sociology of knowledge*, London: Sage (pp. 155–76).

Latour, N. and Woolgar, S. (1979). *Laboratory life: The social construction of scientific facts*, London: Sage.

—— (1986). *Laboratory life: The construction of scientific facts* (2nd edn), Princeton NJ: Princeton University Press.

Laudan, L. (1981). 'The pseudo-science of science?', *Philosophy of the Social Sciences*, *11*, 173–98.

—— (1984). 'Explaining the success of science: Beyond epistemic realism and relativism', in J.T. Cushing, C.F. Delaney and G.M. Gutting (eds), *Science and reality: Recent work in the philosophy of science*, Notre Dame IN: University of Notre Dame Press (pp. 83–105).

—— (1996). *Beyond positivism and relativism: Theory, method, and evidence*, Boulder CO: Westview Press.

Lyotard, J.F. (1984). *The post-modern condition: A report on knowledge*, Minneapolis MN: University of Minnesota Press.

Mannheim, K. (1936). *Ideology and Utopia*, New York: Harvest Books.

Margolis, J. (1991). *The truth about relativism*, Oxford: Blackwell.

Marx, K. and Engels, F. (1963). *The German ideology*, New York: International Publishers.

Maxwell, G. (1962). 'The ontological status of theoretical entities', in H. Feigl and G. Maxwell (eds), *Scientific explanation, space and time*, Minneapolis MN: University of Minnesota Press (pp. 3–27).

McGinn, C. (1989) 'Can we solve the mind–body problem?', *Mind*, *98*, 349–66.

Meiland, J.W. (1977). 'Concepts of relative truth', *The Monist*, *60*, 568–82.

—— (1980). 'On the paradox of cognitive relativism', *Metaphilosophy*, *11*, 115–26.

Merton, R.K. (1948). 'The self-fulfilling prophecy', *Antioch Review*, *8*, 193–210.

—— (1973). *The sociology of science: Theoretical and empirical investigations*, Chicago: University of Chicago Press.

Naess, A. (1972). *The pluralist and possibilist aspect of the scientific enterprise*, London: George Allen & Unwin.

Nelson, A. (1994). 'How *could* facts be socially constructed?', *Studies in History and Philosophy of Science*, *25*, 535–47.

Niiniluoto, I. (1991). 'Realism, relativism, and constructivism', *Synthèse*, *89*, 135–62.

Nola, R. (1995). 'There are more things in Heaven and Earth, Horatio, than are dreamt of in your philosophy: A dialogue on realism and constructivism', *Studies in History and Philosophy of Science*, *25*, 689–727.

Pickering, A. (1984). *Constructing quarks*, Chicago IL: University of Chicago Press.

—— (1991). 'Philosophy naturalized a bit', *Social Studies of Science*, *21*, 575–85.

Pinch, T. (1986). *Confronting nature*, Dordrecht: Reidel.

Plato (1961). *Theaetetus*, trans. F.M. Cornford, in E. Hamilton and H. Cairns (eds), *The collected dialogues of Plato*, Bollingen Series, New York: Pantheon Books (pp. 845–919).

Polanyi, M. (1958). *Personal knowledge: Towards a post-critical philosophy*, Chicago IL: University of Chicago Press.

Putnam, H. (1975a). *Mathematics, matter and method: Philosophical papers* (vol. 1), Cambridge: Cambridge University Press.

—— (1975b). *Mind, language and reality: Philosophical papers* (vol. 2), Cambridge: Cambridge University Press.

—— (1981). *Reason, truth and history*, Cambridge: Cambridge University Press.

—— (1983). *Realism and reason: Philosophical papers* (vol. 3), Cambridge: Cambridge University Press.

—— (1996). 'Irrealism and deconstruction', In P.J. McCormick (ed.), *Starmaking: Realism, anti-realism, irrealism*, Cambridge MA: MIT Press (pp. 179–200).

Quine, W.V. (1951). 'Two dogmas of empiricism', *Philosophical Review*, *60*, 20–43.

Radder, H. (1993). 'Science, realization and reality: The fundamental issues', *Studies in History and Philosophy of Science*, *24*, 327–49.

Rescher, N. and Brandom, R. (1980). *The logic of inconsistency*, Oxford: Blackwell.

Rorty, R. (1979). *Philosophy and the mirror of nature*, Princeton NJ: Princeton University Press.

Scheffler, I. (1980). 'The wonderful worlds of Goodman', *Synthèse*, *45*, 201–9.

——(1986). *Inquiries*, Indianapolis IN: Hackett.

—— (1996). 'Worldmaking: Why worry', in P.J. McCormick (ed.), *Starmaking: Realism, anti-realism, irrealism*, Cambridge MA: MIT Press (pp. 171–7).

Shapin, S. (1975). 'Phrenological knowledge and the social structure of early nineteenth-century Edinburgh', *Annals of Science*, *32*, 219–43.

—— (1982). 'History of science and its sociological reconstructions', *History of Science*, *20*, 157–211.

Siegel, H. (1987). *Relativism refuted: A critique of contemporary epistemological relativism*, Dordrecht: Reidel.

Sismondo, S. (1993a). 'Some social constructions', *Social Studies of Science*, *23*, 515–53.

—— (1993b). 'Response to Knorr-Cetina', *Social Studies of Science*, *23*, 563–9.

Tilley, N. (1981). 'The logic of laboratory life', *Sociology*, *15*, 117–26.

Trout, J.D. (1992). 'Theory-conjunction and mercenary reliance', *Philosophy of Science*, *59*, 231–45.

—— (1994). 'A realistic look backward', *Studies in History and Philosophy of Science*, *25*, 37–64.

van Fraassen, B.C. (1980). *The scientific image*, Oxford: Clarendon Press.

—— (1989). *Laws and symmetry*, Oxford: Clarendon Press.

Wittgenstein, L. (1953). *Philosophical investigations*, Oxford: Blackwell.

Woolgar, S. (1988). *Science: The very idea*, London: Tavistock.

Index

abracadabra theory 50
absolute relativism 132–4
agonistic field 85, 93–5
anti-realism 62–6
archaic data 51–4
Ashmore, M. 7, 68–73, 91, 162
astrological policy 145–6
auxiliary hypotheses 65, 80
Azande 25, 42, 44, 145

Barnes, B. 10, 14–18, 91, 119–20, 126, 136, 138–9, 143–4
Bloor, D. 9–18, 72, 91, 119–20, 126, 136, 138–9, 143
Blurry Image 59–60, 67
Boghossian, P. A. 141
Bohm, D. 39
Boyd, R. 19
Brandom, R. 151
Brown, J.R. 35, 38, 46

Callon, M. 27–8, 60, 62
Cantor, G.N. 39
causal constructivism 21–3
Chomsky, N. 24
chronological constructivism 160–1
Collin, F. 75–9, 86, 91, 121, 140
Collins, H. 6, 9, 18, 29, 82–3, 136, 138–40, 143, 147
conceptual innovation, easy versus difficult 112–13
conjunction argument 63, 65
constitutive constructivism 21–3
constitutive scenario 53–4
constructive empiricism 26, 59–67, 95–6
constructivism 1–4; *see also* causal constructivism; chronological

constructivism; constitutive constructivism; instrumental constructivism; logical constructivism; material constructivism; metaphysical constructivism; metaphysical socialism; reasonable constructivism; scientific constructivism; semantic constructivism; strong constructivism; very strong constructivism; weak scientific constructivism
Constructivist Counterfactual Argument 3
contempocriminality 115–18
contempospin 117–18
credibility 36–8, 41

Descartes, R. 81
Devitt, M. 5, 26
doppelelectron 100–1
double-bind theory of schizophrenia 68–9
Dretske, F. 142, 145
Duhem, P. 80
Duhemian asymmetry 80–90, 146
Durkheim, E. 7, 11

earth, shape of the 81–2
Eddington expedition 82–3
empirical equivalence 39, 42, 64
Engels, F. 7
Epimenides 153
epistemic ethics 56–8
epistemic relativism 4–6, 9–10, 12–18, 32–3, 41, 45, 91, 125–34, 139

facts, varieties of 24–6
Feyerabend, P. 113
Fine, A. 4, 9, 40, 63, 66